Mapping the Territory

Critical Approaches to Welsh Fiction in English

Editor: Dr Katie Gramich, Cardiff University

Contents:

Mapping the Territory

Critical Approaches to Welsh Fiction in English

edited by Katie Gramich

PARTHIAN

Published by
Parthian
The Old Surgery
Napier Street
Cardigan
SA43 1ED
www.parthianbooks.com

First published in 2010
© Contributors

ISBN 978-1-905762-98-9

The publisher acknowledges the financial
support of the Welsh Books Council.
Cover image: *Ruhrrevier I, 1920* by Conrad Felixmuller © DACS 2010
Cover design: Marc Jennings www.theundercard.co.uk
Typesetting by Lucy Llewellyn

Printed and bound by Lightning Source

British Library Cataloguing in Publication Data

A cataloguing record for this book is available from the British Library.

Introduction:

Mapping the Territory

Katie Gramich

The title of the great Welsh historian Gwyn Alf Williams's seminal 1985 work, *When Was Wales?*, was deliberately provocative. The unexpected 'when', as well as the past tense of the verb, immediately made potential readers curious and probably irritated them, especially if they were Welsh. The writer's polemical point was that 'Wales' is and was a variable and varying entity, conceived and imagined in different ways by people, even ostensibly 'the same' Welsh people, at different times. Mapping the 'where' of Wales may be relatively straightforward, Gwyn Alf suggests, but mapping the *when* and the *why* of the country and its culture is quite a different matter. The origin of Welsh fiction in English can be said to have a similarly wavering and disputed history. In fact, its historiography has altered radically in the past two decades. When Glyn Jones, himself an important Welsh poet and fiction writer in the English language, published his pioneering work of literary criticism, *The Dragon Has Two Tongues*, in 1968, it seemed uncontentious to begin his narrative of origins with Caradoc Evans's short story collection *My People*, published in 1915. In this, he was following in the footsteps of his contemporary, Gwyn Jones, also a creative writer, an editor, and a Professor of English Literature, who had published *The First Forty Years*, an account of the origins of Welsh fiction in English, in 1957. Jones, while acknowledging the existence of Anglophone fiction writers before Caradoc Evans, is unabashed in his dismissal of them:

> But with Caradoc Evans the war-horn was blown, the
> gauntlet thrown down, the gates of the temple shattered.
> Or in homelier metaphor, it was as though some new-style

> yahoo had flung a bucket of dung through the Welsh parlour window ... For good (or if anyone prefers, for bad) he destroyed the sandcastle dynasty of Allen Raine and the Maid of Cefn Ydfa, and sank it in the sea.[1]

The terms of Jones's dismissal are themselves interesting and unintentionally betray the misogynistic assumptions which underpin his forthright and absolute judgement. Caradoc Evans is figured as the masculine warrior hero destroying the flimsy literary edifices erected by females. Even the less flattering picture of Evans as yahoo implicitly aligns him with the towering figure of Jonathan Swift, creator of the yahoos and satirist par excellence, like Caradoc Evans himself. Implicitly, it is the genteel domestic domain of ladies which is desecrated by Caradoc's honest, manly dung and – Professor Jones suggests – about time too! However, this accepted narrative of origins has been radically challenged over the past few decades. With the somewhat belated advent of feminist criticism to the academy in Wales in the 1980s, Gwyn Jones's confident denigration of the female forerunners of Caradoc Evans began to be challenged. At the same time, the nature of university courses in English literature was changing in order to admit less canonical writing into the syllabus and abandoning hitherto absolute standards of literary 'worth' and 'value'. This meant that the history of the origins of Welsh fiction in English began to be conceived as including hitherto forgotten, neglected, or denigrated works. In this rewriting of the accepted historiography, Welsh scholars and critics were doing what had already been done in the English and American academy. Mainstream histories of the English novel in university courses once tended to begin indisputably with Daniel Defoe's *Robinson Crusoe* (1719) but today may just as readily identify Aphra Behn's *Oroonoko* (1688) or Thomas Nashe's *The Unfortunate Traveller* (1594) as the starting point of the novel genre in English. Yet, rewriting the history did not lead, and perhaps was never meant to lead, to consensus. Today, some scholars might identify T. J. Llewelyn Prichard's *The Adventures and Vagaries of Twm Shon Catti* (1828) as the first Welsh novel in English (as does, for example, Meic Stephens's authoritative 1997 *Companion to the Literatures of Wales*) but others, notably Jane Aaron and Belinda Humfrey, cite works such as Anna Maria Bennett's *Anna, or Memoirs of a Welch Heiress* (1785) or *Ellen, Countess of Castle Howell* (1794) as earlier works which are indisputably novels with distinctively Welsh characters, settings, and concerns, and thus have arguably an even stronger case for being regarded as the earliest Welsh fiction in English. However, it is unlikely that the beginnings of Anglophone Welsh fiction can be mapped back earlier than the late eighteenth century, since the Welsh language was of course the pre-eminent language of the majority of the people of Wales before that time, and thus the medium of their literary expression. Indeed, despite the tracing back of the origins of Welsh fiction in English to a much earlier date than 1915 (the date of publication of Evans's *My People*) it is important to remember that such fiction was the expression of a small English-speaking minority in Wales up to the twentieth century. This is not the place to trace the history of the decline of the Welsh language in Wales in the late nineteenth and early twentieth centuries, followed by its welcome survival and revival in recent years. Suffice to say that, by the early twentieth century, there came into being in Wales a people for whom Welsh was not their mother tongue, even though it had been that of their parents, grandparents, and many generations before them. These were people of the generation of writers such as Jack Jones (b. 1884), Lewis Jones (b. 1897), Rhys Davies (b. 1901), Glyn Jones (b. 1905), Gwyn Thomas (b. 1913) and Dylan Thomas (b. 1914). These writers began to publish their work in the late 1920s and 1930s and this is where the chronology of this collection of critical essays begins. It is the thirties that are generally considered as the heyday of what Raymond Williams was later to label 'the Welsh industrial novel'. In this collection of critical essays, the genre is represented by Lewis Jones's 1937 novel, *Cwmardy* and its sequel, *We Live* (1939), but Jack Jones's *Black Parade* (1935) or Gwyn Jones's *Times Like These* (1936) would have been equally representative selections.

Other important writers of the early twentieth century in Wales did not come from Welsh families who had 'lost' the Welsh language as a result of migration and social pressures but were themselves of families who had migrated to South Wales in the wake of the boom in iron and coal mining in the nineteenth century. Among these were Joseph Keating, who was of Irish origin, whose underrated novel *Son of Judith* (1901) is an important early work in the establishment of a distinctive Anglo-Welsh idiom in the novel, and B. L. Coombes (b. 1893), who was of English origin but worked for most of his life in the Welsh mining industry and produced a classic autobiographical account of the experience of the coal miner in *These Poor Hands* (1939).

This book of critical essays contributes to the rise in the public profile of Welsh writing in English which has occurred in recent years, both within Wales and in the wider world. This is in part a result of the proliferation of university courses on these texts, greatly helped by the foundation of the Library of Wales series which, since 2006, under the innovative and enthusiastic editorship of Professor Dai Smith, has been responsible for the publication of twenty-nine books, encompassing fiction, poetry, memoirs, reportage and letters.

The series, strongly advocated by all academics in the field of Welsh Writing in English, is published by Parthian and supported by both the Welsh Assembly Government and the Welsh Books Council. This series joins the Honno Classics series, initiated in 1998, which has brought many forgotten texts by Welsh women writers back into the public domain. The availability of texts is really the first requirement for serious study of a body of literature; serious critical engagement with that body is now growing rapidly, and this collection of essays forms part of that new body of critical work, which is needed by a new generation of students approaching the field for perhaps the first time. This book, then, is aimed primarily at undergraduate and postgraduate students and sets out to introduce them to the field of twentieth-century Welsh fiction in English and to demonstrate the varying critical approaches that can be used to analyse these texts.

The essays in this volume offer an approach to twelve texts that have recently been republished in the Library of Wales series, but which were originally published in the period from 1927 to 1975. The texts demonstrate the variety of Welsh fiction in English during this middle period of the twentieth century. They include what has sometimes been regarded as the archetypal work of Welsh working-class, industrial fiction, in Lewis Jones's *Cwmardy* and *We Live*, but alongside those novels, it also reveals some very different and perhaps unexpected literary voices, such as the ironic male ventriloquism of Dorothy Edwards in *Rhapsody* (1927) or the Grand Guignol Expressionism of Gwyn Thomas's *The Dark Philosophers* (1946). Raymond Williams argued in his influential work *The Welsh Industrial Novel*[2] that Welsh writers, emerging from a largely working-class, industrial background in the earlier twentieth century, had, in effect, to reinvent the bourgeois genre of the novel to suit their own experiences. Williams, writing as a novelist himself, was no doubt correct in this diagnosis, but the range of texts represented in this volume shows that the reinvention of form itself was a metamorphosis into a number of different shapes. What is also notable is that the short story has been a particularly attractive form for Anglophone fiction writers, perhaps because of its very malleability.

In keeping with the diversity of the fiction analysed, the

critics who contributed to this volume have adopted varying critical approaches. The first essay, Stephen Knight's "'On Stony Ground': Rhys Davies's *The Withered Root*' (1927) presents a contextualised re-evaluation of Davies's important first novel. Focusing on religion, women and politics, Knight shows how *The Withered Root* can be seen as a subtle and often conflictual response to his origins by a Rhondda writer beginning to forge a space for himself in the literary marketplace. Appearing in the same year as Davies's novel, Dorothy Edwards's volume of short stories, *Rhapsody*, initially appears to belong to an entirely different world. Though Edwards came from a not dissimilar background to Davies, as Tony Brown demonstrates in his essay 'Narrating Marginality: Dorothy Edwards's *Rhapsody*,' she creates, as he goes on to argue in his detailed stylistic analysis, out of her own personal experience of loneliness an unsettling, distinctively Modernist representation of the anomie of the age. Ironically enough, *Country Dance*, which appeared five years later, is much more overtly Welsh in setting and theme, yet it was written by an Englishwoman with strong Welsh affinities, Margiad Evans. Malcolm Ballin in his essay '*Country Dance* (1932) by Margiad Evans: Text, Paratext and Context' initially encourages us as readers to pay close attention to the book itself as object, and to profit from the insights such a materialist approach can bring. He then offers a detailed reading of the text and a valuable contextualisation, where we can see Margiad Evans participating in the newly emerging Anglophone periodical culture of Wales in the 1930s. Lewis Jones's *Cwmardy* (1937) and its sequel, *We Live* (1939), again offer a stark contrast to the neo-Romanticism of Margiad Evans; Alyce von Rothkirch's essay 'Liberty and the Party Line: "Novelising" Working-class History in Lewis Jones's *Cwmardy* and *We Live*" gives an admirably full account of Jones's life as a political activist and the relation between that brief life and the two novels he produced in it. She argues that 'the impact of the novels cannot well be measured by aesthetic criteria alone' and that Jones's achievement in honestly dramatising the tensions between a devotion to the Party and personal liberty is a not inconsiderable one. Gwyn Thomas's style and his representation of life in the South Wales Valleys is very different from Lewis Jones's; eschewing the latter's documentary realism, Thomas forges an idiosyncratic Expressionist style, as Laura Wainwright elucidates in her essay '"A Hell of a Howl": Gwyn Thomas's *The Dark Philosophers* (1946) and "the language of the cry"'. By comparing Thomas's style with that adopted by European visual artists, Wainwright shows how Thomas can be regarded as a Welsh artist in the vanguard of European writing, while also revealing how cross-medium comparison can be truly illuminating. Steve Hendon's essay '"Everything is fluid in me": A Postcolonial Approach to Alun Lewis's *In The Green Tree*' (1948) picks up on one of the most influential recent trends in criticism of Welsh writing, showing how Alun Lewis's work can be understood as the attempts by a Welsh poet and short story writer to come to terms with his anomalous position as a soldier of empire. Another poet's prose work is considered by Matthew Jarvis in his essay 'In and Beyond the City: The Places of Dannie Abse's *Ash on a Young Man's Sleeve*' (1954). Jarvis takes an environmentalist approach to the text, revealing how the places mapped in Abse's autobiographical volume actually take us beyond suburban Cardiff to intersect with rural Wales and the spaces of the Jewish diaspora. A year later, North Wales is the setting of Emyr Humphreys's ferocious Gothic novel, discussed magisterially in M. Wynn Thomas's essay '"A huge assembling of unease": readings in *A Man's Estate*'. Seeing it as, in one sense, a 'classical Welsh Calvinist tragedy', Thomas demonstrates how the novel stems from Humphreys's awakening to his own position as a 'subaltern colonial subject' but, with some understatement, concedes that 'nationalism is not given an easy ride' in the novel. Like Abse's *Ash on a Young Man's Sleeve*, which appears to be so firmly rooted in the Cardiff suburbs, Humphreys's novel so fixed in its North Welsh 'milltir sgwar' is shown to reflect a 'Europe-wide post war crisis'. In a rich contextualisation of Humphreys's work, Thomas also positions him *vis-à-vis* his English contemporaries and shows how the American novelist Faulkner was an important influence. Humphreys has been the most prominent Welsh novelist to embrace a realist aesthetic, one which is also embraced and defended theoretically by Raymond Williams, as Daniel Williams discusses in his essay "Writing Against the Grain": Raymond Williams's *Border Country* and the Defence of Realism'. Published in 1960, but the product of a long and difficult gestation throughout the 1950s, *Border Country* is seen as 'an attempt at substantiating a new realism' through new ways of constructing vision and voice. In this regard, the chapter is valuable also for revealing the congruence between Raymond Williams's theoretical writings and his fictional experiments. Just as 'the problem of form' was a constant preoccupation for Raymond Williams, Brenda Chamberlain can be seen as a writer who transgressed the boundaries of form in her published writings, as David Lloyd argues in his essay 'Against "Journalese": Form and Style in Brenda Chamberlain's *A Rope of Vines*' (1965). He explores the ways in which Chamberlain subverts readerly expectations of the form of the 'journal'; eschewing context and explanation, she 'forces the reader into direct experience of the present'. It is interesting to reflect here that two of the female authors whose work is discussed in this volume both chose the form of the journal or diary to write their fictions (Margiad Evans's *Country Dance* and Chamberlain's *Rope of Vines*). Certainly Evans's construction of Ann's book in her novella can also be said to 'force the reader into direct experience of the present', especially with its distinctive use of the present tense.

However, might the choice of form also be regarded as influenced by gender? One might argue that the journal is a characteristic genre of the private realm, associated with domesticity and therefore, historically, with the domain of women. It may be that women writers even in the twentieth century are still drawn to the genre for these reasons but, at the same time, as the examples of Evans and Chamberlain clearly demonstrate, are more than willing to transform that traditional genre in interesting and challenging ways. The last two essays in the volume both focus on the use and abuse of the body in novels of the 1970s. Sarah Morse's essay '"Maimed individuals": the significance of the body in *So Long, Hector Bebb*' (1970) explains how this multi-vocal novel dramatises how the body of the boxer effects the 'conversion of physical into economic capital', using 'the motif of boxing [to] reveal the infrastructures of society'. Michelle Smith's essay '"It was forbidden, strictly forbidden": Contesting Taboo in Bernice Rubens' *I Sent a Letter to My Love*' (1975), noting the persistently discomfiting nature of Rubens' fiction, shows how taboos regarding language, sexual and gender behaviour, and, especially, disability are constantly challenged in a novel which can be regarded as 'a subversive rewriting that has the capacity to imagine power emanating from the margins'.

The essays in this volume indicate the range and diversity of critical approaches current in contemporary Wales. In the past, autobiographical and biographical approaches have held sway (for example, in Glyn Jones's *The Dragon Has Two Tongues* and in the Writers of Wales series) and biographical context forms an important part of each of these essays. But the critics represented here also show their scholarly, comparative, postcolonial, historicist, psychoanalytical, feminist, structuralist, environmental and, of course, literary credentials, in a collection which we hope will serve both the needs and the aspirations of a new generation of critics of Welsh writing in English.

NOTES
1   Jones, *The First Forty Years* (Cardiff: University of Wales Press, 1957), pp. 8–9.
2   Raymond Williams, *The Welsh Industrial novel* (Cardiff: University College Cardiff Press, 1979).

'On Stony Ground':

Rhys Davies's *The Withered Root*

Stephen Knight

> Behold, there went out a sower to sow. And it came to
> pass, as he sowed, some fell by the way side, and the
> fowls of the air came and devoured it up. And some fell
> on stony ground, where it had not much earth; and
> immediately it sprang up, because it had no depth of
> earth. But when the sun was up, it was scorched; and
> because it had no root, it withered away. (Gospel
> according to St Mark, 4, 3–6)

Producing *The Withered Root*

The Withered Root (1927) was Rhys Davies's first novel,
written some eight years after he left the Rhondda to find
a life in London and literature.[1] Most commentators hurry
over it to discuss his many short stories and the richly
varied novels – notably *Rings on Her Fingers* (1930), a
South Wales Madame Bovary story, the emotive industrial
trilogy *Honey and Bread* (1935), *A Time to Laugh* (1937)
and *Jubilee Blues* (1938), the ironic rural myth of *The Black
Venus* (1944), the Dylan Thomas focused *The Perishable
Quality* (1957) and the posthumously published *Ram with
Red Horns* (1996), a 1960s-set dark comedy: Davies was
a committed and productive writer who commanded sales
and admiration in Britain and America.

Those who do pause over *The Withered Root* tend to
understand it as a preliminary to a simplistic reading of
Davies's later positions, reading him as London-based, anti-
religious and largely apolitical, with a commitment to fine
writing and a general if distant sympathy for Wales, and
clearly, though covertly, homosexual. Accordingly, they read
the novel as being about a sensitive young man with the

same initials as Rhys Davies, who has very little in common with his working-class parents, goes down the pit, hates both it and the industrial culture in general, in compensation over-stresses his spiritual side by becoming a revivalist preacher, as a result is exhausted and disillusioned; he is also recurrently tempted by women, and is finally destroyed when he fails in both religion and passion.

This chapter will argue that such a view of *The Withered Root* is limited and naïve about both the novel and its author, and that in particular his assessment in it of religion, women and politics is a good deal more comprehensive and complex than the standard response to the novel would suggest.

Essentially, *The Withered Root* is a mythic story, about Wales, and talent, and religion, and passion; Reuben Daniels is a figure who wavers between tragic misdirection and self-indulgent culpability. The novel is an elegy for what Rhys Davies did not become, a powerful evocation of the ways in which a context can imprison and destroy talents and feelings in ordinary people, and also extraordinary ones. The partner to *The Withered Root* is *Tomorrow to Fresh Woods*: published in 1941 after Davies had established himself, it tells the story of a Rhondda boy very like himself, who grows up in a turbulent, sensual, ugly – and also fascinating – world that he has transcended as a sensitive young writer. Its title deploys the last line of *Lycidas*, Milton's elegy to a young writer: in both poem and novel the phrase, like Davies's later novel, proclaims the forward-looking confidence of the living writer, where the title of the earlier novel went back to Jesus's parable of the sower for a sense of tragic lost potential – as does the body of the text of *Lycidas*.

But pain can bring power. *Tomorrow to Fresh Woods* is a fine fluent read, and Davies liked it enough to re-use sequences in *Print of a Hare's Foot*, yet its feel-good quality also reduces fictional tension. *The Withered Root* is the stronger novel, a masterpiece of modernist tragic realisation, controlling a raw power like that of Hardy's *Jude the Obscure* through a well-developed four-book structure, with a subtly varying point of view and revelling in rich, pointed language and imagery – for example, the Cardiff tram that scuttled 'along like a green rat'.[2] It was a book good enough to make even D. H. Lawrence want to meet the author.

Readings of *The Withered Root*

The standard readings, working back from the later Davies, and crucially not separating Reuben Daniels from Rhys Davies, find it an inherently negative book, in three main ways, all evidenced in one of the fullest treatments of the novel, an essay by James A. Davies.[3] The commonest response is to see it as 'an anti-religious book', an ultimately hostile account of the Welsh Nonconformist revival of 1904–5,[4] taking Reuben Daniels as a version of the charismatic Evan Roberts, South Welsh miner and preacher extraordinaire who led the revival until becoming exhausted – in ways never clarified.[5]

A second area of negative impact for commentators is that the politics of the novel appear hostile not just to the exploitative character of the mining industry but also to the culture that was produced by that world – labourism, self-education, sport, and singing. James Davies states that in not dealing with the common topics of the South Welsh industrial novel, it shows a 'strange defiance of the Zeitgeist', and Daniel Williams, with reference to *The Withered Root*, says '[u]ltimately, industrialization is itself a profoundly un-Welsh development for Davies'.[6]

A third target of the book, most commentators feel, is women: James Davies says that Reuben has 'a series of confrontations with sexually predatory women',[7] and implies that from his drunkard mother, through the prostitute Ann, the beautiful Eirwen and the religiose and sex-obsessed Catherine Pritchards, he is beset on all sides –

a gay self-justification seems also to be implied by the critic.

All three of these positions are in need of considerable revision and elaboration, both in general terms of Davies's work and in terms of detailed analysis of the novel. This detail will follow in three sections about religion, women and politics, but the general points that question these assumptions might be raised briefly first as a context for the detail.

To start with, the novel does not describe a *rite de passage* out of Wales: Reuben Daniels dies returning to the valley. And his position is hardly that of Rhys Davies, in spite of the initials. The author never went down the pit or had working-class parents – he was a grocer's son, with a schoolteacher mother; he was indeed interested in religion but moved from the excitable Nonconformists to the cooler Church of England and then to atheism, keeping (after one inspection) well away from revivalism.[8] Basically he was interested in literature, which only briefly and ineffectively crosses Reuben's horizon.

In any case, the Revival does not start until half-way through the book: it and Evan Roberts are used as instruments by which Davies explores both the Wales he has left and the forces that lead to what he himself described as 'the disintegration of a young man'.[9]

In terms of politics, Davies later remained strongly sympathetic to the plight and the actions of the miners, as he shows fully in both his industrial trilogy and his non-fiction, *My Wales* and *The Story of Wales*, as well as many stories,[10] but his account, as will be explored below, is different from the sentimental populism of Jack Jones or the communist rigour of Lewis Jones.[11]

The suggestion of being anti-woman is the least credible of these charges. In later life Davies was evidently homosexual but had many long-lasting and close friendships with women, wrote about them with real power and sympathy, and throughout his work used them sympathetically as focal characters in many of his short stories, starting in *The Song of Songs*, in the same year as *The Withered Root*, and continuing through the stories, as Katie Gramich has shown,[12] and notably in two of his most powerful novels, *Jubilee Blues* and *The Black Venus*.

An analysis of *The Withered Root* will show that the simplistic attitudes questioned here are based on misunderstandings and misreadings, generated in particular by a failure to separate the viewpoint of Reuben Daniels from that of the text and, by implication, the author. The text does not by any means endorse the views and especially the actions of Reuben, but rather sees him as making a series of mistakes, partly through the failure of those around him to give him adequate support – in terms of the parable, his roots are too shallow – and also through his own agency – the heat of his own passionate and misguided nature that primarily destroys his shallow-rooted potential for fertile growth.

Re-reading *The Withered Root*

Religion
Rhys Davies himself seemed to invite the reading of the novel as focused on religion when, in *Print of a Hare's Foot,* he described its theme as 'warfare between religious spirit and carnal flesh, with spirit a heavy loser'.[13] However, in the words of the friend he made on the basis of this novel, D. H. Lawrence, 'Never trust the artist. Trust the tale.'[14] The novel shows with some subtlety that the spiritual and the carnal have a good deal more in common than is comfortable, and the real loser is the gifted young man who cannot either combine or control them.

As a young man Reuben Daniels is very interested in religion, and this seems both the result of and an escape from his bleak home life. Religion is present in Reuben's home: at first his father vacillates between chapel and drink; as his mother drinks more, the father becomes increasingly religious, but this basically involves sitting silently at home reading his Bible. Reuben's religion is at first more interactive: when he meets the dying and atheistic Philip he longs to 'bring the love of Christ into his life' (56), and as Katie Gramich comments 'he starts out on his spiritual journey with the idea of attempting "to lessen the sorrows of the world"'.[15] But his spiritual mode is also heavily sensual: walking the dingy streets at night he feels 'There is a wound in the bodies of men, and the blood flows out drop by drop, staining the world' (64). Acceptable as this might seem in the context of affective preaching and charismatic religion, it must remind readers of the eerie sequence of Reuben's interests as a child – at first 'a sullen cruelty' (17) where he drowns and autopsies kittens, cooks a mouse and likes slaughterhouses; calmed by walking on the mountains with his father he is enthused by the minister's excitability and red face and notices that 'the vein on his forehead stood out, I thought it was going to burst' (18). Religion channels his extreme, erratic and potentially cruel sensuality.

When he turns to revivalist preaching, it is, the novel carefully tells us, as a result of rejecting sensual passion at the human level. The key scene is when he and Eirwen – tall, beautiful, also talented, as a singer in her case – go like other couples down 'The Lane'. Reuben muses timidly about their life together: 'Like a little heaven on earth it will be. A home of our own, where we'll have books and a piano and a cat and peaceful meals in the evening' (96). He can only kiss her with 'a gentle, chaste desire' but she is kindled into passion: he is alarmed, seeing her mouth as 'a sucking grimace', a source of 'Evil, evil ...' (97). Eirwen responds, with some credibility, 'Thought you were a man I did' (98).

It is in the very next scene that Reuben is encouraged towards revivalism with the Corinthians, one of those marginal sects that Gwyn Thomas would later mock memorably (as in *The World Cannot Hear You*, 1951), and in a moment of intense, sexualised, sensuality he is inspired to speak: 'through his mind swept flashes of blue light, fiery wheels and phrases printed in lightning. Then his body was pressed between burning stones, wet hair seemed to sway into his mind, and he was entangled in long whorls of curling radiance' (131).

Carnality is sublimated, Reuben takes up his task, and the novel moves into a re-enactment of the revival of 1904–5. At first, the revival seems without negative features: the opening scene in the Corinthians' chapel is both a brilliant piece of emotive realism – Davies has so many skills that his simple power to create an involving scene tends to be overlooked – and also a representation of deeply felt religion: 'Here were people who displayed their religion with proud and fervent emotion, and in their prayers there was the utter abasement of the poor human being before the mystery of the Divine' (107). This is judged from Reuben's viewpoint, but here at least the text does not contradict him.

As the story of the revival develops, however, Davies consistently cuts across religious excitement with dry negation: 'They had come for fire to warm their stale souls and they must not be denied it' (152); the converts 'declare their successful entrance to bliss' (154); a woman writhes on her back 'fluttering little screams of ecstasy', her mouth foams and she writhes 'as though she were in an orgasm of pleasure' (181). Equally gesturing are features like the obsessive counting of converts,[16] the evident self-importance of Reuben's handlers and most specifically the way in which Catherine Pritchards, the over-sized and over-dressed hymn-singer, works herself up in parallel excitement, spiritual and physical. When, overdosed on elderberry wine, she visits Reuben's bedroom, her language of seduction is that favourite of emotive religion from twelfth-century St Bernard on, 'The Song of Songs'.[17]

Reuben has huge success – Morgans, his effective manager, calls him 'a young saint' (255) – but the same promotional care makes him feel like 'an eccentric star performer in a play' (270); that the indoor meetings have 'an awful atmosphere' and that 'people attend as they would at a circus where they'll be able to perform themselves' (263). As a result 'the style of his sermons [became] more stern and sombre' (278) and – he still responds sensually – 'A sick ache surged through him' (282). He finds relief only in nature, bathing naked in a pool and, literally, hugging a tree, but even this, from his unreliable viewpoint, is sensualised: 'The thick jet of desire sprang unappeased within the inner walls of his being ... The rough bark seemed to yield into soft and sleek tissue against his body' (284).

There are several responses he tries to make to his situation. The first denies religion. He visits the home of the child who has been killed in a revivalist stampede and can finally only say to the mother that his prayer for her 'would not bring a shred of lasting comfort to your mourning soul. Deceit, vanity and deceit' (288). Feeling that he is losing these layers of deceit, he goes home and reads a book by the stoic humanist Walter Savage Landor, stating 'The season of life, leading you by the hand, will not permit you to linger at the tomb of the departed' (289); Reuben feels 'he had stayed too long amid the tombs of life' (289) and 'there was a final flame of pure life in the core of the world that he had not pierced to yet' (290). The poem he reads from, 'Pericles and Aspasia', was published in 1836 by Landor: never a mainstream author, he was very highly regarded by Swinburne and Havelock Ellis, whose opinions were likely to have impressed Davies, especially Swinburne, an aesthetically sensitive writer, whose classicism and humanism, even his acculturated radicalism, bear some resemblance to his own positions and those he is expressing through Philip Vaughan.[18] But Reuben is quite unable to engage with this material, either intellectually or in practice.

At once he is offered a chance to practise this model of stoic secular value: called home after his father's death in a pit accident, he assesses the dead man, telling his mother 'He did not think enough of the earth. He looked to Heaven for happiness, and there should have been joy for him here' (300). That seems Landorian enough. But Reuben's own chance of following the advice is ruined, through repeating his previous behaviour to Eirwen in a new and extreme variation. When she visits the house Eirwen says 'I should have waited for you,' and when he visits her, now physically fired up in the absence of his religious displacement, she allows him to seduce her. But the real quotidian world in which she always lives means she still feels committed to the husband she reluctantly married in the absence of any commitment from Reuben. He is rejected by her because of her own fidelity to the results of his previous rejection of her. So the negative power of religion reaches beyond his abandonment of it, and condemns him to his melodramatic, out-of-control final sequences where again he is unable to accept the comfort of partnership with the woman he meets on his deranged journey to Cardiff.

Religion is seen as negative basically as an unnatural sublimation of desire, and through the special lens of the revival and the experiences of Evan Roberts. He too left the crusade, though the reasons have never been clear – he certainly was against the more mechanistic and melodramatic responses of his audience, and undoubtedly suffered from exhaustion, but the self-censorship of contemporary and later accounts has never allowed for an explanation of his withdrawal to Leicester, under the protection of a woman revivalist, nor his lengthy and mostly quiet subsequent life in Cardiff, with only token contact with forms of religion, until his death in 1951. Roberts is only an excellent mechanism for the development of Davies's story, not its topic.

Not all about religion is negative. Rhys Davies seems to remember his youth with at least some positive thoughts, and has respect for some aspects of religion: Reuben's early

keenness to bring relief to the despairing and dying Philip
Vaughan is just the sort of friendship that Landor will later
recommend to him; Reuben's father does achieve a form of
peace in his study of the bible, and is well aware of the
risks of revivalism: he feels it is 'Unnatural' (159) and later
says 'I am afraid for you' (231). Equally, the long-bearded
baker, Morgans (perhaps based on the massively-bearded
Rev. Evan Phillips, who inspired Evan Roberts), who copies
out the Bible much as Reuben's father reads it, clearly
operates in a positive way before his revival involvement.
He bakes his fine bread for the ordinary people as 'a
natural Minister of God' (82), and he twice urges Reuben
to dilute his spiritual intensity with the normality of
marriage – 'God is in that love' he says (81), and later calls
it 'the natural pleasure of man' (267). But Reuben's
translation of the intensity of sexual passion into a religious
mode breaks, as both simple Christians fear, the vessel of
that spirit; Reuben's religion was not deeply rooted enough
and so it withered, and the major cause of that was his
difficulty in relating in a normal way to any of the four
women in his life.

Women
Reuben's mother shapes his negativity. Strong-willed, a
woman of some property, she chose his father as a
satisfactory partner – 'she was no sentimentalist' (80) – and
though 'fond of her child, in her off-hand rasping manner
... did not believe in surrounding a child with the sickly
heat of pronounced affection' (16). When she mocks
religion he bites her in a fury; his apology is met by a brief
caress, 'rare and unexpected from her' (27), and as he
responds warmly, '"Now then baby," she said mockingly,
"get off to school"' (27). His mother's real partnership is
not with her husband but her drinking companion, Mrs
Williams – 'an abundant woman with hefty arms and a
habit of glowering at a man' (8). It seems implied that this
deficit of domestic feeling – especially in the context of

Reuben's volatile nature – fuels the emotionality of his religion, very different from his father's calm faith, and though his mother is eventually, with much hesitation, herself converted, this does not outlast his father's death. Her final impact is at the end when he walks back in delirium to the Rhondda through the snow, feeling his father's spirit urge him home to see her, where 'There would be peace at last' (343). She lurches into the house, drunk, '"Reuben!" she exclaims doubtfully' (345) and he faints, hitting his head against the table, to die two days later.

If Martha's under-sexualised, under-emotionalised presence damages Reuben at the start and end of his life, a similar framing role is played by the over-sexualised Ann Roberts. Thrown out by her father for her activities as a Cardiff prostitute – the hefty-armed Mrs Williams acts as feminist resistance by rebuking him publicly for his own vices and hypocrisy – she runs off and hides. When Reuben says he 'wanted to help you' (39) she takes this sexually, and grins, but he does not understand. So she asks for money anyway, and he runs to fetch some. Responding in the only way she knows, she kisses him, with 'Say you like me' (40). As later with Eirwen, he is both stimulated and alarmed: 'Something sprang into being within him, crept like a flame to his chest, along his arms, to his mouth and eyes. But he kept rigid in her embrace' (40). They separate; he meets a friend who explains what prostitutes do; Reuben 'lay in bed that night with the mind sickened' but after reading his New Testament 'he again found comfort in the life of Jesus Christ' (41).

The sequence clarifies Reuben's qualities and dangers as innocent and over-excitable, generous and naïve, and predicts his leap from human to religious passion. Ann will return to frame his dark story when negative forces have magnified their impact, with the help of other people's exploitation of him. As he lurches, ill and delirious, through Cardiff Bay, in a sequence that appears to draw very effectively on Joyce's Nighttown sequence in Chapter 15 of

Ulysses, he meets Ann and, seeming close to his original innocence with her, with 'an emotion of gladness within him, he recognised her' (327). She looks after him, even though he tries to leave to avoid 'a harlot's pity' (329). Accepting her help increasingly and valuing her innate nobility, he still sees and speaks through the religiosity that has failed him: 'Your soul is as lovely as the dawn' (336) he says. But when she looks at him with 'a bright dreamy regard' and 'would touch him gently and lingeringly' (337) such normal, mildly erotic contact is unbearable: he feels imprisoned and 'one morning he escaped' (337) – the narration presents his viewpoint for judgement in the word 'escaped'. Ann's behaviour has more than matched his own original innocent generosity, but the banal forgiveness of sin and routine inter-human behaviour is unavailable to the hyperbolic Reuben and he makes off to the Rhondda on his last mission of quasi-heroic folly.

Between mother and prostitute, of course, in the litany of masculine stereotyping, stands girlfriend/wife. Reuben is led to meet Eirwen Vaughan only through his encounter with her seriously ill cousin, Philip: he meets him declaiming a Hamlet soliloquy on the hills, very soon after the Ann Roberts sequence. Intense, literary, sickly, seeming like a version of the D. H. Lawrence Davies so far only knew through books, Philip is for literature, against religion and in favour of the simple interactive life that Reuben very occasionally glimpses, through his father, through Morgans and in the Walt Whitman poem Philip quotes: 'I think I could turn and live with animals, they are so placid and self-contained' (113).

Philip's cousin, Eirwen – Davies would have known that her name means 'snow-white', and the implication is purity rather than a troupe of dwarves – is at once attracted to Reuben, and he to her: in his religiose way he sees 'her face was chaste and tender', but he has to insist it is 'a holy love' (77). But there is more to her: he also notices 'the sensuous lips delicately curved' and 'the quivering of her nostrils' (73). Eirwen is alive and capable of passion: at first he merely steps back and she responds to his unnatural behaviour with 'Coy you are' (74), but later his recoil from her responses will make him see her as an over-sexualised and aggressive monster – though that is from his unreliable viewpoint, not the judgement of the text and that is also like the women he sees in his overheated dreams: the negative Eirwen is his creation, not a real assessment of woman.

The novel treats this interaction as absolutely central: it is after the disastrous walk with Eirwen down Lovers' Lane that he is swept into the revival, and even more dramatically it is after he finally enacts his sexuality in a mixture of adoration of her beauty and aggressive assertion of his masculinity that, when she tells him she is still attached to his substitute, her husband, he rushes off on his fateful journey to Cardiff. For, tired of waiting for Reuben – everyone sees them as a fit couple – she has married the pub landlord's son and, in spite of his mistreatment, remains committed to him. Eirwen is very far from a 'predatory woman': the text makes her a woman of real and also everyday beauty and strength, whom Reuben is tragically unable to enlist into his life – his extreme nature and the lack of credible relational models together ruin a life of potent possibility.

Catherine Pritchards to a considerable degree condenses the roles of the soiled dove, Ann Roberts, and the potential wife, Eirwen. A revival convert who has had an illegitimate child by a minister – a previous overvaluing of religion – and a singer whose talents are exploited on the theatrical and manipulative side of the revival business, she is never seen as evil or monstrous. Like Mrs Williams or Morgans the baker, she is a character who occupies a certain position in the text, against which Reuben will define himself – as usual, negatively. Davies uses her to personalise the sensual and sexual undercurrent of the revival and while this is not unfair – the photographs of the

Evan Roberts entourage include several striking women, notably the lead singer, Annie Davies – it is selective: as Gramich notes, in fact women participants made a serious religious and organisational contribution to the revival.[19]

Like Eirwen, Catherine is no monster. She is a less than stable person who is overwhelmed by the secularisation of religion, that element which Reuben disdained, though his managers appear to have promoted. But Reuben's hyberbolic response to sexuality is also indicated, and the text clarifies that Reuben's rejection of Catherine is made from an unjustified, distorted viewpoint: 'he saw how since he had first come into contact with her, she had been subtly casting the net of her piety around him' (258–9). Here, as often, Reuben takes too willingly to the role of victim, though he is correct to remember Philip Vaughan's words about how 'In some natures the impulse of religious worship is mingled inextricably with the sexual impulse' (259): Philip had gone on to say 'especially in women', so Reuben is evidently able to exclude himself, but the text itself shows how his thoughts grow more excitedly religiose as after rejecting Catherine he turns and twists quasi-sexually in his bed, and finally, exhausted, sleeps.

Politics
Though *The Withered Root* is firmly set in the Rhondda, the heart of coal mining in South Wales, it does not share the industrial politics of the 1930s mining novels. But Davies was writing nearly a decade before Jack Jones first published, and when the only existing mining novels were the sentimental romances of Joseph Keating.[20] Davies shows no sign of following this model, nor yet the work of Allen Raine, either her treatment of the revival in *Queen of the Rushes* (1906) or her representation of industrial Merthyr in *A Welsh Witch* (1902). As Philippa Davies comments,[21] his work is more realistic in tone than the preceding Welsh romances, and the models appear to be Hardy and the French naturalists. The only apparent Welsh literary link is with Caradoc Evans:

when he later said that Evans 'had never escaped the chapel',[22] Davies indicated the major difference he felt lay between them – Evans's failure to criticise and move beyond his origins, in, he might have added, the lack of a novel that served that role like *The Withered Root*. Davies's work never has Evans's negative, even bitter, force, but early in the novel and in later fiction, when sketching humble Welsh life he often uses the inverted syntax, with a word brought forward in the sentence to be stressed, by which Evans suggests Welsh speakers' special use of English – but without Evans's mocking exaggerations and perhaps basically because this is what a London publisher and audience would have expected after the success of *My People* (1915).

But though Davies is not in the left-wing valleys novel tradition, there is a form of social politics in *The Withered Root*, as in his later work.[23] It opens with a theme which was to be central in *Honey and Bread* (1935), the grim negation of beautiful nature caused by the coal industry: Reuben's parents settled down in 'a dwelling in one of those naked rows, chiefly occupied by colliers, that rise, shrouded in grey coal-dust, on the Valley hills' (3). The context can occasionally and potently be glimpsed: Davies offers a very early statement of the classic theme of industry set against a defeated nature:

> From the back of the house, beyond the strip of garden, the mountain curved up steeply, a greyish green. In winter the winds swept down fiercely from the wide uplands, and the snow drifted, half-burying the back of the Row. A single railroad track, leading to the pit, was cut on the breast of the mountain and, about half-a-mile from the Row, the pit sprawled, an amorphous collection of dim sheds and structures coated thickly with black dust, the tall chimney stacks rising up barrenly, some issuing from them slowly like black thin banners of submission. (6–7)

The people are also submissive to the forces of industry, in their drinking and in their hopes of escape through the chapel. The difficult lives of the people are a recurrent if marginal presence – Old Morgans revels in that fact that through his skill and devotion to his trade 'the loaves of the hungry people shall come forth brown' (80). Davies shows how their circumstances are a direct cause of their vulnerability to the emotional colour of revival:

> Yes, they were God's children, they would not be orphans any longer, every cell in their bodies loved the Father who sat enthroned above all earthly splendour and promised them rewards more eternal than earth could give. Money, a mansion, holidays, clothes, foreign lands – bah, what were they compared to the bliss in Paradise that they were earning by praying thus on their poverty-clad knees? (152–3)

This uses irony for, not against, the ordinary people, but there is none of either kind in a sequence of naturalism that could come from Davies's much admired Zola: it occurs when Reuben visits a dying man whose wife has accepted revival: 'Near the refuse tip of the colliery is a collection of old, black cottages where live the very poor' (203). As Reuben prays, his 'voice was as clear and resonant as a bell' (205) but the scene explodes very differently in chaos and malice as the children fight, the wife rages and the husband is not improved: 'His peevish eyes looked out cunningly from the grey dough of his puffed-out flesh' (207). Far from the rumbustious events of Jack Jones or the world-changing plans of Lewis Jones, the scene, rather unusual in this hero-focused novel, seethes with the pain and dysfunction of industrial exploitation.

While the novel can at times realise the context, including mining work, it does not go into the socioeconomic why and how of their exploitation. *The Withered Root* has no engagement with the politics of mining or its world at any level: it exemplifies as well as any of Davies's work Philippa Davies's comment, 'the essential dynamic of society for Davies is not the struggle between classes but the struggle of the individual for self-determination'.[24] But Davies did not separate himself from the industry: when, later on, he sought a pseudonym he called himself 'Owen Pitman',[25] and in his books *My Wales* and *The Story of Wales* he shows both a strong awareness of the problems of the depression and admiration of the resistance to it.

Within *The Withered Root* and elsewhere in his work there is another area in which Davies engages to some degree with industry and resistance, but just as the trilogy *Honey and Bread*, *A Time to Laugh* and *Jubilee Blues* tends to move away from organised politics into a politicisation of the self, Davies's sense of politics relates to his own generalised, over-historicised, but clearly strongly felt condensing of modern politics into a long view of Welshness and what it stood for. Presumably it was in this spirit that he changed the spelling of his name from Rees to Rhys, referring no doubt to the Lord Rhys, famous thirteenth-century prince of South Wales.

Davies is fond of tracing events in the narrative back to a distant and valued past that is still felt to be pervasive in what he sees as Welsh attitudes: Eirwen sings to her family 'old Welsh folk-songs – melodies full of Celtic longing and hopelessness, love-songs that seemed to swoon with their melancholy music' (92). In a revival meeting the people 'sang with all the emotional abandonment of the Welsh' (178) and when Reuben preaches 'The old fearful soul of the Welsh recognised him: ever through the ages there had been men such as he – poets, bards, seers, prophets born to the simple, worshipping people, reared among them and at the suitable period arising to open the scroll of their ancient talent' (194). It is a deeply populist, even *gwerin* position, without any functionalist concept like the welfare state or a level playing-field for democratic personal development.

Daniel Williams has written about this telescoping of history as being characteristic of the late nineteenth-century 'Celtic twilight' approach being used by writers like Matthew Arnold, Davies and D. H. Lawrence 'as a means of exposing the narrow materialism of their contemporary societies'.[26]

The position certainly withdraws from any modern rationalist politics, but this does not mean it cannot sympathise with modern resistance: rather, Davies draws on his trans-historical simplifications to link the hunger-marchers with 'their forebears who fought locally for the means to live'.[27]

This is a highly idealist set of politics, and one easily made into a basis for individual consolation rather than collective resistance, but it is not in fact conservative, and has surviving power. Though it seems to act as a writer's retrospective affection for his homeland, it resembles not so much repressive conservative sentiment as the loosely historicist personalised politics of modern post-industrial England, where Henry VIII and Queen Boudicca seem more discussed and more real than the actual founders of British modernity like William Beveridge and Aneurin Bevan.

There is another, related, layer of value-judgement in The Withered Root which has also flourished in modern times. As Reuben leaves the Corinthians' chapel wondering about the call to revival, he walks to his other pole of possibility, Eirwen's family farm. About him wisdom is embodied, but not humanly so:

> The hills crouched like long supple beasts asleep and over them the wide sky stretched in a vast and flawless arch of darkness; tranquil peace lay over the Valley and as he climbed higher his soul becomes more calm.
> He thought: Here the Voice of God is heard best. (109–10)

Similarly, after Reuben's first great success in revivalism, when he sits with 'his eyes strained out and inscrutable' he

> went out and trembled as the cool air touched his burning head.
> The mountains were like black robes flung against the misty sky, and he lifted his head and breathed in the night, conscious of the great pure spaces above him. (188)

Like any modern nature-lover, or ecologist, Reuben can be calmed by nature, but it cannot with any finality heal his inner turmoil, and at the end its fury accompanies his walk to Cardiff and in even worse form his fatal return. Reuben may sense the genial animality of nature, but his own beasts of passion are not supple and will not sleep; the peace that he consistently seeks, finally at home with his mother, will elude him.

Like racial history, the appeal of nature was another of the forces that flowed into the space vacated as religion became less and less convincing in the later nineteenth and early twentieth centuries, and it is another recourse that Reuben cannot make use of, though the novel and Davies offer it here as a potential position of value. In this, Davies differs from the Lawrence to whom he is often linked, and looks in fact towards Hardy and his sense of the immanent power of nature. Jeff Wallace stresses that where Lawrence uses nature as a force that creates or matches drama in the characters, Davies finds in nature a real resolution of conflict – though it is true that in Reuben's fateful odyssey to and from Cardiff a Lawrentian aura of pathetic fallacy dominates the natural world about him.[28] But even the unquestioned force of natural politics cannot save Reuben from his combination of shallow roots and undue heat.

Many may still find it hard to travel with Davies in his imagined post-political world – largely because such a domain has been so negatively realised today – but as to his vision of a world of natural wisdom, of mythically embodied antique wiseness in the ambient world of nature, there would be many today who would share his views. And on the basis of this novel, that is not only because he imagined his themes vividly, but because he had the capacity to write them with such persuasive elegance.

As Reuben lies dead, his mother, who is, like the hills, still there, sees his face as that 'of one for whom life had not yet begun' (345). But for the writer who was Rhys Davies it was the beginning, and a powerful imagining of separation from what he feared a clever young Welshman might be reduced to in a world where, as he saw it, passion only lay in religion and sexuality. Later on he would find positive figures on which to base those values – the calm, literary Penry in *Tomorrow to Fresh Woods*, the larger-than-life yet absolutely real old-world Dr William Price, a modern Merlin who stalks through Rhys Davies' parents' Rhondda in *Print of a Hare's Foot* and recurs in Davies's thoughts. And most of all, and so resolving the crisis of male gendering so powerfully and painfully realised in *The Withered Root*, he found it in the compassionate, amusing, even inspired women who are the foci of most of his later work.

Rhys Davies knew his Bible, as almost everyone in Wales then did. The title is easy enough: Reuben fell on stony ground, he flowered too soon and was consumed in his own fires. Later characters would be deep enough to flourish, either in their Welsh past or in Rhys Davies's delving imagination. But the novel's key force is the mother, and here coincide Davies's understanding through reviewing his own life and that from his reading in psychology of what it meant that she was still there at the end. Reuben was the oldest son of the patriarch Jacob, but he was disinherited when he had sex with Jacob's own concubine, the mother of his step-brothers. In both the Old Testament and *The Withered Root*, Reuben's life was sowed on bitter ground; but his own passionate seed itself fell on stony ground and both Reubens were destroyed by one sexual adventure, though the modern writer needs euphemistically to split the one woman into mother and potential wife.

As Freud was to show, psychology is very close to literature.[29] Though Reuben is a preacher (where Penry will be a writer), the novel is still haunted by literariness, well beyond the Bible. Philip Vaughan preferred the cool head of Hamlet and the steady mind of Emerson, but when Reuben in the same vein dallies with Landor's classical humanism, it has no meaning, for he cannot enact its message that there is 'a final flame of pure life in the core of the world that he had not pierced to yet' (290). Morgans in his bakery, his father at his Bible, even the fated Philip with his books, may have touched supreme simplicity, but Reuben cannot achieve such self-sublimation. Reuben Daniels is not only tragic, hyper-passionate, over-assertive and over-sensitive at the same time: he also has the thin skin and the deep imagination of a writer: Davies wrote to his friend, Charles Lahr, that Reuben was 'one of those elemental poets'.[30] But where he is a failed writer, destroyed by his over-emphasis on feeling and his fear of sexual commitment, and so never able to access his personal grail of peace, by constructing him and charting his errors of passionate commission and humane omission, Rhys Davies was able, at first through the negative construction of the failed RD, to establish himself as a long-lasting, deeply insightful, endlessly charitable writer, whose own root struck deep and long flourished in European culture, including that of Wales.

NOTES

1   The dates of Davies's travels, first to Barry and Cardiff and then London, are not certain: his account of the early years in *Print of a Hare's Foot* (London: Heinemann, 1969) is deliberately vague. It is clear that he was born in 1901, not 1903 as he sometimes suggested; it appears he left home in Blaenclydach soon after the end of the First World War, as Penry the future writer does in the autobiographical novel *Tomorrow to Fresh Woods* (London: Heinemann, 1941).

2   Rhys Davies, *The Withered Root* (Cardigan: Parthian, 2007 [1927]), p. 325. All further references to the novel will be given parenthetically in the essay.

3   James A. Davies '"Love ... and the Need of it": Three Novels by Rhys Davies', in Meic Stephens, ed., *Rhys Davies: Decoding the Hare* (Cardiff: University of Wales Press, 2001), pp. 191–204.

4   The 'anti-religious' comment is by James Davies, p. 193. The

dramatic 'Revival' involved emotional preaching and mass conversions across much of Wales, starting in the south; there had been a famous instance of the same phenomenon in 1859 as well as a number of minor revivals. One outbreak of the revival was depicted with some coolness by 'Allen Raine' in *Queen of the Rushes* (London: Hutchinson, 1906: reprinted Dinas Powys: Honno, 1998), which Davies presumably knew, but the two novels are very different. The wide range of writing about the revival in Welsh and English is discussed by Katie Gramich, 'Dehongli'r Diwygiad: ymateb awduron Cymreig i Ddiwygiad 1904–05' *Taliesin*, 128 (2006), pp. 12–28; as 'Gender, National Identity and Religion in Wales: Literary Representations of Welsh Religious Revival' this paper was given in English at a conference in Cardiff in 2008.

5   Davies reads the novel as fully based on Evan Roberts, the leader of the 1904–5 revival, in the same way that Davies's *The Painted King* (1954) is based on Ivor Novello; see Davies, in Stephens, ed., 2001, pp. 191–96.

6   Davies, in Stephens, ed., 2001, 191; Daniel Williams, 'Withered Roots: Ideas of Race in the Writings of Rhys Davies and D. H. Lawrence,' in Stephens., ed., 2001, pp. 87–103 (98).

7   Davies, in Stephens, ed., 2001, p. 193.

8   For his brief and unimpressed glimpse of revivalism, see *Print of a Hare's Foot*, pp. 63–4.

9   In a letter to Charles Lahr in 1929, quoted in J. Lawrence Mitchell, '"I Wish I Had a Trumpet": Rhys Davies and the Creative Impulse', in Belinda Humfrey, ed., *Fire Green as Grass* (Llandysul: Gomer, 1985), pp. 96–111; reprinted in Stephens, ed., 2001, pp. 147–61 (147).

10 Dai Smith discusses the stories as 'an engaged account of this people's swirling life' based on an inherently political understanding of their lives in 'Rhys Davies and his "Turbulent Valley"', in Stephens, ed. 2001, pp. 29–39 (36).

11 For a discussion of Davies's attitudes to the coal industry in Wales see Stephen Knight, '"Not a Place for Me": Rhys Davies's Fiction and the Coal Industry', in Stephens, ed. 2001, pp. 54–70.

12 Rhys Davies's *The Song of Songs* (London: Archer, 1927), a small collection of stories, has as its main theme how women cope in a spirited and often cunning way with their

circumstances. In the title story a strong woman who cares for an ill father chooses her own future by marrying a meek but wealthy shop-owner, having chosen to be impregnated by a large handsome miner. On the stories see Katie Gramich, 'The Masquerade of Gender in the Stories of Rhys Davies', in Stephens, ed. 2001, pp. 205–15.

13 Rhys Davies, *Print of a Hare's Foot* (London: Heinemann, 1969), p. 119.

14 The famous comment is variously worded by commentators but this is how he put it in *Studies in Classic American Literature* (New York: Selzer, 1923), p. 3.

15 Gramich, 'Dehongli'r Diywgiad', p. 25: the author's translation.

16 Davies is simply reporting a fact: newspapers carried scores of them linked to places. Blaenavon had 1200 but Bedwas as few as 50; merely 45 for Porthcawl but 509 in Penarth. See Kevin Adams and Emyr Jones, *A Pictorial History of Revival* (Farnham: CWR, 2004), unpaginated.

17 Mitchell describes Davies's use of 'The Song of Songs' here and as the title of his 1927 collection of short stories as 'a linguistic bridge from divine to human love'; see p. 149. However, the short story of that name is a darkly ironic use of the title as the woman 'beloved' is briskly, and liberatingly, self-serving; see note 12.

18 Algernon Swinburne, whom Davies would surely have found interesting as a sensualist and technically brilliant poet with strong French interests, wrote the essay on Landor for the 1882 9th edition of the *Encyclopaedia Britannica*, while Ellis – whose sexological interests may also have attracted Davies's attention – wrote a fulsome 'Introductory Note' on Landor's major prose work *Imaginary Conversations* (London: Scott, 1886), pp. vii–xxiv in *Camelot Classics*, a series edited by Ernest Rhys, whom Davies very probably came to know in Welsh circles in literary London.

19 Gramich, 'Dehongli'r Diwygiad', p. 13.

20 For a discussion of these authors see Stephen Knight, *A Hundred Years of Fiction, Writing Wales in English Series* (Cardiff: University of Wales Press, 2004), pp. 25–28 and 75–82.

21 See Philippa Davies, 'Introduction' to *Ram with Red Horns* (Bridgend: Seren, 1996), pp. 5–10; on p. 8 she speaks of Davies as dealing with life which is 'average and commonplace'.

22 *My Wales,* p. 217.
23 On this aspect of Davies's work, see Stephen Knight, '"Not a Place for Me": Rhys Davies's Fiction and the Coal Industry', in Stephens, ed., 2001, pp. 54–70.
24 Philippa Davies, p. 8.
25 Owen Pitman, *Two Loves I Have* (London: Cape, 1933).
26 Williams, p. 94.
27 Rhys Davies, *My Wales* (London: Jarrolds, 1937), p. 138.
28 Jeff Wallace, 'Lawrentianisms: Rhys Davies and D. H. Lawrence', in Stephens, ed., 2001, pp. 175–90, see pp. 184–88; 'pathetic fallacy' is a somewhat old-fashioned term for the trope where the natural world is used to realise the feelings of the individual as if involved in a sort of sympathy.
29 Davies's relation with Freud's theories remains unstudied: he is unlikely to have been unaware of the impact of psychology on modern writing – Virginia Woolf's essay called, in its revised form, 'Modern Fiction', which asserts, among more general ideas, the importance for the novel of 'the dark places of psychology', appeared in *The Times Literary Supplement* in 1925.
30 Quoted in Mitchell, in Stephens, ed., 2001, p. 148.

Narrating Marginality:

Dorothy Edwards's _Rhapsody_

Tony Brown

Dorothy Edwards was born and spent her early years in Ogmore Vale, near Bridgend in Glamorgan, a village which at the time of her birth in 1903 was a thriving mining community, its life governed by the social and economic rhythms of the South Wales coal industry. Her father, Edward Edwards, however, while an active socialist who counted Keir Hardie, the pioneering Labour MP for Merthyr, among his many political friends, was not a collier but a primary school headmaster who had married the daughter of a well-known Baptist minister.[1] In this respect, Dorothy Edwards's situation paralleled that of a number of the first generation of Welsh writers in English – Rhys Davies, Glyn Jones, and Alun Lewis – in that they were born and brought up in a working-class mining community, knew that community from the inside, but were the offspring of parents who were by virtue of their profession middle class. These writers, in other words, were _of_ these working-class communities but not wholly a part of them.[2] Like Lewis, Dorothy Edwards's cultural distance from her home community was exacerbated by her attendance at a prestigious school, in her case Howell's School in Cardiff, whose values were essentially those of the English middle classes, and then by study at university.

The death of her father when Edwards was in her late teens, before she started at university, must have been a particularly harsh and difficult event. They had evidently been close and, given the vigour of his personality and his ideals, her father had been an influential presence in his daughter's life; the traces of this disorientating loss are present in her fiction and one might argue that her tendency to be drawn into somewhat dependent relationships with men older than herself – the fraught and finally painful romantic relationship which she had at university with a lecturer, John Thorburn, was the first – has the same origin.[3]

While Edwards thrived in the intellectual life of what was then the University of South Wales and Monmouthshire in Cardiff, and made close female friends, after her graduation in 1924 with a degree in Greek and philosophy her isolation grew. Her college friends moved away to other parts of Britain, several of them to become school teachers; though visits were exchanged, the friendships continued mainly by letter. Edwards herself was determined not to become a teacher, one of the few careers open to a young woman with a degree in the arts, but to become a writer. Outside the university, literary life in Cardiff was, however, virtually non-existent – there were no publishers, no journals in which to publish, no literary societies – and Edwards initially tried to maintain links with student literary activities and clubs.

Following her father's death, Edwards and her widowed mother had moved to Rhiwbina, Cardiff's recently built 'garden village', and it was there that Edwards lived for most of her remaining years. She did in 1925–27 go abroad, spending some six months in Vienna, living with a socialist bookseller and his wife, apparently teaching them English in exchange for her board, and then some nine months in Italy, which she in part financed by undertaking translation work.[4] These were enriching periods, filled with visits to museums, art galleries and concerts; after such experience, the sense of quiet mundanity and cultural isolation of life alone with her mother in suburban Cardiff must have been especially acute. Moreover her mother, neurotically anxious about their finances – they were living on Mr Edwards's pension and what Dorothy Edwards could earn by reviewing – clearly felt, and presumably said, that her daughter could have been more profitably employed as a teacher than as a writer. The tension Edwards was feeling is evident in her letters to her university friends, Beryl Jones and Wilfred Kelly, who were teaching in Yorkshire: 'if I started to write one article a week to pay the rent etc., we should be in exactly the same state that we are now – i.e. she would be asking – not without justice – for more and I should be slinking about weighed down by furtive guilt'.[5]

It was, however, in these years that Dorothy Edwards was writing the stories that she collected in *Rhapsody* (1927), stories about a world far, it would seem, from the suburbs of Cardiff and, of course, strikingly far from the frequently harsh and shabby life of the mining valleys of South Wales in which the short stories of contemporaries like Rhys Davies, Glyn Jones, and Alun Lewis are set. Indeed, with the exception of 'The Conquered', the stories in *Rhapsody* are set far from Wales in an England which is invariably rural, in houses which are usually in remote locations, far from cultural centres. In 'Rhapsody', for instance, despite his love of music, Mr Everett lives with his invalid wife in 'the country, some way out of London' and the events of the story take place when the narrator is invited to the even more remote house which the Everetts have rented for the summer, evidently in the far north, and on a hill 'far from the village', its roof 'just visible above the trees'.[6] In 'A Country House,' the remote location of the eponymous house is an essential source of the tensions of the story: 'I cannot go to any concerts, we are so far from everywhere,' says the wife to the visiting Richardson, as he is about to leave her to carry on her unfulfilling life with her insensitive husband (40); in 'Sweet Grapes' the protagonist, Ferris, consciously seeks solitude and rents a house 'somewhere in the Peak district, and situated ... right on top of a hill' (111). In the later story 'Mutiny' events take place at the summerhouse of an old abbey which is, again, in the countryside, several miles' walk from the nearest station.

That word 'events', however, needs qualifying, for not a lot actually happens in 'Mutiny', or indeed in any of these stories, if by 'events' we are looking for the kind of

action in the external, social world that we would normally
term a 'plot'.[7] Indeed, the middle-class characters of
Edwards's fiction rarely seem to do much beyond reading
books or playing music, visiting each other for meals or –
in story after story – going for walks in the surrounding
countryside. In a number of the stories the characters are
on holiday; certainly, other than writing, few of the
characters seem to work. As Glyn Jones commented, rather
pungently, 'Usually in Anglo-Welsh writing the only people
who do no work are the ones on the dole'.[8] But in Dorothy
Edwards's enigmatic stories, there is no reference to
current events in the post-war world beyond these remote
and curiously non-specific locations: no reference to
politics or economics or international events.

But to look for these things in Edwards's stories is
fundamentally to misconstrue their nature, and the nature
of the place we encounter when we enter into Edwards's
fictional world. For that world is very much her own place,
a place far from her study in Rhiwbina, but having no
direct relation to any geographical location; as Christopher
Meredith argues in his introduction to *Rhapsody*, the
'England' of these stories 'is largely an invented emotional
space. Houses, townscapes and landscapes become
dreamlike representations of inner states' (xiii). What we
have is a world which projects moods and states of feeling
with which its creator was all too familiar; these are stories
characterised by the beauty of the natural world in its
seasons, by a yearning for the deep emotions evoked and
communicated by music, and by impulses of feeling
between people which can rarely be expressed. It is a
world, thus, of emotional constraint, suffused with a
profound sense of isolation, feelings of marginality and
frustration, especially (though not solely) on the part of
women; it is a place in which beauty and content are
fleeting and elusive. The world of these stories, moreover,
lacks most of those elements that give our lives security.
There is, for instance, an almost compete lack of family

domesticity, a sense of 'home' and roots. In many of the
stories the houses are merely places which the characters
rent for a period or which characters visit; the episode of
personal interaction is usually brief and finite. (One notes,
too, that a number of the houses, far from being 'homely',
are characterised as 'ugly', including not only the house
which George Morn ('Days') buys in his native village but
also the house in which he was born (155, 156, 163).)
Where there *is* a family, without exception it is incomplete,
a suggestion of the way in which the loss of her father had
contributed to the shaping of Edwards's inner world. The
teenaged Sidney Mihael ('A Throne of Heaven') is an
orphan, lacking even 'a guardian, properly speaking, only
the lawyers' (140), and he spends the holidays alone at his
boarding school; when eventually he is contacted by a
friend of his dead father and invited to stay, almost
inevitably the man is a widower whose daughter longs for
company. To be a young woman in these stories is always
to be bereft of one, or both, parents and thus, like Rahel
('A Garland of Earth') or Primrose ('Mutiny'), to be
vulnerable to the whims and pressures of a remaining
parent or guardian or indeed, like Mary in 'La Penseuse',
to be at the mercy of chance – and the insensitivity of men.
The Rapunzel-like Elizabeth in her tower ('Sweet Grapes')
epitomises the situation of most of the women in
Rhapsody; whether young women or neglected wives,
unfulfilled and marginalised, they lack any real sense of
being at home in their world.

But these are not just stories of domestic or social
loneliness. One might argue that the circumstances of
Edwards's own life unconsciously sensitised her to the
spirit of the age, to the spiritual outlook of her generation
which, after the meaningless chaos of the First World War,
no longer had faith in an overarching spiritual order, a faith
which gives the individual a sense of meaning in life. In
other words, not only do Edwards's characters lack familial
parental assurance, they seem to inhabit a universe in

which human events lack any sense of lasting significance. One senses an essentially modernist emptiness beyond the edges of the stories.

In entering the world which Dorothy Edwards creates in *Rhapsody*, then, we enter a place which is a personal, idiosyncratic version of reality. The tone of the stories does in fact vary but, as in dreams, Edwards's world has a sense of being 'not-quite-real': as I have noted elsewhere, the characters have somewhat odd, often un-English names: Mertris, Delcage, Chenery, Trenier, Froud, Gallon, Sorel – and on occasion the detachment with which the physical appearance of the characters is described again renders them curiously unreal, almost cartoon-like: Mr Wendover ('Treachery in a Forest') has 'small and wistful blue eyes, and a grey moustache that drooped down on either side of his mouth like the horns of a cow' (61); Alexander Sorel ('Days') is 'a little man and there is something doll-like about his clothes. His collars always look very high' (158); in 'Rhapsody', Elliott, the narrator, observes Everett on his first appearance: 'His face wore a curious expression, as if he were listening all the time to something intensely illuminating but scarcely audible ... and he seemed to be imploring you "please don't interrupt me for a moment; it will soon be over"' (1–2).[9] The sense of unreality which makes reading these stories so unsettling is often added to, as Meredith notes, by the rather stylised register which Edwards uses in her dialogue (xi). When Mr Everett meets the narrator for the first time, at the railway station, Everett is anxious about not missing his train: 'There was no means of ascertaining the time at the concert this afternoon, and I regret to say that I came out of it earlier than necessary' (2). Even allowing for the fact that they have not met before, the formality of 'ascertaining' and 'I regret to say' seems odd, even though we later realise that the mixture of formality and fussiness is not uncharacteristic of Everett.

The idiosyncratic tones of the stories – comic, sardonic, ironic, enigmatic – are, however, predominantly created by the position of the narrators in relation to the events which they are relating, and that positioning is worth careful examination. 'Narrators', of course, for we quickly realise in the opening stories that we are not listening to the voice of the author, or even a performative version of the author, but, in several of the stories, the voice of a male persona. The narrator of 'Rhapsody', for instance – we eventually learn that his name is Elliott – is a man who has recently arrived in England from Egypt; 'a little depressed and lonely' (1) in a London in which he seems to know no one. He is an outsider from the beginning of the story, an observer of the episode in the lives of the Everetts that he relates. At the same time, it is his attitudes to the events, and especially to the actions of Mr Everett, that guide our response; it is his decency which gradually provides a moral context for Everett's behaviour.

Elliott is initially prepared to be amused by Everett's 'most diabolical plot' (8) to hire a young woman who is, while ostensibly a governess for the Everetts' son, clearly being hired to provide Everett with the musical pleasure which his invalid wife can no longer provide. Elliott is even prepared to become involved in the little 'conspiracy' (9) by taking Mrs Everett on a walk while the 'governess', Miss Trenier, is being interviewed. His feeling 'desperately wicked and conscience-stricken' (10) as he does so is merely a pang of conscience at practising what he sees at this point as a minor deception on a woman who is evidently quite unwell. Mrs Everett's 'abruptly' asking Miss Trenier, as soon as the husband is out of sight, 'Why did you apply for the post?' (11) suggests Mrs Everett's uneasiness from the outset, but the narrator makes no comment; he merely notes that, as the four of them have tea, 'Mrs Everett did not speak, and looked across to the woods' (12). The reader is left to pick up Elliott's comment and to reflect on what might be passing through Mrs Everett's mind. (It is a gesture that recurs in a number of these stories, a character withdrawing from a social situation into his or her own reflections, and on each occasion no explanation is given by the narrator.) Elliott at this point is still willing to be a somewhat detached observer of the game Everett is playing, Elliott 'a little maliciously' prompting Antonia Trenier on her ostensible need to teach arithmetic to Vincent (12).

The tone of Elliott's attitude, and thus of the story, gradually changes as his feelings towards Mrs Everett develop; he sits and talks to her 'partly because no one else did so, and partly because I liked to' (14). He becomes increasingly aware of her isolation, imagines what she must be feeling as she hears the music which her husband and Antonia Trenier are enjoying together elsewhere in the house. Initially, as elsewhere in *Rhapsody*, music is the means by which personal feelings, especially covert erotic feelings, can find expression, but when Everett hears Antonia's beautiful singing voice for the first time, takes her hands and presses one of them to his cheek, the direct expression of affection confirms to Elliott the true nature of what has evolved from Everett's 'plot'. Elliott's narration has never taken Everett very seriously – he is described as 'pirouetting' across the garden and 'scurrying off' to arrange tea (10, 11) – but now the tone becomes more hostile: Elliot notes that Everett sings 'in a ridiculous thin whisper of a tenor voice' (17). As his compassion for Mrs Everett has grown, Elliott realises that the 'plot' he has become involved in is in fact altogether more serious and, for Mrs Everett, painful.

When Mrs Everett, ill as she is, reminds Antonia of the need to make preparations for Vincent's departure to boarding school, it is Elliott who has the sensitivity to realise the likely consequences for Vincent of arriving at school after the other boys, to imagine the loneliness and homesickness Vincent might experience (19). Elliott's decency – 'for my part I was chiefly concerned about Vincent' (20) – makes Everett's lack of concern all the more unattractive; the casual, placatory way in which Everett gives his son his expensive watch to take with him Elliott sees as having something ultimately 'unfriendly' about it, and now his feelings are directly expressed to the reader: 'somehow it annoyed me' (20). He responds 'angrily' to the Everetts' lack of concern for the practicalities of their son's journey from Scotland to London on his own and it is Elliott who takes the boy as far as the change of train in Glasgow.

As Mrs Everett's health worsens and it is evident to Elliott that her husband and Antonia are merely waiting for her to die, the painful depth of her sense of loneliness and emptiness which her husband has caused becomes clear when she asks Elliott to ensure that her body is taken 'home': 'don't let *them* bury me anywhere near here' (24, my emphasis). When, after her death, Everett, with Antonia on his arm, comes to wave Elliott off as he returns to Egypt, Everett's face has a look of 'intolerable joy' (25); primarily the reference is to the intensity of Everett's feelings for Antonia, but it is perhaps a joy that is 'intolerable' in quite another way to Elliott.

'A Country House' is another story with a male narrator, one whose character is perhaps the most fully developed in the collection. From the outset of the story, the nature of this man, who is more centrally involved as a participant in the events of the story than Elliott, is revealed to the reader not just by what he tells us but also by *how* he tells us. While in the opening paragraph he tells us that his wife has always 'been my first consideration', his defensiveness and insecurity, crucial to what follows, are already evident:

> When I met her she was a mere child, with black ringlets down her back and big blue eyes. She put her hair up to get married. Not that I danced attendance on her. That is nonsense. But from the very first moment that I saw her I allowed all those barriers and screens that one puts up against people's curiosity to melt away. Nobody can do more than that. It takes many years to close up all the doors to your soul. And then a woman comes along, and at the first sight of her you

push them all open, and you become a child again.
Nobody can do more than that. (27)[10]

It is a brilliantly revealing piece of writing by Edwards. The
speaker's emotional inadequacy is immediately evident;
this is a man who seems as a matter of course to assume
that maturity is a matter of constructing barriers around
the self. Being emotionally open to others is associated with
being childish and thus vulnerable, and it is the intrusion
into a man's life of 'a woman' that renders him thus. We
note his anxiety – revealed by the strength of 'nonsense' –
not to be thought to have 'danced attendance' on his young
wife; presumably to behave thus would be unmasculine.
The notion that a marital relationship might consist of an
equal relationship between two people who are able to
express their feelings one to the other, openly and maturely,
seems not to occur to him. Throughout the story 'a
woman', and he is invariably referring to his wife, seems
almost to belong to a different species to a man, with
different responses to life and, above all, with access to
modes of feeling of which the narrator is incapable and by
which he thus feels threatened. His repetition of 'Nobody
can do more than that' reveals an anxiety that he is in fact
open to the charge that he *could* have been more sensitive,
more open, in his marriage. And, given that the story is
narrated by the husband, a man whose limited capacity for
sensitivity is all too obvious from the outset, we never have
direct access to what his wife is thinking and feeling,
though her sense of isolation and marginality – the house
is again, we remember, in a remote rural situation – is all
too evident to the reader.

The narrator's emotional insecurity manifests itself in
his possessive attitude towards his wife (whose name he
never tells us) and to the house in which they live: 'I have
lived here since I was born. I can find my way about in the
dark. But it is natural that a woman would not like it' (28).
When he brings in Richardson, an electrical engineer, to

plan the construction of a water turbine system to provide the house with electricity – the car turns into '*my* gate' (29, my emphasis) – the husband seems curiously intimidated by Richardson's self-containedness and by his deep voice which the narrator mentions several times; he sees Richardson, we assume, as having a natural masculine authority that he himself feels he lacks. The rather staccato syntax with which he describes Richardson – 'At this point I ought to describe his appearance. He was tall, about forty years old. He had blue eyes, and grey hair brushed straight up' (28) – is typical of the husband's style of expression throughout and again symptomatic of his inhibition. To articulate one's feelings is to render oneself vulnerable; this is a man who can say of his wife, 'I do not know how to describe her' (29).

Richardson, it emerges, shares the wife's love of music, though that love is rarely able to be fulfilled by going to concerts: 'We were so far from everywhere here' (36). On the first night of Richardson's stay she plays an emotional Chopin nocturne; her husband is shocked, though initially his reaction, expressed to the reader, is not spoken aloud:

> Now I could watch girls dancing to Chopin's music all day, but to play Chopin to a stranger that you meet for the first time! What must he think of you? ...to choose to play [the nocturnes] when she is meeting someone for the first time! That is simply wrong. ... Night is a distorter. These nocturnes come of [Chopin's] never having spent his nights alone, of spending them either in an inn or in someone else's bedroom. (32)

There may of course be some element of emotional longing in her performance, but her husband's immediate association of her choice of music with sexual misconduct is a manifestation of his own insecurity both about areas of feelings with which he feels uneasy and threatened (night, he thinks is 'a vapour rising from the depths of the earth and perhaps bringing many things with it', 32) and about his wife's feelings. The first stirrings of sexual jealousy become evident as, when Richardson asks her to play another nocturne, the husband exclaims aloud: 'Night isn't like that. Night is a distorter' (32). He records that 'My wife looked into the darkness outside the window'; we have no access to his wife's thoughts, but we notice the echo of the silent gazing of Mrs Everett, another woman trapped in an unrewarding marriage.

Without directly expressing his growing suspicions to the reader, the narrator's hostility becomes all too evident, despite his protestations that he does not consider Richardson 'a villain' (34): he watches Richardson with his notebook 'as though he were making some very serious calculations. I do not suppose he was for a moment' (34); 'I know all this, because I watched him' (36); 'I noticed him very particularly' (39). The final scene between Richardson and the wife on the eve of his leaving is overheard by her husband as he lurks in the garden. It is evident that, though Richardson has developed feelings for the wife, he has decided not to act on them: 'People do not change their lives suddenly. That is, they don't except in literature' (40). Even as related by the husband, Edwards conveys a sense of the deep emotion with which the scene is charged, emotions which – in this piece of literature – will remain, characteristically, stifled. As Richardson leaves, the narrator is raising a flag, supposedly for his birthday, though the triumphalism is clear; but what is evident to the reader, though not to the narrator, is the emptiness which resonates in the final lines of Edwards's story, a suggestion of the bleak years of unfulfilment which the couple face: 'Up above the flag waved senselessly in the wind' (43).

The first-person male narrator of 'Sweet Grapes' is comparatively less developed as a character, nor is he a participant in the story he tells. But the presence of his narrating voice – 'one gathers', 'you know' (113, 115) – and the perspectives he brings to the search of 'My friend

Hugo Ferris' for a summer of solitary reading and his flirtation with the young girl, Elizabeth, who lives with her cousin in the remote tower which Hugo rents, is crucial to the reader's response to the story. Logically, the unnamed narrator can only actually know what Hugo has told him and that is, of course, a subjective view. Thus, we assume that Ferris has told the narrator that Elizabeth 'made at first no impression whatever on him', but presumably, and revealingly, Ferris has also told him that he noticed her 'rather pretty earrings' (113); there seems no point in the narrator having made up such a detail. The fact that Elizabeth looks pretty, 'particularly when she looked down' (114), has also come from Ferris (the narrator quotes him as saying it on p. 119), an observation which again belies Ferris's supposed lack of interest. The narrator's account of the girl's kissing the 'astonished' Ferris on the tower again contains details which seem likely to have come from Ferris himself, especially the reference to his kissing of 'a rather nice salt-cellar in her neck' (121), and his recalling such details again suggests the effect that Elizabeth did have on him.

'I should imagine that the place was very suitable' for the solitude that Ferris was seeking, says the narrator (112), and of course we need to be aware that some of the details of the story are indeed imagined, albeit based on Ferris's account. We might take it that the sexual tension between the girl and Ferris in the pub, for instance, owes something to the narrator's imagining what the scene must have been like, since it seems unlikely that Ferris would have recreated it for his friend in quite these terms (118). (What we have again, of course, is Edwards's remarkable ability to portray pent-up feeling.) In fact, at several points in the story it is evident that the narrator holds views about young women that are essentially similar to those of his friend, the gender values of young men of their class – 'It is astonishing how young girls have not the faintest conception of the pleasures of solitude' (117) – and, when the girl smiles at a casual comment from

Ferris, the narrator comments that she was 'probably, you know, gratified by his interest' (115). Ferris has professed himself as having been bored by the encounter – Elizabeth 'did not provide any suitable conversation' – but the narrator comments that 'one would think that a young girl growing up there, with her soul opening out, so to speak, hanging on the lowest bough waiting to be plucked and all that sort of thing, would be rather nice. But of course that is quite a different thing' (123). The gestural vagueness of 'all that sort of thing' assumes that the narrator is speaking to someone who knows what he means, shares his attitudes, would be willing to accede to the idea that a young, evidently lonely girl like Elizabeth is available for 'plucking' by an educated young man like Ferris, or himself. However, this expression of shared masculine values makes those points at which the narrator's perspective is rather different from that of Ferris all the more telling. The narrator at times seems slightly more aware, more understanding. He seems to be more sensitive to Elizabeth's situation – 'when a young girl has lived so much alone without friends and has dreamed about the future and about love ... and then suddenly someone who is not only a dream but also a fact comes into this world' (113); he professes to 'see Ferris's point of view', but is also aware of the emotional tension Elizabeth must have been feeling in the scene in the pub, faced by Ferris's ambivalence and then impatience: 'I suppose, she felt rather like crying' (119).

No doubt, given her situation, Elizabeth might indeed have been incapable of engaging Ferris in 'sophisticated' (119) conversation. But when Ferris departs for home at the end, leaving Elizabeth, his emotional incompetence, his utter insensitivity towards the young woman, is all too evident to us, and to the narrator:

> 'You won't be able to kiss me then, you know,' she said, smiling, but with a very anxious look in her eyes.
> For some reason Ferris thinks this was very funny. He laughed then, and he laughed very much again when he told me.

'Won't you be sorry?' she asked gently.

He became serious, and reflected for a moment. 'No, on the whole, I shall not,' he said truthfully. (124)

That 'truthfully' is surely more the narrator's awareness, and judgement, than Ferris's. The narrator is no doubt right in sensing that Ferris was embarrassed at the scene, but the narrator's compassion is at the end, for all the limits of his masculine perspective and similes, fuller than that of his friend, as Elizabeth joins Edwards's gallery of marginalised, lonely women:

> I do not think that it has occurred to him that she probably cried in the night. Of course it was all very awkward for him ... and yet it seems a pity that something so like a flower, like a young rose, you know, should have to cry all night. (124)

A similarly haunting atmosphere is created in another story in the volume *Rhapsody*, 'A Garland of Earth'. Again we have a remote location, Coleman's house and laboratory on a hill above a small coastal village, surrounded by open countryside. The sense of isolation is echoed and endorsed by the presence of both a ruined tower perched on a cliff and an enigmatic, unfinished black tower at the end of the pier that juts out from the village, which is visited by the narrator, Mr Leonard, and the other characters in the story.[11] Again we have a lonely young woman: Rahel, the seventeen-year-old daughter of Coleman, spends her time assisting her father and the mysterious young man, Mr Froud, in the laboratory; Coleman asserts that his daughter, a botanist, is 'another Curie' (128) but the narrator sees 'something strange and sad' about this 'pale and strained' young girl (132, 134). In many ways, though, it is not Rahel who is at the centre of the story, but the narrator himself. Mr Leonard tells us immediately: 'I am an old man now, and I do not know whether I am able any longer to tell a story without making unnecessary observations ... it must be the fault of the old that they see too little in life, not too much' (125).

His narrative is not, indeed, without detours and he reminds us repeatedly of his age: he enjoys a walk with Rahel and her young brother, Jimmy, 'although I think that I walked a little too slowly for them' (130). His attitudes to gender are predictably conventional. As a gift for Jimmy, Leonard brings 'a book by Herman Melville' (126), presumably *Moby-Dick* because it is at one level a story of sea-going adventure; in the event, unsurprisingly, the eleven-year-old boy can make very little of its 'filosophy' (130). For Rahel, however, Leonard brings 'a very beautiful fan'; she accepts it with a smile of what seems genuine pleasure, commenting 'Nobody has ever given me a present like this before' (129). However, she simply puts the fan into her pocket: 'She did not hold it up to her face before the mirror.' Leonard expects her to behave in the way that young ladies of her class usually behave, but Rahel's world is not one which is concerned with the conventions of feminine appearance: she is being trained as a scientist. Later, on a walk with Leonard, she comments on how she is 'making a map of the flora of the district' (130); her elderly companion replies with a comment about 'pressing flowers', to which Rahel responds with impatience. For Rahel, who carries a specimen case, botany is a science, not just a genteel pastime for 'young ladies'. Here and later, when he urges the pale, strained young woman not to spoil her 'pretty head by too much studying' (134), Leonard can only assert plaintively that he is in fact 'no opponent of the higher education for women' (130).

In fact, her studies may not be the only source of strain. This latter scene immediately follows Leonard's observing her, on the beach, with Mr Froud, the rather odd young man who is Coleman's laboratory assistant: 'He was standing talking to her with his hand held out in a strange, absent-minded way, as if he had meant to take hers and had forgotten half-way' (133). On Mr Leonard's approach, Froud leaves with an expression of what Leonard can only term 'stupidity'. The old man is puzzled by the episode: 'I have had a long life, but there is very much that I have not seen' (134). It would seem that on this occasion Leonard has seen but not understood, for it is evident that not only is Rahel isolated from friends and companionship but she is experiencing some sort of emotional attention and pressure from Froud.

But the narrator does come to see more. Leonard's relationship with Rahel grows: 'she ... showed an affection for me, and talked to me and even sought my company as if I were her father' (133). While Leonard does not comment on the reasons for this (they are all too apparent to the reader), the relationship seems to bring a growth in understanding and awareness in him which makes this one of Edwards's most moving stories. On their walks it is Rahel who opens his eyes to the exquisite, intricate beauty of the flowers that she studies, flowers that Leonard confesses 'had always been too small for me to notice' (132). Leonard relates how one afternoon he sits on the rocks above the beach, with Rahel beside him:

> I looked round at the little bay and the chess castle at the other end, and the rocks and the waves of the sea, and at the lovely little flower on one side of me, and the girl with her pale fair hair and her pale face and her pale grey eyes. Ah, that was a moment of the greatest beauty!
> After this I did not see anything so clearly. (135)

It is an epiphanic moment and, despite that last statement, one senses that Leonard's awareness has been subtly altered. Near the end of the story, as the characters walk on the exposed headland above the bay, 'a great black cloud' gathers. It reminds the classically educated Leonard of the coming of the Erinyes, bringing 'vengeance for some blood-guiltiness, but as if it, too, felt the horror of the doom it brought' (136). Ultimately, though, the scene is suggestive less of the characters' vulnerability in the face of some sort of retributory order than, as the storm builds, of their smallness and insignificance in a vast impersonal universe. Jimmy's comment in the discussion about perspective is more apt than he realises: 'It makes *me* feel small, so I don't know what a *ship* must feel like.' This episode as much as the earlier epiphany colours our response to old Mr Leonard's reflection, back in his room, in the final lines of the story:

> These few years that I have yet to live will bring something
> as new and strange to me as anything these children have
> before them to see. One comes, an old blind man, like old
> Oedipus at Colonos, leaning on the arm of a girl, looking
> down with blind eyes on the earth, and suddenly one sees
> little pink flowers, like children looking up to the sky. One
> may not rest yet, one may not rest yet. (138)

The resilience, even optimism, in such a world is unexpected and poignant, born it would seem of the experiences he has undergone during his stay, especially the way in which Rahel has opened his eyes.

Other first-person narrators in *Rhapsody* are not developed as actual characters, though our sense of the presence of the narrator's voice, the tone which s/he adopts and what s/he chooses to tell us, or not tell us, remains crucial to the emotional effects of the stories and ultimately to their meaning. The presence of the first-person speaker in 'Treachery in a Forest', for example, is signalled throughout by the way the narrator directly addresses the reader, thereby engaging him/her in the story: 'As you know, Shelgrove Forest has become very popular as a centre for motorists' (61); 'You would not have thought when you saw them' (64); 'By the way,' (64); 'You must picture him' (69); 'And you know' (70). The fanciful description of the trees in the forest as Mr Wendover goes for a walk – 'their tall upright trunks and their crowns of foliage on every branch look like great warrior poets who have received chaplets for victory in all the categories of poetry' (62) – one also takes to be that of an imaginative, observant narrator, rather than anything of which Mr Wendover is capable of imagining. Wendover is essentially *observed* by the narrator with a detachment which contributes to his appearing a slightly comic figure. The narrator's description of his moustache drooping like 'the horns of a cow' (61) we have noted, and when he toddles from his house to that of the Hardings, the couple he has met, carefully carrying in his hands the three fresh eggs he hopes to share with them, 'People who passed him, especially people who passed in charabancs, laughed at him' (67–8). Here, however, the narrator steps in to observe that 'there was really nothing to laugh at' (68).

For ultimately the story achieves a delicate balance: Wendover appears as both comically naïve and fussy and at the same time as lonely and poignantly in need of friendship with Mr and Mrs Harding; this balance is essentially achieved by the tone of the narrator. Although there is narrative detachment from Wendover, the story is narrated from his point of view; we never see the Hardings without Wendover being present, nor does the narrator tell us anything directly about their marriage. We are allowed to see only what Wendover observes, though, as so often in Edwards's stories, what the narrator allows us to deduce from what is observed is fuller and more subtle than the character, in this case Wendover, is capable of. There are clear suggestions that temperamentally the Hardings are rather different from one another; for example, Mr Harding is rather elegant, fastidious about his clothes and about cleanliness (62, 68), while his wife pays no attention to her 'soiled white blouse' with its pinned cuff (62, 70, 72). There is evident tension in the Hardings' relationship and it seems likely that fussy Mr Wendover's persistent attempts to make friends does not help the situation. When Wendover makes what turns out to be his last visit to them, Harding calls his wife, 'Here is Mr Wendover to see *you*' (73, my emphasis), before 'in a most strange way' sitting down and looking 'past Mr Wendover along the road'. When they finally accept his invitation to tea at the cottage he is renting, again Harding behaves 'most strangely all evening', staring out of the window – that motif again – and 'once or twice he passed his hand over his eyes as though he had a headache' (75). The tension is evident, and is noted – but not explained by the narrator (whether Wendover even notices is not related). The repressed feelings burst out just once: when Wendover offers Harding a Turkish cigarette, commenting that he recalls that this is what his guest smokes, Harding abruptly exclaims, 'The fact is, Mr Wendover, you think they suit my character. You think I am a Bluebeard, who will chop my wife's head off' (75). It is a bizarre – and again unexplained – moment, born, the reader assumes, not only of irritation at Wendover's persistently seeking their company but of Harding's sense that Wendover is in some way critical of his attitude to his wife. Clearly, he overestimates Wendover's powers of perception, and the outburst is in fact the result of Harding's own awareness of what *might* be said of the way he behaves towards his wife. The Hardings' leaving the next day, earlier than expected, and without seeing Wendover, is presumably at Harding's instigation; the fact that Mrs Harding inadvertently signs her apologetic note to Wendover with her maiden name is evidence, we assume, of her own unhappiness in the marriage.

Even when Dorothy Edwards utilises third-person narration, as in the superb story 'Days', where the uncharacteristically bleak landscape reflects something of the sense of emotional distance and unfulfilment of the central couple, the obliqueness of the narrative, what we are *not* told, is also crucial to the effect of this dark-toned story. The sense of pent-up feeling is, as we have seen, characteristic of Edwards's fictional world. Seemingly far removed from the actualities of the world around her, these fables of loneliness and marginality are not only rooted in tensions and repressions with which Edwards was all too familiar, but also express a sense of human marginality which extends beyond the merely biographical and social to express modes of feeling which are distinctively modernist. These stories may not initially strike us as experimental but, in their emotional resonance and in Edwards's profoundly subtle manipulations of narrative technique, these stories are among the most skilful pieces of fiction to come out of English-speaking Wales in the twentieth century.

NOTES

1   For a detailed account of Dorothy Edwards's life and background, see Claire Flay's forthcoming study in the Writers of Wales series (University of Wales Press) and my own essay '"A personal isolated odd universe": Dorothy Edwards and her short fiction', *Moment of Earth: Poems and Essays in Honour of Jeremy Hooker*, ed. Christopher Meredith (Aberystwyth: Celtic Studies Publications, 2007), pp. 140–58.

2   Rhys Davies's parents ran a grocery shop in Blaenclydach, the very name of which, 'The Royal Stores', perhaps indicates something of their social outlook; Glyn Jones's mother was a teacher before her marriage and his father a clerical worker with the Post Office in Merthyr; both of Alun Lewis's parents were teachers of English at Aberaman, near Aberdare.

3   Harold Watkins, a neighbour in this period, recalls her after the break with Thorburn, walking the hills nearby 'alone for hours at a stretch, day after day, week after week, working off her 'nerves', trying to find calm'. See Harold M. Watkins, 'Dorothy Edwards', *Wales* 6 (1946), p. 47. The nervous stress and the isolation were recurring characteristics of the years that followed.

4   Watkins, p. 44.

5   Letter to S. Beryl Jones and Winfred Kelly, 4 September (c.1929). The letter is in the collection of Edwards material, primarily letters and a journal, held in the Archives Department, University of Reading.

6   Dorothy Edwards, *Rhapsody* (1927; Cardigan: Parthian, 2007), pp. 5, 22, 13. Further references are to this edition and are included in the text.

7   It is worth noting that when Edwards does attempt a story with a plot, 'La Penseuse', the means by which she seeks to bring the characters back together after years apart is utterly unconvincing. Even accepting the coincidence that the post as housekeeper for which Mary applies is with her old friend Sidney Mertris, it seems very odd that throughout the whole appointment process Mertris's name is never mentioned. Moreover, Mary does not see the brass name plate at the gate of the house and misses seeing his bookplates when she looks at his books while waiting in the Library: all to ensure the shock of the actual confrontation. She does, however, pick up a book by their friend Richard Warnham and a few weeks later Richard turns up, from Tibet. As Sidney comments, it's 'a queer thing' (p. 207) and one rather assumes that Edwards's sense of the crudeness of the plotting was one of the reasons why she did not collect the story in *Rhapsody*.

8   Glyn Jones, *The Dragon Has Two Tongues: Essays on Anglo-Welsh Writers and Writing*, ed. Tony Brown (Cardiff: University of Wales Press, 2001[1968]), p. 52.

9   'A personal isolated odd universe', *Moment of Earth,* p. 151.

10   See also Christopher Meredith's reading of this opening passage in his foreword to *Rhapsody* (p. xii).

11   In his perceptive pioneering essay on Edwards, Meredith analyses the scene in which the characters visit the tower, which has one window facing out to sea and one facing inland: 'This bleakly absurd scene ... might stand for the human predicament as Edwards sees it all through the book. The stunted tower is her most pared away image of an emotional prison. The rest of humanity can be observed but, apparently, not reached. The other view is out to sea and nothingness.' See Christopher Meredith, 'The Window Facing the Sea: The Short Stories of Dorothy Edwards', *Planet* 107 (October/November 1994), pp. 64–67.

Country Dance (1932) by Margiad Evans:

Text, Paratext and Context

Malcolm Ballin

Paratext

Pick up the Parthian edition of *Country Dance*.[1] This reprinting of Margiad Evans's first published work repays close reading. The reader holds a lean artefact, just over a hundred pages, with a colourful cover – a couple linked together, the woman in a low-cut, yellow and red floral print dress, the man in a dark brown coat, booted, with a neckerchief, serious-faced, apparently dancing. (Later this will be found to be derived from the author's own depiction of Gabriel, one of the central characters, not dancing with Ann, the story's main protagonist, but walking with Margiad, his later girlfriend, titled 'They walked up and down'.)[2] In the cover version the picture has a superimposed green, leafy background suggesting something pastoral and idyllic. The back cover has another picture, captioned 'He takes me by the shoulders', a version of another authorial illustration (14); this time the man is dressed in working gear, the woman in an apron, with onlookers registering alarm. Later this is seen to represent Ann's other suitor, Evan ap Evans, her shepherd-father's master, in an early confrontation about a scorched chimney.

The prospective reader is told that 'At the heart of *Country Dance* is Ann Goodman, a young woman torn by "the struggle for supremacy in her mixed blood", Welsh and English.' It is a 'story of passion and murder'. Derek Savage says that it is 'written with a terse incisive power'. The book is marked 'Library of Wales'. The reader turns to the frontispiece: the figures formalised, not unlike the style of children's cut outs, in bright primary colours, this one captioned 'Evan ap Evans and the gypsies'. Once again, the male figure is dominant; the gypsies appear reactive, one in leopard-skin shirt, two of them striking pugilistic poses. Alongside the man appears an observing woman in a hat and long skirt.

Next, there is an account of Margiad Evans. She was born Peggy Whistler in Uxbridge in 1909; lived in the Border area near Ross-on-Wye and adopted the nom-de-plume Margiad Evans 'out of a sense of identity with Wales'. She studied art and continued to paint and draw throughout her life, though this became secondary to her writing. *Country Dance* is her first novel, dated 1932, and other works of fiction followed in 1933, 1934, and 1936. The listing includes short stories and poetry. There is a seven-year gap between *Creed* in 1936 and her next work, *Autobiography*, in 1943. Her final book, *A Ray of Darkness*, appeared in 1952 and is 'an account of her experience of epilepsy'. She died in 1958. The illustrations are by Peggy Whistler.

A Foreword by Catrin Collier opens with her recollection of 'a set of beautifully bound diaries' discovered in Hay-on-Wye. They were 'perfumed with the scent of long dead, pressed summer flowers' and described 'the narrow confines of rural life in Wales during the first half of the twentieth century' (ix). Collier's account emphasises the isolation and restricted horizons of such a life, where domestic excitements, marriage and courtship were the main incidents. Collier says that the 'novella' (the first use of the term) opens with an account of Ann Goodman (x). She pictures Peggy Whistler stumbling across the ruin of Ann's house and imagining the figure of 'the shepherd's daughter looking to the Welsh mountains, thinking of her lovers' (x). 'Ann's Book' is penned in the present tense, written in 1850, when her fiancé, the Englishman, Gabriel, gives her the book as a parting present as she sets off for England – 'to write in it all I do, for him to see, until we shall be married' (xi). The book 'begins to chronicle the minutiae of farming life that changed little between the setting of *Country Dance* in 1850, and 1932' (xi). Collier emphasises the sense of foreboding that exists throughout. 'This simple story of lovers' rivalry mirrors the conflict between Welsh and English', Celt and Saxon, who nevertheless share 'the rural life doomed to disappear with the advent of mechanisation, (xii). The work 'gives us a glimpse of old rural Wales and life in the border country even more potent than the faint scent of flowers pressed over a century ago' (xii). Collier reflects on the way in which Evans's work initially received 'critical and popular success' but faded from sight after the 1950s. Evans was wholly absent from Collier's own reading formations but Collier looks forward 'to revisiting her world in future'. The tone of Collier's Foreword is a little sentimental, the motif of pressed flowers signifying her desire to recover a lost world and to pay tribute to the neglected past of a lost society and a lost writer.

There are further preliminaries, this time of the author's own contriving. An 'Old Song' in Welsh:

> *Dod dy law ond wyd yn coelio*
> *Dan fy mron a gwylia 'mrifo*

is translated:

> Place thy hand, unless thou believest me,
> Under my breast and beware of hurting me;
> Thou shalt hear if thou listen
> The sound of the little heart breaking.

This is taken, like other songs that appear later, from the oral tradition, marking the significance of Welsh life and language in the tale and setting a melancholy register.

Now follows an 'Introduction' (3–5) signed by Margiad Evans. This opens with the assertion, quoted on the cover, that 'The struggle for supremacy in her mixed blood is the unconscious theme of Ann Goodman's book.' The reader is to expect, then, the working out of a theme of which the protagonist is 'unconscious', as she writes about her English shepherd, Gabriel, and her father's master, the Welshman, Evan ap Evans. These men are respectively 'jealous and sullen' and 'violent and successful'. Olwen Davies is also to feature: someone of 'strange whimsical beauty'. Ann Goodman is to be a 'country woman to her backbone', with an English father and Welsh mother. Evans wants to recover the memory of Ann from the 'curiously nebulous and unreal' character that has obscured it. She comments on Ann's literary style, choosing only the present tense, adding 'strength and vividness' to her account. She seeks to defuse any readerly surprise that, in this historical and social setting, Ann appears so literate. So Ann, Evans's fictional creation, is presented as in some sense historically 'real', but as being, however sophisticated a writer, 'unconscious' of the forces moulding her destiny, ending in a dramatic death which has 'picked ... out with horrible distinctiveness' the memories of her lovers.

This introduction creates deliberate authorial distancing from her subject. The chosen timescale is at least one clear generation before Evans's own lifetime. The characters are in some way beyond the writer's control, driven by their 'blood'; they are mythic in scale and they impact fiercely on their own imagined society, making even their creator 'uncomfortable' in eavesdropping on their reality. Their social setting is exotic, rural, close to the earth. Readers are to be given a passport to an enclosed world where they, too, will be intruders. The events are to be tragic, having national as well as local significance. Margiad Evans's artful framing of her novella invites sympathy for Ann and underlines the dramatic character of the events she is to describe.

Text

At last, the reader is admitted to the main text. The narrative technique is established, and the nature of the main characters and the springs of action are economically set up in the first dozen pages (9–21). Titled 'Ann's Book: First Part: 1850', the opening words establish Gabriel as a figure of authority: 'Gabriel gives me this book, telling me to write in it all I do, for him to see until we shall be married ... I am to leave Twelve Poplars and look to my mother' (9). The journey is cold and long; she has to prepare her father's breakfast at five o'clock. Ann does not, at this stage, act as an independent agent but behaves as dictated to by others. The harshness of Evan ap Evans's character appears. She notes her father's opinion: 'the master can never hold his tongue or his temper'. The parson calls and discusses her with her mother: Gabriel is an Englishman living in Wales and Evan is a Welshman, living in England. The Sexton's daughter (not yet identified as Olwen) is led a hard life by her father (12). Ann scorches a chimney and Evan 'takes me by the shoulders before all the world' so that Ann will 'hate Evan ap Evans from this day and wish Gabriel had been here to shake the life out of him'.

The Sexton is drowned by suicide and Ann finds his daughter, Olwen, 'soaked to the bone' (13); she 'can't go farther, I'm too affeared'. This archaism occurs frequently.[3] 'Come home and you shall sleep the night with me.' An episode with the gypsies (15) leads to conflict as Ann refuses to support Evan, 'master or no master', in his authoritarian stance: 'Those who won't work shan't live.' When another chimney falls in the wind, Evan accuses her of bringing bad luck: 'Are you a witch, Ann Goodman?' (16). Her father is prone to 'grumble and find fault with all that I do' (16). She has to sweep the chimney and the dirt 'forces me to take a bath in the wash-tub' (17). When the parson calls again she is working in the garden with her skirts tucked up. She is 'more than decent, but I burn with shame'. The sexual undertones hinted at in the dirt, the bath and the disordered dress are reinforced by the parson's description of her as 'a very pretty gypsy with your curls down' (18). Evan always speaks to her in Welsh (though

Evans translates most of his words). At a dance in the barn
(at one level the obvious source of the novella's title) he is
dressed in 'a very fine waistcoat, with silk flowers' and tries
to persuade her to dance with him. 'He sings softly, in the
voice that the English have not, an old Welsh song that I
have sung round the fire at night' (20). Eventually, 'Willy-
nilly', she first dances the lively jig 'Black Nag' with him
and then dances again to the tune 'A-hunting we will go'.[4]
She resists the temptation to box his ears. When she returns
home she finds Olwen asleep in the kitchen:

> Such a beautiful face I have never seen. I carry her up,
> lay her on my bed and take off her clothes. She wakes:
> 'Oh Ann,' she says. 'Good night,' and sleeps again. (21)

These passages touch on the unresolved and unacknowledged
sexual impulses in Ann's nature, masked by anger in the case
of Evan, infused with tenderness in relation to Olwen.

By now, the reader has a good idea of the way Ann
relates to the demanding nature of Gabriel and the potent
figure of Evan, to her sick mother and patriarchal father, to
the smooth-spoken parson and to the lonely and beautiful
Olwen. The remaining ten pages of Part I deal with her
violent quarrel with Gabriel, who becomes jealous both of
Evan and of the Parson when he reads about them in her
book – and her consequent reclamation of the book as her
own (24). There is another tender scene with Olwen (27)
and a further confrontation with Evan (29), this time
centred on his role as the master, and explicitly raising the
Welsh/English duality:

> 'Thou art very saucy for a shepherd's daughter: very high
> and haughty thou art, Ann Goodman: had thy father not
> been such a good shepherd, thou mightst have had cause
> to rue it before now!'...
>   'No,' I tell him, 'I am English. I was with English folk
> in Wales, and I hate the Welsh and all their shifty ways
> of dealing. "Taffy was a Welshman, Taffy was a thief."'

'Ay, among Englishmen I'd cheat the log-heads out of
every penny. Thou hatest the Welsh, dost thou? Is
Myfanwy an English name?'

For once I cannot answer. (29–30)

The translation renders the intimate pronouns in Welsh as
quasi-biblical English archaisms. Later, we discover that
Myfanwy is her mother's name. Olwen tells Evan that
Gabriel has quarrelled with Ann on his account and he
decides, despite Ann's opposition, to ride into Wales to
speak to him (34). Ann has a bad dream, with a wagon
dripping in water bearing a coffin (35). Book I ends
forebodingly, with the ruin of the hay harvest.

Ann's Book: Second Part opens with another folk song:

Gwyn ac oer yw marmor mynydd,
Gwyn ac oer yw ewyn nentydd
...

White and cold is the marble of the mountains,
White and cold is the foam of the rivers,
White and cold is the snow on Berwyn,
Whiter, colder is the breast of Ann.

The book starts dramatically: 'My mother is dead.' Her
dying words are in Welsh (not spoken by her since her
marriage) and Ann teaches her father, brought from the
fields in haste, to say 'Rwyf yma wrtheich ymyl' (I am here
with you) to her in her last moments. He will fulfil a
promise to take her body back to Wales and Ann is to write
to her cousin, Mary. 'I takes the pen in my hand' (43) (a
childish, untypically ungrammatical, English construction).
Ann tells Evan (45) 'I'm not coming back' and bids him
'Ffarwel'. As in her dream, her mother's coffin is borne
through a river on a wagon, dripping with water. After the
burial (46) her father tells her, immediately and brutally,
'now your mother is dead I have no use for you ... You
make trouble with the master, you would lose me my

shepherding by your saucy ways. All the parish sees he is sweet with you; if you won't have him, stay here till his blood cools ... don't you set foot over the border without I send for you. You will not be welcome' (46).

The theme of 'blood' recurs again. Later he underlines the parting: 'Once I am out of Wales I stay out of Wales, (47). Ann sends her 'dear love' to Olwen (48).

The action moves to the Welsh side of the border, balancing the earlier book's setting on the English side. Ann attends the Welsh-speaking chapel, afraid to attend church in case she meets Gabriel, who has 'no use for the Welsh, nor for their way of speaking' (49). Mary describes the fight between Evan and Gabriel and probes the relationship:

> 'Perhaps, seeing you were his shepherd's daughter –
> though you were as good as he is by blood and better by
> behaviour – he thought nothing of a kiss here and there.'
> 'There were no kisses.'
> 'Well,' says Mary, 'there is no telling what a Welshman
> means by what he says.' (53)

Ann encounters Gabriel again (56). He catches her in his arms and tries to kiss her but she resists him.

> 'You would not take my word,' I says slowly in Welsh.
> Gabriel scowls at the tongue.
> 'Loose me.' (57)

The language asserts her identity and difference, in a precise parallel with her former insistence on English with Evan. But soon afterwards she takes his hand and he puts his arm around her. Later they meet at the fair:

> 'When will you marry me – when the mourning is done?'
> 'It is too soon to talk of that.' I says. (57–8)

He visits her in the evenings – 'But it is not like old times together' (58).

'Will you marry me in the spring, Ann?'
    I cannot answer. (59)

After the tensions of a 'mixed' wedding in the village,
Gabriel and Ann meet at night on the mountain, Craig Ddu.
He is training his dog for the trials at Pentredwr and Ann
agrees to attend. 'We stop at the pool where we was used to
catch trout' (60). As the moon rises, Ann's language takes on
romantic intensity:

'Have you seen the Roman soldiers marching through
Craig Dinas and the White Lady that drowned herself in
Llyn-tro?' (61)

Gabriel has not; he is preoccupied with domestic
problems. He tries to make love to her, taking the pins
from her hair. She resists and he accuses her of still loving
'that Welshman' (62). Ann becomes 'affeared' and they
part in anger. August brings farming troubles and Gabriel
is training his dog for the trials. Ann has a further sense
of foreboding:

For my part, I cannot see deep water, running or still,
without a shiver, like some harm will come to me from it,
and the sight and sound of a waterfall is full of terror. (64)

Conflicts come to a climax at a supper at Tan y Bryn where
Gabriel is described as 'glowering on the company' (66). A
Welshman proposes a toast:

'I drink to Wales!'
    Gabriel roars:
    'And I to England!' And stands facing the other across
the table. ... Mary looks serious.
    'There'll be trouble in a minute, the men are hot as
coals,' she whispers.
    Gwen purses up her lips.
    'I give the Border,' she says, very quiet. (67)

The passage illustrates Margiad Evans's chosen style for 'Ann's Book': simple sentences, monosyllables, direct exchanges, superfluous detail elided. Gabriel seems to accept Ann's rejection and takes up with Margiad: 'three times they walk slowly up and down beneath the poplars' (67).

But in the aftermath of the trials, after Gabriel wins the cup (humiliating Ann's father), Gabriel and Evan fight again and Evan knocks him out: 'Cymru am byth!' Ann attends to Evan's wounds and feeds him milk from Gabriel's silver cup:

'Cariad, have I won the cup after all?'
'Drink', I answer, 'and never come here again. I wish one of us three were dead!' (74)

The symbolism and the ominous wish are both significant. Ann will not marry Gabriel:

'If you are an Englishman, Gabriel Ford, then from this day I'll count myself as Welsh. You are a jealous, unreasonable man, and I pity the woman your choice falls on.'
'You'll have need to.'
'You now look ripe for murder.' (75)

Gabriel stoops to kiss her before departing. She is 'half choked with rage'. It is the last occasion they are described as speaking to each other.

There are rick fires; a child dies from consumption; 'the harvest has begun' (78). News of Gabriel's planned departure at Christmas arrives and Ann's fortune in the tea-leaves is doom-laden: 'tears, tears, tears ... you are standing near a great misfortune, and soon you shall hear of a death' (80). Gwen, who is 'very fanciful, like most of the Welsh folk' (81), sees a great dog and thinks it is the devil and is frightened of Llyn-tro where 'the white otter swims'. Ann comments thoughtfully: 'I think the Welsh are fanciful folk that frighten none but themselves by their tales' (83). There is an incident with a bull that escapes and threatens Ann. A shepherd's crook is found at the scene, suggesting Gabriel's presence (85). Ann decides to 'go home by the longer way – affeared' and to take care to 'slide the bolts very early'. A message arrives to ask her to go to her father's assistance: his sheep have scab; he has taken to the bottle (87) and neglected them and his house. The action moves back to England. Ann prepares ointments for the sheep, though it is not 'work for a woman' (90). She hides from the Parson's visit. Mrs Somers is doleful:

> 'What a deal of dying there has been this year! ... Half the parish looks ready for the grave with all the rain we've had.'
> 'It might be our turn next,' I says. (91–2)

Olwen returns from Monmouth and appears again as a source of spontaneous affection:

> She throws her arms around my neck tight enough to throttle me. ... She is more lovely than anything I have ever set my eyes on. (92–3)

They discuss Evans ap Evans's rough language and behaviour and the contrasts between Welsh and English ways, leading to the revelation that Ann's father was born in the workhouse and that 'he brought his wife there out of Wales' (95–6). Though 'a hard man in many ways, he [Evan] would never get rid of John Goodman' (96). This revelation provokes a strong reaction from Ann:

> I do not know what comes over me that I cry out:
>   'Ni fedrwch gael ei debyg yn Lloegr!'
>   [You won't find his equal in England!]
> Olwen stares at me.
> 'Why, what does that mean?'
> 'I hardly know myself.'
> At dusk I pass the master in the fields.
> 'Nos da, Ann Goodman.'
> 'Nos da, Evan ap Evans.' (96)

This passage, typically spare in expression, is crucial, marking a thaw in Ann's attitude to Evan. It is reinforced when her father is found lying drunk in the field. Ann starts to undertake his work and Evan insists on taking over from her (97). Ann decides not to return to Wales and she watches Evan ploughing. He speaks to her 'in the tongue he was born to' (98):

> 'What art thou doing there, all alone?'
> It is the truth that I answer.
> 'Waiting for thee.'
> It is dark when he leaves the plough, and, coming to me, looks down in my face:
> 'Fy nghariad, the waiting is over,' he says and with his two hands draws me to him.
>
> We shall be married before the trees are bare, for there is no need of waiting.
> In a letter Mary tells me Gabriel left Tan y Bryn last week without warning.
> Autumn has come: her sheep are from the mountains, and Morgan is threshing the barley in the long evenings. It seems like some peace at last!
>
> (END OF ANN'S BOOK) (99)

Clare Morgan remarks that Ann's capitulation to Evan reinforces 'the macho myth of Welsh sexual potency' and she sees this passage as stereotyped and reflecting a relatively superficial understanding of the Welsh language and of the borders.[5] But the further use here of heightened, near-biblical language for translation from Welsh is plangent and effective. The coincidence that marriage was to re-name her as Ann Evans, the same as Margiad Evans's grandmother, may add some private significance. The expected marital union subsumes earlier conflicts in a conventional but touching act of closure. This apparently happy ending to 'Ann's Book' is reinforced by the seasonal metaphor of harvest and fruition.

The last four pages, untitled, are written in conventional English in the past tense, implying Margiad Evans's authorial voice. They coldly resist the pastoral fantasy:

> Evan ap Evans was never married to his shepherd's daughter; before the trees were bare, she was lying in Salus churchyard, and his name and Gabriel Ford's were on the lips of all the countryside. (101)

'On her temple was a great wound that cried aloud for justice' (101). The border society never wholly resolves the question of guilt. The narrator says that 'Gabriel was undoubtedly the murderer' (102). He is never seen again. Evan is distressed by the village gossip; he leaves the area and dies in Canada. 'The little ruled book where Gabriel is branded and where a darker pen runs beside Ann's quill' conceals a 'subtler underlying narrative', the product of 'a mind which though clear in itself was never conscious of the two nations at war within it' (102–3). The action represents the history of the Border which 'tells of incessant warfare'. Margiad Evans is still intent, throughout this apparently objective conclusion, on reinforcing the fiction that these events actually happened, though she concedes that

> All old stories, even the authenticated, even the best remembered, are painted in greys and lavenders – dim, faint hues of the past which do no more than whisper of the glory of the colour they once possessed. Yet live awhile in these remote places where these pale pictures were painted, and some of their first freshness will return to the (103)

The novella ends, then, on an attempt to engender a late romantic haze. If readers could only live for a while in the Borders, their understanding would be assured. Her desire to insist on the significance of the Border and to invest her novella with linked historical and psychological meanings seems to lead Evans into some contradictions. In her book, despite the authorial denials both in the introduction and in the conclusion, Ann is actually presented as being highly conscious of the oppositions between Wales and England within herself and others and of the significance of the Border. Her story is marked more by sharp realisations of the harsh realities of rural life than by misty shades of lavender and grey. The colourful illustrations that Peggy Whistler supplies alongside the text are anything but subdued and pale. Clare Morgan describes them as theatrical and dramatic, 'positively balletic ... the stuff of mime'.[6] Indeed, the events throughout *Country Dance* are designed to suggest life, vitality, labour, urgency, fear, anger – actualities only briefly offset by moments of relaxation, tenderness and peace. The final, softer mood music deployed by Margiad Evans does not altogether succeed in defusing the tensions and touching the realism of the central content with the signs of more distant myth or folktale.

In the end-papers, a formal note on the Library of Wales by Dai Smith positions *Country Dance* within the 'the rich and extensive literature of Wales which has been written in English'. The closing paratext thus situates Margiad Evans among the acknowledged creators of 'the voices and actions of the human experience that has made us, in all our complexity, a Welsh people'. It is followed by advertisements for selected publications from the series, including Raymond Williams's *Border Country* and Lewis Jones's *Cwmardy*. This literary context demands some formal analysis.

Context

Country Dance is the story of an imagined book: it 'begins and ends with the book' (103). Indeed, an early reviewer of *Country Dance* in the *Manchester Guardian* appears to believe that the fictional 'Ann's Book' actually existed:

> In reproducing [Ann's Book] she has presumably rehandled
> it, but she has done it so skilfully that the naïveté and
> unconscious dramatic quality of the original have either
> been preserved or reconceived. ... Nevertheless it is a
> curious document which takes us close to the folk-life of
> the Welsh Borders as it was till recently. And its
> unpretentious truth contrasts strangely with Mrs Peggy
> Whistler's pretty and mannered illustrations.[7]

Her illustrations are seen as somehow less authentic and
'curious' than Margiad Evans's fictional character's own
imagined writing. Ceridwen Lloyd-Morgan says that the
use of the present tense is typical of the style of Welsh
storytelling and that it 'never sounds artificial'.[8] It is
probably this that preserves the illusion of 'unpretentious
truth' – a tale flowing directly from its heroine's consciousness. The occasional interpolations in Welsh and the use of
archaisms – 'thou', 'dost' – add to the suggestions of
historical authenticity. Ann is represented as not merely a
mediator between the Welsh and English; she is sometimes
both a commentator and a teacher.

Robert Herring described Margiad Evans as 'best
known for her shattering sincerity': a noted feature of her
documentary and confessional work as well as her fiction.[9]
However, as Katie Gramich insists, *Country Dance* is not a
simple text:

> Margiad Evans complicates the simple binary opposition
> between the two countries, for Welsh people are found
> inhabiting English soil, and vice versa. Beneath the
> apparently simple narrative, rigid demarcations regarding
> national and gender identity are being radically
> questioned.[10]

The novella is the site of interwoven contexts: personal,
literary, historical, social and political.

Peggy Whistler's 'premonition of passion' for the
Herefordshire countryside and her pleasure in life at her

aunt's farm near Ross-on-Wye were formative moments
that led to what Lloyd-Morgan calls 'The Birth of Margiad
Evans'.[11] Stephen Knight remarks that she became 'Welsh
by choice'.[12] However, she was at pains to define herself
more precisely and to deny, despite her 'drop' of Welsh
blood, ever having posed as Welsh: *'I am the border* – a very
different thing.'[13] She wrote to Herring emphasising her
Home Counties origins: 'I love Woking. I was born in a
suburban maisonette called "Rusholt".'[14] The emphasis on
the liminal elements in the mentality of Ann Goodman
flows from the context of Margiad Evans's preoccupations.
This may have appeared more potent because of the
emphasis in the psychology of the time on the importance
of the undivided self. Contemporary anxieties about such
divisions can be seen, later in her life, in *A Ray of Darkness*
(her testament of her life as an epileptic):

> Has not every one of us a mental image of himself, which
> he watches ceaselessly, which he must watch, and which
> must not, for his health's and sanity's sake, deviate from
> the self seen by everyone else?[15]

Barbara Prys-Williams provides a moving account of the
fissions that perturbed her development, leading to the
'adoption of a fictional mode [that] gives Margiad Evans
particular freedom in patterning her experience poetically,
symbolically'.[16] In *Country Dance*, the Kleinian fears of
'splitting' that Prys-Williams identifies are worked out in
parallels with Ann Goodman's fictional experiences. These
align Ann's relationships with some of Margiad Evans's most
intimate experiences involving her father (feckless, alcoholic,
oppressive, possibly abusive, often loved), her mother
('powerful and ungentle', often infuriating), and at least one
passionate same-sex attraction.[17] Rivalries between
competing images of home and territory and the demands of
rival suitors become embroiled with personal tensions.

These conflicts comprise a part of what Katie Gramich
describes as a 'feminist cultural geography', a context within

which 'Wales itself is conceived ... as a place in which Welshness and womanhood can be lived and performed'. Gramich regards Evans as interrogating 'the structural forces that shape human experience'.[18] The Border conflicts in *Country Dance* perform a variation on the pattern of Welsh self-imagining. In her choices of self-definition, sometimes on one side of the Border, sometimes on the other, and in her battles to control her own social relations, Ann often exerts personal agency, even when it appears inappropriate by the standards of her time. After the encounter with the gypsies, she refuses to comply with Evan ap Evans's demand that she act as a witness and 'bursts out, fairly furious, master or no master. ... His mouth falls open.' Her defiance amazes him, just as in other contexts it disturbs her father and Gabriel. Her recalcitrance is sometimes represented as stemming from her Welshness by English characters (Gabriel or her father) but from her Englishness by Welsh participants (such as Evan). The fact that both her lovers have themselves been displaced from the land of their birth intensifies and complicates their national allegiances, in a way characteristic of immigrants into host societies. This partly accounts for the deliberate 'relentlessness' of the emphasis on national traits in the work that has been remarked on by John Powell Ward.[19] Inhabiting a pre-feminist world where women's labour is at once essential and disregarded, the story of Ann is conceived, in Ceridwen Lloyd-Morgan's words, as 'an act of recovery of women's lost history in a world where it is men who are individualised and remembered'.[20]

Country Dance has its literary precursors. The genre of the novella is not well defined but it provides a context for poetic compression of events within prose fiction. Early twentieth-century examples available to Evans include Joseph Conrad's *Heart of Darkness* (1902) and Thomas Mann's *Death in Venice* (1913). In both these cases, as in *Country Dance*, a limited cast of characters is placed in a location signifying a concentrated atmosphere of threat and foreboding. The novella's concentrated space helps Evans to highlight the ceremonious structures in *Country Dance*. These are noted by both Gramich and Lloyd-Morgan: the dance-like 'criss-crossing' between Wales and England – a formal patterning that is reflected in the lives of the characters and underlined by what Lloyd-Morgan calls the 'sculptural quality' of Peggy Whistler's illustrations.[21]

Margiad Evans has things in common with the style and interests of fellow writers of the 1930s. Several commentators have identified the period's interest in recovering lost communities, especially in appealing to 'a virtuous culture divorced from commerce and the market'.[22] Valentine Cunningham notes how, within the context of Ireland and Wales, writers became involved in a search for a 'post-British identity' and how 'a confused awareness of conflicting needs for the preservation of tradition coexisted with a frantic search for novelty'.[23] He goes on to remark on the creation of what he terms 'a genuine literature of the provinces', often writing in language other than the BBC English of 'the ruling élite', in attempts to 'give the workers a voice'. In general, Cunningham argues, most writers failed in such attempts to write in a proletarian style and were irresistibly drawn back to earlier literary models such as the Brontës.[24] Margiad Evans in *Country Dance* (probably not known to Cunningham) both exemplifies some of these characteristics and defies the generalisations implicit in them. There is an Arcadian quality in the Border territory celebrated in her novella, notwithstanding the sturdy realism of her representations of rural labour. Clare Morgan identifies a 'nostalgia for a kind of Edenic relation between man and nature', that she associates with the influence of Wordsworth, Blake, Burns and Keats.[25] 'Ann's Book' experiments with a demotic style distinct from received English, accompanied by occasional untranslated words of Welsh. Evans thus attempts to bridge the 'aphasic cultural gap' identified by Kirsti Bohata as occurring among Welsh writers in English.[26] But she also has heavy debts to earlier English models.

For example, Evans's decision to place *Country Dance* in 1850, a clear generation from her own time, parallels Brontë's dating of *Wuthering Heights* in 1801, fifty years before her time of writing. The openings of both works establish this temporal distance in their very first lines. The framing personal narrative is also discovered in Brontë's novel, as is the device of the 'found' diary of a young girl.[27] Lloyd-Morgan records Margiad Evans's fascination with Byron and the Brontë sisters, clearly demonstrated in Evans's essay on them in *Life and Letters To-Day*.[28] In another essay in the same journal she remarks that 'Wordsworth's verses *are* the earth ... Burns was gnarled as a rock, fluent as rock water, strong as a gale.'[29] In *Wuthering Heights*, Cathy's love for Heathcliff 'resembles the eternal rocks'.[30] The influence of Wordsworth appears in Evans's later *Autobiography* (not a conventional account of her life story but a celebration of her diurnal experience of country life and spiritual experiences on the Welsh borders). This contains intuitions of formative moments in her internal life written in terms reminiscent of *The Prelude*:

> Oh exquisite, uncommunicable time! I was eleven years old then, on that day my vision began. It lapsed, it failed, but it always came again, renewing my being, filling my breast like a fountain, opening my eyes.[31]

This 'patient record of impassioned observation', to quote a review of *Autobiography* in Gwyn Jones's *Welsh Review*, further illustrates the Romantic influences on Margiad Evans's literary history.[32]

Evans was, however, a twentieth-century, professional writer, self-conscious about her literary life and publishing career. She had regular correspondence and contacts with Basil Blackwell at Oxford, with Gwyn Jones and *The Welsh Review*, with Keidrych Rhys's *Wales*, with David Garnett, with Robert Herring and his patron, Winifrid Annie

Ellerman (known as 'Bryher') and their magazine, *Life and Letters To-Day*.[33] Her literary life was lived in the intellectual context of the metropolis as well as the Borders.

Some of her later writing expresses the critical values that inform her style in *Country Dance*. In the second of her two articles, 'Arcadians and Barbarians', for *Life and Letters To-Day* – a commentary on English folk songs – she describes the song 'Sweet Nightingale' as 'tender, delicate, clear, clever, … [it] pleases equally the naïve and the sophisticated'. These epithets of approval would describe 'Ann's Book'. Of the song 'Tom Bowling' she writes: 'There is not a single "poetic" or transcendent phrase in it, not a single image, and but one steady metaphor: the language is limited, not fervent, yet it gets to the interior of things.'[34] Her critical preferences reflect the virtues of her own early writing.

A tragic dimension suffuses *Country Dance*, usually as a sense of foreboding, underlined by such devices as the prefatory Welsh songs, the experiences of being 'affeared', the frequent references to 'blood' and incidents involving drowning. The account of the pressures that a rural society exerts on a woman's life and of Ann's assertion of her own will against them is at once dramatic, poignant and ultimately liberating.

However, none of this would allow the original reader in 1932 to suspect the underlying issues about Margiad Evans's own health that were to influence much of her later work. Her piercing descriptions of cystitis as a fox gnawing at the vital organs of her character Arabella in her later novel, *The Wooden Doctor*, must be among the most potent and direct representations of a woman's physical suffering in the language.[35] *A Ray of Darkness* (together with her unpublished essay, 'The Nightingale Silenced' – written in hospital in 1954) delineates her experiences of an undiagnosed brain tumour that produced epileptic symptoms and the damaging effects on her capacity to write, brought about by prescribed medication. *A Ray of*

Darkness is so accurate and moving that it has recently been recommended to neuro-surgeons as 'a brave and positive book' on the topic.[36]

In *Country Dance*, though, Margiad Evans anticipates by almost half a century Raymond Williams's description of Welsh culture as encompassing a 'hard, fierce, internally contending yet bitterly communal feeling'.[37] *Country Dance* justifies her latest positioning in the context of the Library of Wales's newly reconstructed canon of 'forgotten' Welsh Writers in English.

ACKNOWLEDGEMENT: I am grateful to Katie Gramich for introducing me to the work of Margiad Evans, for making available a number of helpful essays, and for her assistance on points of detail.

NOTES

1   Margiad Evans, *Country Dance*, (Cardigan: Parthian, 2006 [1932]).

2   *Ibid.*, p. 78. Further references to *Country Dance* are incorporated in the text.

3   The *OED* refers to frequent use of 'afeard' [*sic*] in Shakespeare and suggests the word is still current in dialect.

4   Both dance tunes come from English traditional sources. 'The Black Nag' is a jig, dated from 1657. See <Black-Nag 1997-09.pdf application> published by the Folk Dance Federation of California South> accessed 28 August 2009.

5   Clare Morgan. 'Exile and the Kingdom: Margiad Evans and the Mythic Landscape of Wales' in *Welsh Writing in English,* VI, 2000, pp. 89–118 (106).

6   *Ibid.*, p. 105.

7   H. Pa. F., 'A Country Tragedy; [review of] *Country Dance*', in 'Book of the Day', *The Guardian*, 28 November 1932, p. 5. http://archive.guardian.co.uk, accessed 1 September 2009.

8   Ceridwen Lloyd-Morgan, *Margiad Evans* (Bridgend: Seren, 1998), p. 30.

9   Robert Herring, 'Golgyddol' [Editorial], *Life and Letters To-Day,* March 1940, pp. 217–20 (220).

10 Katie Gramich, *Twentieth-Century Women's Writing in Wales: Land, Gender, Belonging* (Cardiff: University of Wales Press, 2007), p. 86.

11   Lloyd-Morgan (1998), pp. 8 and 18.
12   Stephen Knight, *A Hundred Years of Fiction* (Cardiff: University of Wales Press, 2004), p. 124.
13   Moira Dearnley, *Margiad Evans* (Cardiff: University of Wales Press, 1982), p. 13; Lloyd-Morgan (1998), p. 32.
14   'Notes on Contributors', *Life and Letters To-Day:* Welsh Number, March 1940, obverse of front cover.
15   Margiad Evans, *A Ray of Darkness* (London: John Calder, 1978 [1952]), p. 40.
16   Barbara Prys-Williams, *Twentieth-Century Welsh Autobiography* (Cardiff: University of Wales Press, 2004), p. 37.
17   See Prys-Williams, pp. 45–6 for parental relations. See Lloyd-Morgan (1998), p. 44; p. 45 for relations with mother; p. 55 for lesbian relationship; pp. 66–7 for relations with father. For possible abuse, see Sue Asbee, 'Margiad Evans's *The Wooden Doctor:* Illness and Sexuality', in *Welsh Writing in English*, IX, 2004, pp. 33–49 (35).
18   Gramich, pp. 3–5.
19   John Powell Ward, 'Borderers and Borderline Cases', in M. Wynn Thomas (ed.), *Welsh Writing in English: A Guide to Welsh Literature, Vol. VII* (Cardiff: University of Wales Press, 2007), pp. 91–119 (101).
20   Lloyd-Morgan (1998), p. 28.
21   Gramich, p. 86; Lloyd-Morgan (1998), p. 24. See also Ceridwen Lloyd-Morgan, 'Portrait of a Border Writer', in *Planet*, October/November 1994, pp. 45–57 (52).
22   Paul Delaney, *Literature, Money and the Market: from Trollope to Amis* (Basingstoke: Palgrave, 2002), p. 171.
23   Valentine Cunningham, *British Writers of the Thirties,* (Oxford: Oxford University Press, 1988), p. 36.
24   *Ibid.*, pp. 315–21.
25   Clare Morgan, p. 91.
26   Kirsti Bohata, *Postcolonialism Revisited* (Cardiff: University of Wales Press, 2004), p. 106.
27   Emily Brontë, *Wuthering Heights* (London: Wordsworth Classics, 1992 [1847]), pp. 1, 13.
28   Margiad Evans, 'Byron and Emily Brontë', in *Life and Letters To-Day,* June 1948, pp. 192–216. Also see Lloyd-Morgan (1998), pp. 33, 50–1, 112.
29   Margiad Evans, 'A Little Journal of Being Alone' in *Life and Letters To-Day,* March 1940, pp. 255–68 (256).

30 Brontë, p. 59.
31 Margiad Evans, *Autobiography* (Oxford: Basil Blackwell, 1943), p. 78.
32 M. W. Kelly, [Review of] *Autobiography,* in *Welsh Review,* March 1944, pp. 66–68 (66).
33 See, for examples, Lloyd-Morgan (1998): for Gwyn Jones pp. 72–3, 76, 93–5; for Keidrych Rhys p. 72; for David Garnett pp. 67–8; for Robert Herring p. 79, 91; for 'Bryher' pp. 115–17.
34 Margiad Evans, 'Arcadians and Barbarians: Remarks on Some old English Songs', in *Life and Letters To-Day,* June 1949, pp. 184–99 (184–6).
35 See Margiad Evans, *The Wooden Doctor,* ed. Sue Asbee (Dinas Powys: Honno, 2005 [1933])
36 A. J. Larner, ' "A Ray of Darkness": Margiad Evans's account of her epilepsy (1952)', in *Clinical Medicine,* April 2009, pp. 193–4 (194).
37 Raymond Williams, '*The Welsh Trilogy* and the Volunteers: an interview with *New Left Review*', in Daniel Williams (ed.), *Who Speaks for Wales: Nation, Culture, Identity: Raymond Williams,* (Cardiff: University of Wales Press, 2003), pp. 112–42 (136).

Liberty and the Party Line:

'Novelising' Working-class History in Lewis Jones's *Cwmardy* and *We Live*

Alyce von Rothkirch

> Lewis Jones was a Communist. This was the central fact of his life, the philosophical pivot around which his stormy political career and volatile temperament revolved. His politics shaped his life and coloured his writing because of his deep ideological commitment to them as the only release for a trapped society. ... In every respect, although hemmed in by extremely restricting public and private circumstances, Lewis Jones personified individual choice.[1]

Lewis Jones occupies a special place both in British working-class fiction and in Welsh industrial writing in English. Although he wrote only a few short stories and two novels, *Cwmardy* and *We Live*, both published by the left-wing publisher Lawrence & Wishart in 1937 and 1939 respectively, his larger-than-life personality and his impact on the social and political landscape of South Wales have become legendary. In this essay I will briefly look at biographical information insofar as it relates to the two novels under discussion, I will then discuss the controversial issue of the literary merit of the two novels and, finally, I will undertake a close reading of the two novels, paying particular attention to the main character Len Roberts's political education in *Cwmardy* and the tension between his essentially anarcho-syndicalist views and what I term the Party Line in *We Live*.

Lewis Jones was born in Blaenclydach in Clydach Vale in 1897. An illegitimate child, he was orphaned young and brought up by his grandmother. At the age of twelve he went to work underground in the Cambrian Colliery, later part of the Cambrian Combine owned by D. A. Thomas, Viscount Rhondda, who became the model for Lord Cwmardy in the novels. He married at the age of sixteen. Among the many incidents that shaped his political outlook, a few stand out, such as the 1910/11 strike, which ended in a humiliating defeat for the miners, and the Tonypandy riots sparked off by the strike. During the riot the stipendiary magistrate, D. Lleufer Thomas, called for assistance, which was provided by troops sent in (reluctantly, some say) by the Home Secretary, Winston Churchill.[2] Anarcho-syndicalism, a radical labour movement emerging at that time, had a profound influence on Jones's thinking. Anarcho-syndicalists argued for transferring the means of production into the hands of the workers and for overthrowing the capitalist system by revolutionary means.[3] Jones's political views were probably more influenced by the philosophy of anarcho-syndicalist direct action and by such pamphlets as *The Miners' Next Step* (1912) and *Industrial Democracy for Miners* (1919) than by theoretical Marxism.[4] In 1918 Jones was elected the youngest ever Chairman of the Cambrian Lodge of the South Wales Miners Federation (SWMF). After having given up his evening classes in mining engineering, he was sponsored by the SWMF to attend the Central Labour College (CLC) in London between 1923 and 1925, where, according to Dai Smith, 'he seems to have widened his reading, especially of literature, but to have been less interested in the formal study of Marxist economics and philosophy'.[5] While in London, he joined the Communist Party and, on his return to Wales, became checkweighman at the Cambrian Colliery. In 1929 he lost his job because he refused to work with blackleg labour and remained unemployed until his death in 1939. Jones's political activity increased after he became unemployed. He became an organiser for the National Unemployment Workers' Movement, a political speaker and an organiser of demonstrations. Most famously, he led hunger marches to London in 1932, 1934 and 1936.[6] In 1936 he became one of two Communist Party councillors on the Glamorgan

County Council, 'sign[ing] on at the Labour Exchange in Tonypandy before catching the bus down the valley to Cardiff'.[7] When he died in 1939, *We Live* lacked a few last chapters. Mavis Llewellyn, the model for Mary Jones in the novels, a schoolteacher and generally euphemistically described as a 'close friend' of Lewis Jones, finished the remaining chapters and saw the novel through to publication.

Lewis Jones traces the genesis of his novel *Cwmardy* back to Arthur Horner's suggestion that 'the full meaning of life in the Welsh mining areas could be expressed for the general reader more truthfully and vividly if treated imaginatively, than by any amount of statistical and historical research'.[8] Choosing a largely documentary realist style, he used autobiographical experiences as well as stories and anecdotes told to him to '"novelise" … a phase of working-class history'.[9] As Dai Smith has shown, this does not mean the faithful retelling of historical events but a reorganisation and reinterpretation of events according to a particular vision of dialectical historical development. Most of his main characters have real-life models: Len Roberts is clearly partly based on Jones himself but also partly on his friend Jack Jones, a founder member of the British Communist Party, a contemporary of Jones at the CLC and later imprisoned with him in 1926.[10] The miners' leader Ezra Jones is based on Noah Rees, a trade union activist, one of the student rebels at Ruskin College who founded the CLC, and co-author of *The Miners' Next Step*. Later, during a dispute at the Cambrian Colliery in 1923/4, Rees 'advocated caution and compromise' and was 'denounced by more militant leaders'.[11] In Ezra one can also detect a distant echo of the nineteenth-century trade union leader and Liberal MP, William (Mabon) Abraham. Mabon was a successful miners' leader in his time, but in 1875 was brought to accept the Sliding Scale, a scheme which linked workers' pay to the selling price of coal and, thus, put workers at the mercy of international markets. Ezra's phrase, 'half a loaf is better than none', is usually attributed to Mabon, which means that Ezra is immediately identified as an old-style Lib-Lab sympathiser. And finally, Arthur Horner, another founder member of the British Communist Party and President of the SWMF, became the model for Harry Morgan.

While the novels certainly are important documents of their time, the question of their quality as literature is more difficult to answer. Flaws include the narratives' sentimentality, the narrator's tendency to over-explain events and their significance, rather 'stilted dialogue' and the

> failure to imagine fully a group of relationships. The only development that matters is Len's ... At times the sketchiness matches Len's limited discoveries [in *Cwmardy*] ... but mainly it represents a lack of full imaginative realisation.[12]

Perhaps one reason for these flaws is the tension between Jones's wish to paint a rich and realistic portrait of a community while at the same time superimposing a political interpretation, which means that plot and characters are subordinated to the development of the central argument. This interpretation is supported by Douglas Garman, who, as Jones's editor at Lawrence & Wishart, knew the manuscripts well. His editorial work was substantial: he cut at least 50,000 words from a sprawling manuscript of about 200,000 words and may have tactfully rewritten sections.[13] Lewis Jones acknowledged Garman's work in a letter:

> In the circumstances that have developed since the first draft it is misleading to name myself as the author because yourself and the other comrade have at least as much responsibility for it ... I want you to know how much I appreciate your efforts that made an idea into a fact, reminiscences and emotions into a book.[14]

In his obituary of Lewis Jones, Garman notes that writing was not an end in itself for Jones but 'only one of many modes of political activity simultaneously exercised'. He argues that the novels are 'dominated by the unfolding of an idea in terms of mass action'. which leads to the problem that 'a writer [can] disregard the individual development of his characters and ... concentrate on the unfolding of the action'.[15] In other words, the idea and the novel's structure come to dominate the plot at the cost of the motivation and development of characters. Robert Tressell's *The Ragged-Trousered Philanthropists* (1915) is an interesting comparison because this novel, too, is a 'novelised' argument for organised labour politics. The satirical 'speaking' names of his characters, such as Mr Rushton, owner of a painting and decorating business who is known to rush jobs, J. Didlum, purveyor of furniture at extortionate prices, or old Philpot, a workman fond of his drink, indicate that they are representative rather than fully developed characters. Similarly, Lewis Jones's characters are either lively stereotypes, such as Len's parents, Big Jim and Siân, or they function as mouthpieces for particular viewpoints and class interests, like the shopkeeper Cardi Evans, father of Len's schoolfriend Ron. Ron himself breaks the mould of class expectation but is given no more scope to develop than his father.

Defenders of the novels have claimed that they explore a new aesthetics in which a collective, communal identity replaces bourgeois models of realist character development and that *We Live* 'dispenses with the traditional representation of individual character in the realist novel'.[16] This strikes me as far-fetched not least because of Simone Weil's apt objection that 'Several human minds cannot become united in one collective mind, and the expressions "collective soul", "collective thought" ... are altogether devoid of meaning.'[17] While Jones wrote about a close-knit community based on a shared occupation and did include several vivid crowd scenes, the action is, nevertheless, channelled through a circle of main characters. John Pikoulis also argues that the novels do not 'dismiss character in favour of community'.[18] But, like Tressell's novel and contrary to other contemporary industrial novels such as Gwyn Jones's *Times Like These* (1936), Jack Jones's *Black Parade* (1935) or Harold Heslop's *Last Cage Down* (1935), merely portraying working-class life is not Jones's main goal. The novels are also a call to arms, another weapon in the activist's arsenal to persuade a UK-wide audience of the rightness of his argument. Dentith points out that 'In Lukacsian terms, [*Cwmardy*] is confidently narrated; all the multiple details of the novel are subservient to the central narrative, whose overall trajectory and significance becomes cumulatively apparent.'[19] This is a considerable achievement. The novels' style also makes them particularly interesting to historians, who cite them for their documentary value.[20] There is a strong suggestion that, for Lewis Jones, novel-writing was a continuation of political activism by other means, and perhaps the impact of the novels cannot well be measured by aesthetic criteria alone.

Lewis Jones inhabited and wrote about a South Wales that has vanished, along with the industries that sustained it. It was a world in which communal solidarity based on class and an implacable hostility towards members of the other classes pervaded all areas of life. The 'frontier spirit' which had welded together communities of workers and owners of mines during the nineteenth century when the majority of mines were sunk had given way to an ever-widening gap between owners, agents acting on their behalf, and workers. Compromise seemed impossible to politically radicalised workers. The radical anarcho-syndicalist pamphlet *The Miners' Next Step* would in 1912 openly propose that 'The old policy of identity of interest between employers and ourselves be abolished, and a policy of open hostility installed.'[21] Matters were not helped by the attitudes of some mine owners, such as the famously capricious D. A.

Thomas, Lord Rhondda, who wrote in *The Western Mail*: 'I have given up politics for the time being, and I am now immersed in commerce ... I believe in getting as much pleasure and happiness out of this world while you are in it, so long as you do not interfere too much with the happiness and pleasure of other people.' Even to those in the middle class who were socially concerned, like the civil servant Thomas Jones, who, using the pseudonym *Beatis Pauperes*, took this quotation as a basis for a hostile article against 'Lord Rhondda's Religion' in the Liberal periodical *The Welsh Outlook* (November 1916, p. 341), this sounded like hedonism pure and simple, which contrasted badly with the widespread poverty of the mineworkers and their families.

Len's political education and political activism lie at the centre of the novels. However, I would agree with Pikoulis's interpretation that 'Len's politics are what come to him – he does not go out to them; he is a reluctant politician, one who would much rather consult his own interests',[21] if by that he means that Len is reluctant to subordinate his political instincts to the interests of the party machinery. At the core of the novels lies the struggle of the working-class characters for freedom, for living a life free from oppression and for the basic dignity of being able to decide their fate. Liberty is fundamentally important but it is at odds with the logic of capitalism, which deprives workers of freedom because it chains them to the means of production while not allowing them any control over them. Jones presents the case for the organisation of the working-class labour movement in *Cwmardy*, and, in *We Live*, the Communist Party is shown as the only credible organisation for that task. At the same time, there are oddly discordant notes, which reveal Len's – and perhaps the author's – uneasiness at placing Communist Party resolutions above his own political judgement.

Liberty, by many understood as an inalienable right, is closely linked with the exercise of political power. According to Hobbes, being unfree means that an outside agent denies one the power to act.[23] Isaiah Berlin, in 'Two Concepts of Liberty', later defined this concept as 'negative liberty', namely the freedom from oppression or coercion. He contrasts 'negative liberty' with 'positive liberty', in which liberty, rather than being defined by what it is not (i.e. lack of oppression), is positively defined as the freedom to act according to one's wishes.[24] These terms are related but are not the same. Even though Berlin worked in the liberal rather than a Marxist tradition, his terminology has become influential and will be used here. Marxist philosophy is much preoccupied by analysing the various ways in which the capitalist state and bourgeois society systematically remove or curtail the liberty of the working class. A preoccupation with liberty, which is concerned with removing oppression and with allowing people to achieve a degree of control over their lives and act freely, clearly lies at the heart of the political analysis that informs *Cwmardy* and *We Live*. The novels describe capitalism as a system in which inequality and lack of freedom are inbuilt, which means that it is both unjust and immoral.[25] For Jones, the system was beyond repair, and he had no patience with gradualist reformers like the Fabian-dominated Labour Party of the 1930s, which, in turn, was deeply suspicious of the anarcho-syndicalism emanating from the South Wales valleys.[26] The argument presented in the novels is that freedom can only be restored by a revolutionary shift of power over the means of production from owners to workers.

It is interesting to note that, in Jones's analysis, the lack of freedom generated by capitalism encompasses workers and owners. Lord Cwmardy is sentimentally attached to the valley: he enjoys presiding over the local *gymanfa ganu* in the manner of a nineteenth-century coalowner-patriarch, for example.[27] But, more importantly, he is as tied to an exploitative capitalism as the workers are. He has a choice, of course. His fault is that he is weak, without imagination, and allows himself to be led by a manager and a financial advisor, Mr Higgins and Mr Hicks.[28] Hicks is the more formidable enemy and is doubtless based on William Joynson-Hicks, Conservative Home Secretary between 1924 and 1929, an authoritarian figure who reputedly took particular pleasure in putting down the miners and in prosecuting some of them after the general strike in 1926.[29] At the other end of the spectrum are the workers. Their life is utterly dominated by their work and the way the mines are managed deprives them of almost all agency and humanity.

Cwmardy describes Len's and, by implication, the village community's educational journey towards political consciousness from the late nineteenth century through to the 1920s. The first step of this journey is for Len to experience and reject the formal, rigid and arbitrary authority of an overwhelmingly powerful institution: school. Len and his friend Ron play truant sometimes. Len's mother, Siân, is called in to see the schoolmaster, Mr Vincent, who proceeds, first, to humiliate her and, second, to teach Len a lesson by beating him in front of the whole class. Len, never having been beaten before, is terrified. Instinctively, he pulls his hands back as the cane descends, with the result that it comes down painfully on Mr Vincent's own shin. The children start laughing and an infuriated Mr Vincent brutally beats Len's head with the cane. A punishment routine for the time turns into a display of baseless tyranny. But then the children stage a spontaneous revolt: Mary flings her ink bottle at the schoolmaster, who, momentarily blinded, fails to see where the missile came from. The children sit 'motionless and every eye looked straight in front' (*Cwmardy* 33). Helpless, Mr Vincent turns and leaves the room.

Len learns several important lessons that day. First, he learns about the value of courageous leadership in the face of tyranny and the power of a group united against a more powerful enemy. Second, his struggle against an arbitrary display of power is an emblem of the larger social struggle against oppression. Third, he comes to reject a school which, far from instilling a love of learning, exists only to instil discipline and to act as a social sorting machine that determines life chances according to parental class status. As will become obvious later in the novel, Len does not reject learning. What he rejects is the oppressive 'apparatus' of the education system (in the Althusserian sense). Gallingly, Ron is not punished at all because his parents are middle class and he is destined for college (*Cwmardy* 27). Interestingly, Mary appears far more willing than Len to find her place within organisations: in school she keeps her head down and succeeds; later, she quickly rises through the ranks of the Communist Party while Len remains a party activist.

Len's next lesson about oppression and lack of freedom arrives when his teenage sister Jane, for whom the boy entertains increasingly confusing feelings, has a brief fling with the son of Evan the Overman, a colliery official, and becomes pregnant. Deeply embarrassed, for it is not easy for them to take the moral high ground when they themselves are not married, Big Jim and Siân try to force Evan and his son to acknowledge the pregnancy and 'do the decent thing'. Instead, they are insulted by Evan and have to return home without a promise of marriage (*Cwmardy* 65–7). In the end Jane dies in childbirth, a private tragedy which is structurally juxtaposed with a collective tragedy, namely a pit explosion. Again, grief is borne privately, helplessly, even though there is a culprit: the men have known for a while that pit safety had deteriorated. In these pre-trade union days, however, the men are powerless to do anything except try to restore their pit to a semblance of safety (*Cwmardy* 116). There is no redress and, despite Big Jim's bravura performance at the inquest (*Cwmardy* 124–31), the owner and a collusive JP manage to shift the blame onto a dead workman. These two linked incidents teach Len that the powerless are not granted justice. Jane's death also makes him alive to women's sexual as well as economic exploitation by men, a point sometimes missed by critics.[30] He comes to associate sexuality with death, which makes him avoid

sexual relations with women in adulthood.[31] Another set of
linked incidents is connected to the work underground. The
descriptions of the workplace are among the best in the
novel, perhaps because, in Garman's words, the pit 'has a
tremendous fascination for [Jones], much as the sea has for
other writers. He writes about it as though it were a
personality.'[32] The pit soon takes over Len's life: 'Slowly he
came to regard himself as a slave and the pit as his owner
... Not that he had any objection to the work, but the
thought that he was tied to the pit horrified him' (*Cwmardy*
160). He cannot yet put into words what he dreads, but, a
few years after starting work, his education is about to leap
forward when he meets Ron again, who lends him books on
socialism. Len, cursing his defective schooling, cannot
understand much of the books and the weary toil of working
underground by day and reading for much of the night takes
its toll and he falls ill. The 'loss of his wages [plays] havoc
with the domestic budget' (*Cwmardy* 166), and Len learns
to his dismay that his family cannot afford for one of the
wage earners of the family to be ill. 'The books he had been
reading, in addition to improving his vocabulary, had also
explained why the family could not meet the obligations
incurred during his enforced period of idleness' (*Cwmardy*
168). Regular work heavily curtails his 'positive' liberty, but
'idleness', this powerfully inappropriate word for enforced
unemployment used at the time, immediately throws the
family into debt. His increasing political knowledge makes
Len realise that Big Jim's complacent fatalism ('That's just
how it be in this old world, boy bach', *Cwmardy* 168) is
misplaced. Seeking further guidance, he finds it for a while
in a somewhat unlikely father figure, the miners' leader,
Ezra Jones.

The first test of Len's new learning – recently
augmented by Council-run night-school classes in
engineering (*Cwmardy* 188) – comes when the men decide
to go on strike. Due to Len's intervention, the strike is
being fought for a minimum wage and the right to form a

trade union. The strike described is based on the 1910–11 strike, which resulted in violence and in the police and troops being sent into the coalfield. Jones is somewhat free with the chronology of events: he presents them as an argument for unionisation, while the real SWMF had been in existence for at least twelve years by that time.[33] Len now espouses a new political conviction, namely that 'While it is true that our bodies belong to the pit, so also it is true that this makes us masters of the pit' (*Cwmardy* 269). *The Miners' Next Step* phrases this anarcho-syndicalist principle thus:

> Every industry thoroughly organised, in the first place, [is] to gain control of, and then to administer, that industry. The co-ordination of all industries [falls to] a Central Production Board, who, with a statistical department to ascertain the needs of the people, will issue its demands on the different departments of industry, leaving to the men themselves to determine under what conditions and how, the work shall be done. This would mean real democracy in real life, making for real manhood and womanhood. Any other form of democracy is a delusion and a snare.[34]

Seizing the means of production would, in theory, bring liberty to the people. Workers were to secure decision-making powers in how mines were run. In the words of *The Miners' Next Step*: 'On that vote will depend in a large measure your safety of life and limb, of your freedom from oppression by petty bosses, and would give you an intelligent interest in, and control over your conditions of work' (1912, n.p.). Agency and, therefore, dignity and humanity depend on liberty. Bit by bit, the community is politicised.

The political argument in the novel may be straightforward, but it does not lack complexity. Not all collective action is beneficial, for instance. The way the First World War is referred to in *Cwmardy* provides an interesting contrast between mass action based on rational criteria and mass action based on emotional manipulation. As the war starts, Len, by nature a pacifist, finds himself alone in his opposition to the war. True to type, Big Jim immediately joins up and Mary, the principled daughter of her father, wishes fervently she could do likewise (*Cwmardy* 327 and 333). Len finds he cannot resist the pressure, attempts to join up but is refused on health grounds. What then follows is an increasingly critical, class-based analysis of coercive recruiting practices and demagoguery. The colliery recruiting office holds a rally. Lord Cwmardy, Hicks, Ezra and assorted village worthies share a platform and whip up people's emotions so much that they recruit 510 men in one day:

> Both Mary and Len were overcome by the fervour of the whole proceedings. The lights, emphasising the glamorous colours of the decorations, seemed to dance in the vibrations of the mass singing and swept the people forward on waves of hysterical emotion. (*Cwmardy* 347)

Even as normally rational characters like Mary and Len are drawn in, the narrator remains sceptical: 'Waves of hysterical emotion' were not going to sustain the women and children left behind by these men. And while young and middle-aged workmen are alternately cajoled and pressurised to join up, there is no expectation that men like Lord Cwmardy's son, Hicks or even Ezra do likewise. Len begins to question the grounds for war and invites an anarcho-syndicalist lecturer to speak on the case against war. Despite threats of victimisation from Hicks and some disapprobation from Ezra and Mary, who both believe in the justness of the war, the lecture goes ahead. Unfortunately, the lecturer addresses his audience by – as the narrator notes reprovingly – using the same methods of emotional appeal:

He had appealed to the people through their emotions,
had played on their feelings and their deep subconscious
desire for the war to end. But, after lifting them to heights
of emotional enthusiasm, he had left them dangling with
no foundation for their feet. He had not told them what
they could do to end the war. (*Cwmardy* 369–70)

Because the speaker told Len what he wanted to hear, he is
disappointed when he is later revealed to be a man unable
to stand by his principles (*Cwmardy* 379). This incident
completes Len's political education as he, somewhat
painfully, realises that the basis for the exercise of positive
freedom lies in the rationality of the choices made.
Henceforth, he distrusts emotional manipulation by
demagogues, regardless of political colour, even as he revels
in the positive feelings generated by collective action.

Cwmardy, thus, by means of significant incidents such
as colliery accidents, the 1910–11 strike, and the First
World War, as well as through educational endeavours such
as the informal study circle Len and Mary set up (*Cwmardy*
305–6; 319 *et passim*), establishes that there is a need for
a centralised political organisation, which goes beyond local
trade unions. *We Live* begins where *Cwmardy* leaves off,
both chronologically and in terms of the main argument
proposed. The action of *We Live* begins in 1924 and takes
the reader through to the mid-1930s. The novel documents
worsening labour relations, which are partly the result of a
slump in international coal prices after the war and the
hardening of battle lines between labour and capital. The
reader may be forgiven for seeing *We Live* as a seemingly
never-ending chain of industrial disputes (including a lock-
out, the general strike of 1926 and an example of a
particular South Walian form of protest, the stay-down
strike), as well as party meetings, mass meetings, street
meetings and demonstrations. Len is now increasingly
active in the service of his political convictions: he joins the
Communist Party (*We Live* 416) and transfers his political

loyalties from Ezra, who is now presented as a spent force, to the Communist Party leader, Harry Morgan. The first part of *We Live* is devoted to Len persuading his initially reluctant wife, Mary, over to his point of view. In some sense, Mary's joining the Communist Party functions as a symbol for the radicalisation of the whole community. One incident is symbolic of the change: Ezra and Mary go to a Labour Party meeting, which, unbeknownst to the organisers, has been infiltrated by Communist Party members. Len is absent because he is imprisoned at the time. A speaker is disrespectful towards Len and, by implication, towards Communists in general. Mary indignantly storms the platform with Ron and Harry Morgan at her side, the councillors and speakers melt away and the meeting is taken over by Communist Party activists. Mary joins the Party that same evening (*We Live* 654-5). The radicalisation of Cwmardy and the neighbouring villages proceeds in an almost revolutionary way:

> *We Live*, with its fierce, often schematic, tabulation of political lessons culminates in a wide acceptance of the logic of Popular Front [the political alliance of socialist parties, including the Labour Party and the Communist Party] policies impelled by the dynamism of a locally rooted Communist Party.[35]

The way the novel is plotted to put forward this argument has been documented elsewhere (e.g. by Smith, 1982). Instead, I want to focus on moments of unease that seemingly contradict the main argument, namely Len's disquiet about how the Party works as an organisation. Historical accounts of Lewis Jones show that he did not always toe the party line. Hywel Francis recounts an often-repeated anecdote about Jones, which illustrates this:

> I spoke to Billy Griffiths, close friend and comrade of Lewis ... Imagine, ... he said, attending the Seventh

World Congress of the Communist International in Moscow in 1935. Stalin arrives. The thousands in attendance rise. Everyone except Lewis, who was one of the small band of British delegates. He was sent home in disgrace and disciplined by the British Communist Party.[36]

Francis interprets this anecdote to mean that Lewis Jones took a principled stance against the personality cult that had developed around Stalin. Another possible explanation is that he resented Communist Party rules and the implied claim to total obedience. Simone Weil has argued that 'As soon as a party finds itself cemented not only by the co-ordination of activities, but also by unity of doctrine, it becomes impossible for a good militant to think otherwise than in the manner of a slave.'[37] And, as Dai Smith observes, Lewis Jones was certainly no 'slave':

It never seems to have occurred to Lewis Jones that his conduct might just not be politic. It was unthinkable not to be political and he never wavered from his commitment to the Communist Party as the most advanced section of the working class; though, like Arthur Horner, his insistence on also adding his own views to the current party line did not always endear him to those who were, first and foremost, party organisers.[38]

Similarly, Len, although never questioning the primacy of the Communist Party, finds it difficult to submit to party discipline. As Stephen Knight has pointed out, 'Len ..., like Lewis Jones, remains committed more to the emotional immediacy of resistance than to the elaborate and centralized authority of Communist Party decision-making.'[39] In fact, Len is repeatedly flattered, cajoled and on occasion coerced into accepting party decisions which seem to flatly contradict the original purpose of political action, namely to achieve liberty. There are many examples worth discussing, but I am going to limit myself to three.

The first is a criticism of the way in which the party supersedes individual will and thus sacrifices individual freedom of action. Just before the General Strike in 1926, Harry Morgan decides to send Len to 'the city' to speak on behalf of the miners. Len is flattered but, feeling uncomfortable at the thought of leaving his village, he wants to refuse. When flattery does not work, Morgan practically orders Len to go: '"Your place is where you are wanted most," he declared sharply' (*We Live* 578). Attempting to temper the harshness of his order, he then waxes enthusiastic about Len's importance in the struggle:

> Harry went on in this strain for a long time, giving Len no chance to say a word until he had finished, by which time he had drawn a word picture of such immensity that it frightened Len, although the logic of his life experiences forced him towards it. (*We Live* 578)

The sense of coercion in this passage is inescapable, even though Len learns from the experience. Harry does not convince Len so much as overwhelm him. He brooks no dissent and Len gives in.

Second, the party line occasionally goes against Len's convictions, such as when the Communist Party decides to abandon the stay-down strike and order the men out of the pit. True to his anarcho-syndicalist principles, Len advocates a continuation of the strike as long as the men wish to continue with it. Harry objects because he regards a strike involving only a few of the men in one pit as amounting to 'anarchy' (*We Live* 814). Mary, by now a dedicated member of the Communist Party and a councillor, responds to Len's doubts by saying: 'Right or wrong, it is the line and we have to be true to it' (*We Live* 815). Party discipline is put above individual judgement and there is no room for differences of opinion. Again, Len gives in, but not out of conviction. In the end, the men decide to go on with the strike and win a victory, thus belatedly vindicating Len's stance.

Lastly, perhaps the most significant incident demonstrates that the party also sometimes removes agency and therefore positive liberty from party members: the party holds a meeting to discuss the Civil War and with a view to sending an activist to Spain to fight for the Republican cause. Len, still essentially a pacifist, is quiet throughout the meeting, but soon senses that he is meant to volunteer. This becomes obvious when Mary asks on his behalf if only men with war experience can volunteer, which is denied. She sighs – a signal that she is prepared to part with him, if reluctantly. From that moment, a decision has been reached. Len does not speak until after the meeting when Harry comes to tell him that he has to leave within three days. Len speaks 'with a face hard as stone': '"That's all right. It'll give me nice time to square things here. What do you say Mary?" She squeezed his hand proudly in hers and looked at Harry. "Whenever the Party says, we'll be ready"' (*We Live*, 842). His question, which might be read as a last plea for leniency, is answered with Mary's now characteristic unquestioning loyalty to Party decisions. There is no way out for Len and he, taking his responsibility seriously, fights bravely and ultimately dies in Spain. The incident is chilling in its depiction of the coercive power of the Party. The obvious signals sent out by Len's silence are ignored and he is 'volunteered' without him ever formally assenting. To be clear, it is not the cause that occasions this disquiet: Lewis Jones was a vocal supporter of the Republican cause in the Spanish Civil War. He died after addressing some thirty Spanish Aid street meetings, although it may be doubted whether he really managed to squeeze all of these meetings into one day, as Garman and Francis claim.[40] However, Francis also shows that Lewis Jones was alive to the 'personal anguish' caused by the deaths of young volunteers and grieved at 'the Communist Party recruiting young men for what appeared inevitable death', asserting that the party had no right to expect such a sacrifice.[41] In the novel, Len shares this ambivalence but is coerced into accepting his assignment.

In these last chapters it is impossible to know which sections were written by Lewis Jones and which by Mavis Llewellyn. Her words might have reinforced the internal contradiction and increased the complexity of the chapter or they may have smoothed them out. I also do not want to give the impression that Len turns from Paul to Saul in *We Live* or that most of the novel is given over to criticisms of the party line. However, they reveal the political commitment expressed in the novels to be idiosyncratic and complex. These complexities make the novels more interesting because they express something of the internal conflict experienced by a free spirit who grapples with the strictures of an organisation he himself has helped to its position of power. *Cwmardy* is perhaps a less complicated novel in this respect because the threats to liberty are overwhelming, the motivation is clear and the goal is far away. In *We Live*, it appears that the price of collective liberty may be won at the cost of individual liberty, which appears to be as grating to Len Roberts/Lewis Jones as it was to Simone Weil in rather different circumstances.

Cwmardy presents the development of political consciousness and the need for political organisation. The goal is to achieve negative and positive liberty for the collective and thereby for the individual. By requiring its members to toe the party line for the sake of political expediency, the Communist Party in *We Live*, though, is revealed to have a rather more complex relationship with liberty than first imagined. Not to shirk from dramatising this tension and the complex emotional and rational responses to the party may turn out to be Lewis Jones's greatest achievement.

NOTES
1   Dai Smith, 'Introduction', Lewis Jones, *Cwmardy* (London: Lawrence and Wishart, 1978), n.p.
2   Kenneth O. Morgan, *Rebirth of a Nation: A History of Modern Wales* (Oxford: Oxford University Press, 1998 [1982]), pp. 146–7.
3   M. G. Woodhouse, 'Mines for the Nation or Mines for the Miners?', *Llafur* 2: 3, 1978, pp. 92–109.
4   Stephen Knight, 'Anarcho-syndicalism in Welsh Fiction in English', in *'To Hell with Culture': Anarchism in Twentieth-Century British Literature*, eds Gustav H. Klaus and Stephen Knight (Cardiff: University of Wales Press, 2005), pp. 51–65.
5   Dai Smith, *Lewis Jones*, Writers of Wales Series (Cardiff: University of Wales Press, 1982), p. 14.
6   Douglas Garman, 'A Revolutionary Writer', *The Welsh Review* 1: 5, 1939, pp. 263–7 (263); Smith, 1982.
7   Garman, 1939, p. 263.
8   Lewis Jones, *Cwmardy* (London: Lawrence & Wishart, 1978), n.p.
9   Jones, 1978, n.p.
10 Archives Network Wales. 'Jack Jones.' Online: http://www.archivesnetworkwales.info/cgi-bin/anw/fulldesc_nofr?inst_id=35&coll_id=11680&expand (accessed 13 May 2009); Smith, 1982.
11 Smith, 1982, pp. 14–5.
12 Philip George, 'Three Rhondda Working Class Writers', *Llafur* 3:2, 1981, pp. 5–13 (7); see also Smith, 1982, pp. 36–37.
13 Christopher Hilliard, 'Producers by Hand and by Brain: Working-Class Writers and Left-Wing Publishers in 1930s Britain', *The Journal of Modern History*, 78, 2006, pp. 37–64 (47).
14 Letter to Garman, n.d.; quoted in Hilliard, 2006, p. 47; the 'other comrade' presumably refers to Mavis Llewellyn.
15 Garman, 1939, p. 264.
16 Carole Snee quoted in Smith, 1982, p. 35.
17 Simone Weil, *Oppression and Liberty*, trans. Arthur Wills and John Petrie (London: Routledge, 2006 [1955]), p. 78.
18 John Pikoulis, 'The Wounded Bard: The Welsh Novel in English. Lewis Jones, Glyn Jones, Emyr Humphreys', *New Welsh Review*, 26, 1994, pp. 22–34 (24).
19 Simon Dentith, 'James Hanley's *The Furys*: The Modernist Subject Goes on Strike', *Literature and History*, 12: 1, 2003, pp. 41–56 (52).

20 For example, Hywel Francis, '"Say Nothing and Leave in the Middle of the Night": The Spanish Civil War Revisited', *History Workshop Journal*, 32, 1991 pp. 69–76; Julie-Marie Strange, '"She cried a very little": death, grief and mourning in working-class culture, *c.* 1880–1914', *Social History* 27:2, 2002, pp. 143–161.

21 *The Miners' Next Step*, 1912, n.p.

22 Pikoulis, 1994, p. 24.

23 Quentin Skinner, 'What is Freedom?' Lecture, CamTV (Cambridge: Cambridge University, 2006). Online: http://mediaplayer.group.cam.ac.uk/component/option,com _mediadb/task,view/idstr,CU-Alum-AWE06Skinner _audio/Itemid,35 (accessed: 1 January 2009)

24 Isaiah Berlin, 'Two Concepts of Liberty', *Four Essays on Liberty* (Oxford: Oxford University Press, 1969), pp. 118–72 (131).

25 Berlin, p. 125.

26 Knight, 2005; see also Roy Hattersley, *The Edwardians* (London: Little Brown, 2004), pp. 241–2.

27 Lewis Jones, *Cwmardy* and *We Live* (Cardigan: Parthian, 2005 [1937/1939]), pp. 434–5, 448. Further references to the novels will be included parenthetically in the essay.

28 Jones appears to confuse these two characters. In *Cwmardy*, Hicks is the manager and Higgins is the financial advisor. In *We Live* their roles have reversed.

29 Morgan, 1998, p. 284.

30 e.g. Joseph Pridmore, 'Gender and Community in 1930s Working-Class Writing', *Key Words*, 5, 2007, pp. 43–55 (45).

31 Pikoulis ,1994, p. 24.

32 Garman, 1939, p. 265.

33 Smith, 1982, p. 62; Morgan, 1998.

34 1912, n.p.; see also Knight, 2005, p. 52.

35 Smith, 1982, p. 34.

36 Hywel Francis, 'Foreword', Lewis Jones, *Cwmardy* and *We Live* (Cardigan: Parthian, 2006), pp. ix–x; see also Smith, 1982, p. 8.

37 Weil, 2005, p. 29.

38 Smith, 1982, pp. 8–9.

39 Knight, 2005, p. 59.

40 Garman, 1939, p. 263; Francis, 1991, p. 74.

41 Francis, 1991, p. 74.

A Hell of a Howl:

Gwyn Thomas's *The Dark Philosophers* and 'the Language of the Cry'

Laura Wainwright

In *Politics of Modernism: Against the New Conformists* (1989), Raymond Williams casts a critical eye over Expressionism – a movement and technique in European literature and visual art, which came to prominence in Germany in the first decades of the twentieth century.[1] Literary Expressionism, Williams avers, is 'the language of the cry':

> In some later Expressionist work the cry is a consciously liberating, indeed revolutionary moment: the cry can become a shout or the still inarticulate cry of protest; that cry which fights to be heard above the news bulletins, the headlines, the false political speeches of a world in crisis.[2]

We might question the relationship between the three novellas that comprise Gwyn Thomas's *The Dark Philosophers* – often viewed by critics as examples of Thomas's idiosyncratic brand of social realism – and a modernist aesthetic such as Expressionism. Indeed, this essay will aim to address this matter directly. But Williams's analysis of the Expressionist 'cry' clearly resonates with these narratives, all of which are concerned with exposing individual, social and political abuses of power. For all their comic excursions (a feature which I will return to later), these works 'fight to be heard' above the clamour of the first half of the twentieth century – 'the news bulletins, the headlines, the false political speeches' – crying out about the social and economic 'crisis' that befell the industrialised valleys of South Wales during the Great Depression of the 1930s and early 1940s: a period when, Thomas, who was born and brought up in the Rhondda, later recalled, 'we saw lunacy established among us as an apparently normal stable companion. We saw, but we didn't quite believe.'[3]

One of the earliest examples of what later became known as Expressionism is Edvard Munch's appositely titled painting of 1893, *The Scream* (*Figure 1*). In this work, an androgynous figure stands on a bridge, open-mouthed, his hands raised to his mask-like face, apparently screaming in horror, while an abstract scene churns behind him, the undulating sky streaked with red and yellow. The figure's environment seems to enact the tremor and commotion of his (and the complicit artist's) mind, conforming to the Expressionist principle that

> if the creative individual is a conscious and active participant in the structure of the reality of which he forms a part, then his will manifests itself by representing, criticising and changing that structure by means of self-expression, since his subject, in an aesthetic sense, represents objective reality. Therefore objective reality emerges through his subject, and the objective social goal through his art.[4]

In *The Scream*, moreover, as in all Expressionist art, 'the objective representation of reality disappears, behind the vision, which is called upon to express a deeper truth, a more essential insight'.[5] The nature of Munch's 'vision' or 'social goal' is clear. The figure's defamiliarised, almost ghoulish, appearance alienates him from the civilised, social world, represented in Munch's painting by the comparatively tangible bridge and respectable couple walking calmly behind; and Munch completes the figure's isolation by preventing the spectator from witnessing what has so alarmed him. In essence, Munch develops a *visual* 'language of the cry' by Expressionistically objectifying a shuddering modern consciousness of the solitude and unreliability of the self in the world. Indeed, his image of

Figure 1: The Scream by Edvard Munch

the aghast figure on the bridge seems almost to anticipate Jean Paul Sartre's existential epiphany: '*nothing* compels me to save my life, *nothing* prevents me from precipitating myself into the abyss. The decisive conduct will emanate from a self which I am not yet.'[6]

This kind of anguished 'subjectivism', which the Marxist critic Georg Lukács denounced in his essay 'The Ideology of Modernism' (1958) as 'rooted in the experience of the modern bourgeois intellectual',[7] might seem a long way from Gwyn Thomas's accounts of destitution and social decline in the working-class communities of the South Wales valleys. Yet Thomas's style is often far closer to Munch's than to realist accounts of working-class life seen, for instance, in Lewis Jones's *Cwmardy* (1937), Walter Greenwood's *Love on the Dole* (1933), or Robert Tressell's *The Ragged-Trousered Philanthropists* (1914). As M. Wynn Thomas argues, in many of his early works of fiction, Gwyn Thomas 'seems to have evolved what might be described as a Rhondda Expressionist style of writing, perfectly suited to the deranged phantasmagoria of the Depression period';[8] and this is exemplified at the beginning of *Oscar*, the opening novella of *The Dark Philosophers*, where we encounter Lewis, the text's narrator, waiting for his employer to emerge from the local pub:

> The rain bounced down from the chutes about six inches from where I stood. Beside me was a lighted window, small. The light from that window was very yellow and had a taste. Behind that window were about a dozen drunks, singing. Among those drunks was Oscar. I could tell that Oscar's voice if I was deaf. There was a feel about it, a slow greasy feel. Oscar was a hog.[9]

It transpires that Oscar is a wealthy, self-centred and exploitative industrialist and landowner, who resides in a commodious house on a mountain, waited on by Lewis, his errand-boy, and his browbeaten house-keeper, Meg, while his tenants and workers – the ordinary people of the Terraces – live in poverty in the valley below. And just as, in *The Scream*, the familiar world fades into a lurid visualisation of the trauma of modern selfhood, in the above extract from Thomas's novella, external reality is similarly inflected by a 'deeper truth' – a more 'essential insight' into the nature of the raucous drunk behind the pub window, and, most importantly, into the contemporary capitalist hegemony that he represents. Thomas's narrator identifies Oscar not as man but as 'a hog', introducing a line of imagery that is sustained throughout the text: elsewhere, for instance, he intimates that 'for a hog, Oscar did very well out of being a man' (6), and states that 'I wiped Oscar's mouth and eyes with my sleeve, which was thick and rough and made him grunt' (19). Indeed, Oscar displays many traits commonly associated with pigs: he is enormously fat and greedy; at one point, Thomas writes that his 'huge ... body poured over the sides of the chair on which he sat' (15). And his gluttony ranges beyond food to money, land or 'dirt' (6), beer and sex. As Lewis remarks, Oscar 'never saw a woman without wanting her, never wanted a woman without getting her' (44), and, in this regard, Oscar also seems to function as an emblem of the insidious patriarchal substructure of the social hierarchy. Nowhere is this more apparent than at the novella's conclusion, when Oscar seduces and preys, with 'skilled and solemn ecstasy' (p. 95), on Hannah – the despairing widow of a man whose death he had caused only days earlier. And Thomas displays an equivalent sensitivity to the distress of disempowered and mistreated women in the third novella of the collection, *Simeon*. In this final story, Simeon, another villainous landowner (discussed in more detail below), incarcerates his daughters in his 'nice big roomy house',[10] skirted by a 'plantation of oaks' (243), 'surrounded by some two acres of [rich] cultivated land' (p. 243), and situated on a mountain above another indigent South Wales community. There, he subjects his progeny to appalling psychological and sexual abuse until eventually, as in *Oscar*, his victims seek revenge.

From one perspective, we might see Oscar as a capitalist counterpart to the tyrannical pig Napoleon in George Orwell's famous satire of Stalinism, *Animal Farm* (1945). Indeed, the subtitle of the volume in which *Oscar* was first published, *Folk Tales from the Modern Welsh*, also calls to mind Orwell's text, which is subtitled 'A Fairy Story'. Thomas's narrative, however, does not operate in the same way as Orwell's. *Animal Farm* is, fundamentally, an allegorical fairytale, which relies on 'the active participation of the reader'[11] in its generation of socio-political meaning. Thomas, by contrast, is concerned with 'maintaining ... the primacy of the social *image* [my emphasis] through its subjective expression',[12] and presents the reader with a distorted yet, at the same time, pellucid and instructive social reality. As the following exchange between Lewis and Macnaffy, a young woman from the Terraces, evinces, Oscar is always, manifestly, both 'hog' and landowner, in an *expression* of outrage at an insatiable and inhumane capitalist system and its consequences in South Wales:

> 'How the hell do you feed him [Oscar] up to that size?' The girl's face was angrier and more savage as she asked that as if she herself had never had anywhere near enough food, and disliked the idea of Oscar wolfing more in a day than she had to get through in a lifetime in Brimstone Terrace, or wherever it was she lived. 'What do you feed him on?'
> 'Acorns. And twice a year I bathe him in swill.'
> 'Looks like it.' (16)

Here again, Thomas espouses the Expressionist premise, as delineated by José Ortega y Gasset in his 1925 essay, 'The Dehumanization of Art', that 'we [that is, artists] do not move from the mind to the world. On the contrary, we give three-dimensional being to mere patterns, we objectify the subjective, we "worldify" the immanent.'[13] Oscar is a three-dimensional holler of political dissent – 'that direction in language sought, in its own terms, to intervene in the social process and to change reality by struggle'.[14] Like Edvard Munch's painting, he is a 'worldified' scream, or (in the words of another Modernist, Katherine Mansfield) he is an objectified *'cry against corruption'*.[15]

Like Munch's 'endless scream passing through Nature',[16] Thomas's Expressionistic cry is both penetrating and reverberant. In the extract from the beginning of *Oscar* cited previously, the narrator informs us that the 'light from the pub window' in which Oscar drinks has 'a taste',[17] connoting incipient social decay, cognate with the gradual souring of milk. The light's 'very yellow' colour, reminiscent of the disquieting sallow shades of *The Scream*, also generates this impression, associating Oscar with a sickness in the valley that is both metaphorical and literal: Lewis subsequently reveals that Oscar's workers spent their days 'getting their guts turned half solid with coal dust and their limbs occasionally knocked inside out by ... small rocks' (51); that 'a thick belt of redness showed' on Meg's 'neck and the top part of her back' (27) under Oscar's lascivious gaze; and that his mother, confined to her dilapidated house in the Terraces, wore 'a distant look' that made her seem 'elsewhere all the time' (38). Indeed, as John Davies notes, 'from the mid-1920s onwards ... the health of many inhabitants of the [South Wales] coalfield was deteriorating', with cases of malnutrition, anaemia, tuberculosis and mental illness all increasing during the 1930s.[18] In Thomas's novella, even the topography of the region evokes an ailing, wounded body, as Lewis apprehends a 'fierce, yellow stream' (23) 'that cut into the ravine's bed' (28) – an image that calls to mind 'the yellow smoke that slides along the street' (l. 24) and 'Linger[s] upon the pools that stand in drains' (l. 18) in T. S. Eliot's modernist poem of individual and urban stagnation, 'The Love Song of J. Alfred Prufrock'.[19] This, also, faintly Joycean 'diagnostic realism'[20] re-emerges in *The*

Dark Philosophers novella itself, which is set in a mining community crippled by the legacy of another despotic (though, in comparison with Oscar, more realistically portrayed) 'coalowner', Mr Dalbie.[21] In this work, Thomas's 'socially conscious' (233) narrator tells how 'the Terraces crawled' (103) – afflicted by 'a bewildering scale of plagues like rickets, leaking roofs and hearts that lay in perpetual shadow' (113).

As in *Oscar*, Thomas adds Expressionistic touches of colour to the brooding landscape of *The Dark Philosophers* – the narrator, at one point discerns his companion Ben's 'deep voice' as 'a bluer streak in the shadow' (197) – inviting comparison, once again, with the visual arts and, in particular, with Conrad Felixmüller's affective representations of the industrialised Ruhr area of Germany. In *Industrie-Reglandschaft* (1922) or 'Rainy Industrial Landscape', for instance – a title that recalls the inclement opening scene of *Oscar* – Felixmüller also employs a palette of cold blues, greys and blacks to convey the austerity of a particular working-class locale, and in *Ruhrrevier I* (1920, *Figure 2*) he invokes a dull yellow (which also marbles the sky in *Industrie-Reglandschaft*) in order to educe a 'deeper truth' of human suffering and social inequality. In fact, the parallels between Thomas's style and European Expressionist painting are extensive. While, on the one hand, as Stephen Knight argues, we can construe Oscar as a modern incarnation of the hostile giants of Welsh mythology,[22] we can also regard him as a figure analogous to the grotesques that populate German Expressionist visual art: those in Otto Dix's *Prager Strasse* (1920) and *The Skat Players* (1920, *Figure 3*), for example, whom Dix deployed to rail against German militarism and expose the corruption of the Weimar Republic. And Oscar would also merge seamlessly into what George Grosz described as the 'hellish procession of dehumanised figures'[23] in his dismayed visualisation of contemporary metropolitan society, *Dedicated to Oskar Panizza* (1917–18). Grosz claimed that he painted this scene

Figure 2: Ruhrrevier I by Conrad Felixmüller

Figure 3: The Skat Players by Otto Dix

in 'protest against a humanity that had gone insane',[24] evoking the 'lunacy' that Thomas felt characterised the Depression period in South Wales. Indeed, Simeon, whom Thomas introduces in the following terms, might also be assimilated into Grosz's bizarre *danse macabre*:

> He [Simeon] had a red, round face as a rule. But it was thin and pale that night. His eyes looked sunken in and there was black around his eyes that looked like the puckered black blouse my mother wore when she was burying a relative. Simeon was stooped a bit, too, and walked on a stick. His lower lip was fat and stuck out, and you noticed it more with the rest of his face all sunken like that. And his stomach stuck out as well in an upward sort of way. I never saw a stomach like Simeon's. It looked built on a slant. He wore a corduroy coat and thick tweed trousers, brown as October leaves. (247)

Here, Simeon seems more than just a 1930s re-embodiment of Ysbaddaden Bencawr:[25] he is also an expostulatory manifestation of a privileged, introspective and antiquated landed class – another imaged 'exclamation'[26] of social disdain – and his cultured, bourgeois sensibilities are also implied through his veneration of English poetry. As Ben, Simeon's impressionable teenage helper, and the text's narrator, reveals:

> Simeon was strong on a man called Shelley. It [his poetry] was as deep as any I'd heard. It had a fine beat, the way Simeon said it, like the shadow of a song ...
> 'You understand that?' Simeon would ask. 'That clear, Ben?'
> 'No.'
> 'One day you'll understand. Light grows, boy.' (260)

The reader is invited to contemplate which of Shelley's poems Simeon intones to the narrator here; it is tempting, given his incestuous desire for his daughters – it becomes apparent that he is the father of their children – and his Dionysian proposition that he and Ben 'drink to Venus' (280), to imagine him declaiming verses from *Laon and Cyntha* (1817), Shelley's notorious epic poem centred on a romantic relationship between a brother and sister.[27] This exchange, however, also has an ironic sting: Shelley is well-known for his campaigns for social reform and his support of the working classes, yet Simeon, while reassuring Ben that 'Light grows', does nothing to 'illumine' his own 'tempestuous day'.[28] On the contrary, he is, like the Reverend Emmanuel in *The Dark Philosophers*, a 'secluded thinker' (*Philosophers* 194), preoccupied with 'the cosy little subtleties of the inner heart' (204). In the words of one 'dark philosopher', Arthur, he 'stands to one side and [in reality] gives not a damn about his neighbours providing his own skull is whole' (193).

Arthur's stark reference here to the condition of the Reverend Emmanuel's 'skull' pertains to a violence that ripples through Thomas's prose, and which is similarly evident in *Simeon*, when the narrator notices that 'the smile left his [Simeon's] face as if his swinging stick had smashed it off' (276). Indeed, this brutality, which reaches its apotheosis in *Simeon* during the exaggerated moment of Simeon's death, again connects Thomas's style with Expressionist art, which is itself notable for its 'morbidity of theme' and 'element of cruelty':[29]

> I saw Eleanor [Simeon's daughter] pick up a bread knife from the table. She held it stiffly in front of her. I saw Simeon run towards it, his mouth moving like a fish's mouth, his eyes swollen with the crying he was doing and glued to her face, and not seeing the knife that was sticking out in front of Eleanor. I saw his body rush into the knife and I saw the knife slide into his body as if it had been waiting for nothing but that, glad to take it to the hilt.
> I heard a long, choking scream from Simeon. (293)

Sometimes, as in *Simeon* and *Oscar*, cruelty in Expressionist art has a sexual charge. We see this, for example, in Grosz's 1918 painting *John the Sex Murderer* (1918), and in Max Beckmann's chilling critique of post-war Germany, *Night* (1918–19). In Franz Kafka's Expressionistic short story of 1919, 'In the Penal Colony', on the other hand, this motif takes the form of a machine comprising a Bed, a Designer and a Harrow, which subjects prisoners to a protracted and excruciating death. As the Officer, the operator of this apparatus and another agent of an oppressive socio-political system, explains,

> As soon as the [condemned] man is strapped down, the Bed is set in motion. It quivers in minute, very rapid vibrations, both from side to side and up and down. You will have seen similar apparatus in hospitals; but in our Bed the movements are all precisely calculated; you see, they have to correspond very exactly to the movements of the Harrow.
>
> ...
>
> Whatever commandment the prisoner has disobeyed is written upon his body by the Harrow. This prisoner, for instance ... will have written on his body: HONOUR THY SUPERIORS![30]

Objective reality recedes behind a similarly nightmarish, Kafkaesque social vision in *Oscar*, when Lewis observes workers gathering coal from Oscar's tip. 'I had seen the same look on all their faces', he avows,

> the look of people who are being fed in parts through a mangle. And at the handle of the mangle, turning away like blue hell in case anybody should have a little less pain than he paid rent on, stood Oscar. (28)

Echoing many of Kafka's stories, however, as well as a number of Expressionist paintings, Lewis's gruesome vignette also has an absurd and comic quality – a 'gallows humour',[31] as David Smith puts it. Thomas, as so often in his portrayal of Oscar, resorts to the grotesque, with 'its corresponding sense of interchange and disorder',[32] juxtaposing comedy with tragedy, and inspiring both amusement and disgust. Again, this paradigm is also discernible in *Simeon*, when, for example, Ben discloses that, often, Simeon

> would say that something would have to be done about my brain. He'd stand over me when he said that with a glimmer in his eyes that a man wears when he is on the point of getting really busy, as if he were going start dragging my brain through my ears, raw and red like cow liver, and polish off with his sleeve all the mud he'd find on it, a lot of mud, no doubt. (260)

Indeed, Thomas's prose oscillates continuously between the grave and the absurd. In *The Dark Philosophers*, the narrator complains that 'the standard of living [in the Terraces] had for long been so low that people tripped over it and took their time about getting up again' (104), and recalls that

> The last attempt that we [he and his friends] had made at joint letter-writing had been a long message to the local Council on the subject of an increase in burial fees at the local cemetery, an increase so steep it had scared several of the local voters right off dying, and had left them in a jammed position between life and death that was very boring to them and, no doubt, an annoyance to their neighbours. (232)

Similarly, in *Oscar*, Lewis reacts to his employer's splenetic outburst –

> You know those people that pick for me on that tip. They're mine. ... If I told them to get off this mountain, off they'd have to get. They'd be rotting about on their beds having more bastards like themselves. I ought to be able to do as I like to people like that. Don't know what they live for, anyway. (47)

– with 'I did not wish to be in that room if Oscar was going to be taken in such a fashion. I did not know how I would handle a man with a body shaped so much like a whale, and a mind shaped so much like another man's rear' (47–8). The 'cry' that resounds throughout these three texts, then, is often, at once, a cry of pain, of indignation, and of laughter: Thomas presents the reader (to use his own phrase) with 'a hell of a howl' (*Oscar*, 27) – in more ways than one.

In this respect, Thomas's style is especially evocative of a variant of European Expressionism that emerged in 1920 in the form of a play by the Galician dramatist and novelist, Ramón María del Valle-Inclán. This link with Spanish avant-garde theatre is not as surprising as it might sound: Thomas wrote several plays later in his career, and he was also a fluent reader and teacher of Spanish, who obtained a degree in Spanish from Oxford University and, in 1934, spent six months studying at Madrid's Universidad Complutense.[34] Entitled *Luces de Bohemia* or *Bohemian Lights*, Valle-Inclán's play is set amid the social and political maelstrom of Madrid and Barcelona between 1917 and 1922[34] – a background which the text's poet-protagonist, Max Estrella, identifies as 'a grotesque deformation of European civilisation'.[35] Moreover, he opines that contemporary society has become so ludicrously warped, that 'all forms of expression' should be distorted 'in the same mirror that ... contorts the whole miserable life of Spain' (61). This statement indexes Valle-Inclán's own aesthetic in the play – for the Spain of *Bohemian Lights* is indeed 'systematically deformed' (160); and Valle-Inclán calls his dramaturgical vision *esperpento*, meaning, literally, a frightful sight or piece of nonsense.[36]

Comedy, like everything else in *Bohemian Lights*, assumes grotesque shapes in the 'concave mirror' (160) of Spanish society, distending and contorting into a 'macabre humour',[37] which Valle-Inclán invests in his parade of 'frightful' and incongruous characters. There is the avaricious and chimeric bookseller, Zarathustra, for instance – a name that wryly alludes to Friedrich

Nietzsche's *Thus Spake Zarathustra* (1883–84), in which humanity is identified as 'a rope suspended between animal and Superman'[38] – who is introduced as 'a hunched figure with a face reminiscent of rancid bacon' and who chairs a 'literary gathering' attended by a cat, a parrot, a dog and a 'prying mouse' (100). And then there is the corrupt Home Secretary, who goes about his duties with 'his flies ... undone' and his 'glasses hang[ing] from the end of a string like two absurd eyeballs dancing on his belly' (139). Equally memorable are the mourners at Max Estrella's funeral, who reduce the occasion to a tragic farce by speculating that the deceased 'is not dead but merely cataleptic' (171). Moreover, all of Valle-Inclán's characters register what John Lyon elucidates as 'the metamorphosis' in *Bohemian Lights* 'of the heroic into the absurd under the influence of a ... grotesque social context', of an environment where 'social pressures and circumstances have become the controlling agents over the life of the individual'.[39]

This idea of the transposition of potentially heroic individuals into a mass of absurd and puppet-like caricatures not only chimes with Thomas's dark philosophers' 'sacred cause of freedom for the individual and progress for the masses' (*Philosophers*, 235), but also overlaps with his own views about comedy, which he expounded in an interview in 1950. 'People tell me', he commented, 'there are comic undertones in even my most sombre imagery. I can quite believe it. Humour is a sense of the incongruous or absurd, an aggravated contrast between man's divine promise and his shambling, shabby reality.'[40] The 'aggravated contrast' that Thomas describes here is perceptible throughout *The Dark Philosophers*, in the collection's panoply of eccentric characters. In *Oscar*, for example, there is the figure of No Doubt – so called because of his habit of saying 'no doubt' in response to anything anyone says to him, who wears, 'a fisherman's hat ... pulled down towards his neck', giving him 'the look of something growing out of the earth' (40); there is Waldo Williamson, who wears multiple layers of clothing all year round in order to ward off rheumatism, and then visits 'every pub he [passes] to get cool' (7); and then there is Clarisse who has 'lips ... like good chops of meat' (9), and makes a 'glugging sound' which, the narrator decides, she 'must have picked up from the pictures or the chickens' (11). Even the apparently shrewd and debonair Lewis, as Victor Golightly suggests, ultimately embodies a conflict between 'the Hero' and 'the murdering buffoon';[41] and at the centre of this text is the monstrous, and, as the following passage attests, frequently inane and clownish Oscar himself:

> Oscar cleared his plate minutes ahead of me. I [Lewis] was keeping my bacon and kidneys until the last, because I considered these items very tasty and not to be rushed. Before I could get to them Oscar took hold of my plate and ate them for me. I asked him whether he would not like all his food served by way of my plate, but he was too busy eating to pay any attention to all this wit. ...
> 'More for me. More for me. More for me,' he started to shout in a high childish voice, which sounded odd coming from an element with so tremendous a body as Oscar. (72–3)

Furthermore, in *The Dark Philosophers*, not only are the people of the Terraces 'made numb and stupid by poverty' (124), but also the local Public Assistance representative, whose role is to grant relief to those members of this community 'who do not even qualify for the Insurance', is reported as having a 'moustache [that] was so heavy he sometimes toppled over on his face when he was not wearing big boots with thick soles' (185) – a description that calls to mind the Porter in Valle-Inclán's play, who appears sporting 'a moustache and a beer gut, [and] looking like one of those dashing colonels who always manage to fall off their horses during a parade' (129). And the Reverend Emmanuel, before he finally shuns the influence of Mr Dalbie and rediscovers his political zeal, is portrayed in similarly slapstick terms: compared to 'an actor playing the part of somebody very old on stage who has just broken the flour bag over his head' (179). In *Simeon*, on the other hand, Thomas's main character is absurd, 'mad and cruel' (278), and familiar human interactions and relations – particularly those between father and daughter, and adult and child – are oddly and sinisterly disarranged:

> I watched Simeon like a rabbit a weasel. I chuckled once, like an idiot, just to have something to do. Simeon chuckled back. He sounded like an idiot, too. Too many idiots in one small box-room was my way of looking at it. He edged into the bed ... He was so hot. I was cold. It was like mustard and ice-cream mixed. It made you sick. ...
> Simeon's thick, course fingernails tickled me. ... I am very sensitive to this tickling. As with screaming, I don't like it. (265)

Moreover, while we might detect in Thomas's characters a Dickensian comic energy and a Caradoc Evans-like hyperreality,[43] they most strongly evoke the citizens of Madrid and Barcelona in Valle-Inclán's *Bohemian Lights* and the urbanites in Grosz's *Dedicated to Oscar Panizza*: all appear, to varying degrees, distorted and discomposed by the 'concave mirror' or 'lunacy' of their respective milieus. As Lewis insists in *Oscar*:

> You get a lot too much to live on, Oscar, and you get it too easy, and you live among too many people who don't get enough to live on and never get it easy, like my pal Danny. That's mad, Anybody can see that's mad. So you follow suit. You go mad too. Nothing surprising in that, Oscar. (49–50)

In an attempt, in *The Dark Philosophers*, 'to shout a little wisdom and compassion into the world's ear',[44] Thomas transforms individuals into communities of 'shambling' *esperpentos*, 'shabby' misfits and tragicomic puppets –

Expressionistic manifestations of a 'mad' or grotesque socio-political reality, of 'a world', as Raymond Williams suggests, 'in crisis'.

M. Wynn Thomas writes that 'cataclysmic change, of an unmistakable cultural, social, economic and political kind, was the dominant reality of south Wales life between the Wars', and this, he contests, 'is what caused ... Gwyn Thomas to devise a new form of art, capable of portraying the human face of desolating socio-economic process'.[45] As this essay has shown, Thomas's 'form of art' in *The Dark Philosophers* is not, essentially, new; on the contrary, it can be contextualised in relation to a wider trajectory of European Expressionist creativity, reaching back to Munch's sonorous *Scream* of 1893. Yet, equally, Thomas's style *is* new and, indeed, we might argue, modernist, in the sense that it arises out of, and seeks to enact artistically, an unprecedented 'crisis' or 'cataclysmic change' – 'a mighty convulsion', as Tony Conran calls it – in 'the fabric' of early twentieth-century Wales.[46] And although the three novellas collected in *The Dark Philosophers* were published in 1946, more than a decade after what is conventionally regarded as the modernist period, they nevertheless, like all modernist art, constitute engaged and experimental responses to *modernity* or a particular instance of the *modern* – to the 'shock of the new'.[47] As Peter Nicholls discusses in his diversifying study *Modernisms* (and as I hope to have reflected in this essay), 'it is commonplace now to acknowledge that Modernism is not one thing but many and that its divergent forms are profoundly determined by specificities of time and place'.[48] Gwyn Thomas's work cries out, as it were, to be included in this continuing scholarly reappraisal.

Another aspect of *The Dark Philosophers* which can be re-evaluated with this notion of a specifically Welsh modernism in mind is this text's highly distinctive and progressive use of the English language. Thomas's prose is suffused with made-up and mutated words and phrases; in *Oscar*, for instance,

the narrator describes 'the bawl of singing that splurched out
of his [employer's] mouth' (85), observes his friend, Danny,
standing on the coal tip, 'his sack dangling in his hand, the
other hand keeping the mouth of the sack open to admit the
ribblings of coal he picked up' (57), and reveals that his
'mother had greyed off into a fixed quietness since [his] father
died' (29). Thomas appears to be endeavouring in these
examples (to use T. S. Eliot's analysis of the praxis of the
modern poet) 'to force, to dislocate ... language into his
meaning',[49] with 'splurch' evidently originating from 'lurch'
and 'splurge'; 'ribblings' appearing to combine 'dribbling' and
'ribs'; and 'greyed off' collating two unremarkable words that,
together, in this context, produce an almost Brechtian
'alienation effect' within language.[50] This process of linguistic
deconstruction and 'creative reassembly'[51] also has much in
common with Expressionist narratives, which can often
appear 'chopped-up, telescoped or inverted'.[52] Indeed, we
might even view these resonantly unusual words and turns of
phrase as moments at which even language itself has become
disarrayed in the 'concave mirror' of the Depression period –
moments where 'the familiar is deconstructed, as in
modernist art, in order to be reconstructed in all its ...
unpredictable gratuitous strangeness'.[53] Thomas's approach
is, perhaps, most evocative, however, of Joyce's modernist
novel *Ulysses* (1922) – a text which, as the following passage
illustrates, flouts the rules of English in a comparable way:

Men, men, men.
    Perched on high stools by the bar, hats shoved back,
at the tables calling for more bread no charge, swilling,
wolfing gobfuls of sloppy food, their eyes bulging, wiping
wetted moustaches. A palled suetfaced young man
polished his tumbler knife fork and spoon with his
napkin. ... A man with an infant's saucestained napkin
tucked round him shovelled gurgling soup down his
gullet. A man spitting back on his plate: halfmasticated
gristle: no teeth to chewchewchew it.[54]

At the same time, Thomas's narratives are propelled by strikingly unconventional and, often, wildly inventive metaphorical language. In *Oscar*, for example, Lewis claims that 'around her [Meg's] face the time was nearly always night-time' (25), and states that 'I was full of wailing songs that passed through zones of light and dark inside me, and went from very high to very low in their sad, sickening passage' (96). Analogously, in *The Dark Philosophers*, the narrator muses that his friend Willie's 'brightness had undoubtedly been a bit cotton-woolled by the Rev. Emmanuel' (161), and describes how a 'scratch' on the Italian café owner Idomeneo's gramophone record 'went up and down to a certain beat, like a hoarse ghost following the music about, quarrelling with it' (124). In *Simeon*, too, Thomas's 'mind' – to cite Glyn Jones – 'shoots up all its material ... into massive and spectacular fountains',[55] as Ben recounts how he left a sleeping Simeon

> to his dreams, in which he probably went chasing himself around the moon like mad just for the sake of being able to tell himself that being out of breath was a hell of a thing, and the moon was a hell of thing for being there to tempt you to go chasing around it. Simeon was getting a lot too deep for me. (285)

In all of the above examples, we might deduce that Thomas recognises what Gilles Deleuze and Félix Guattari describe in their 1975 study *Kafka: Toward a Minor Literature* as the latent 'revolutionary conditions' of a literature, such as that of Anglophone Wales or Ireland, 'within the heart of what is called great (or established) literature',[56] and embarks on a fresh and distinctive 'utilization of English' – on 'setting up ... a minor [and, in this respect, potentially transformational and even ground-breaking] practice of a major language from within'.[57] Indeed, the 'conditions' of early twentieth-century Wales were, arguably, especially conducive to such verbal plasticity and novelty. This is because many Anglophone Welsh writers – Dylan Thomas,

Glyn Jones and Idris Davies, to name just a few – were first or, at most, only second-generation English speakers, who, as Conran emphasises, were 'essentially dealing with a new language'.[58] Certainly Gwyn Thomas was among the first in his large Welsh-speaking family to grow up speaking English alone, and he recalled his childhood home as follows: 'Our kitchen, about the size of an average hutch, was a busy, bi-lingual bomb of a place. The first six children spoke Welsh, the bottom six English, and all at the same time.'[59] Thomas's work, then, points towards a 'logical slippage'[60] between 'the minor', or 'the marginal', and 'the Modernist' – a nexus which should encourage us to consider more Welsh writing in English from the 1920s, 1930s and 1940s in relation to modernism – that is firmly grounded in both 'temporal' and 'cultural specificity'.[61] Moreover, in this light, the language of *The Dark Philosophers* reveals itself (to return to Raymond Williams's *Politics of Modernism*) as 'a consciously liberating, indeed revolutionary moment': not just as a 'howl' of condemnation and disenchanted laughter, but as a *rallying cry* to the Anglophone writers of Wales, in the absence, as yet, of a wholly distinct, affirming 'Anglo-Welsh' literary tradition,[62] to find their voice – to 'make it new'.[63]

NOTES

1   The Expressionist movement originated in Germany around 1910. The first group of Expressionist painters were the Dresden-based *Die Brücke* group, comprising Ernst Ludwig Kirchner, Emil Nolde, Karl Schmidt-Rottluff, Max Pechstein, Erich Heckel and Otto Mueller. The Munich-based *Blaue Reiter* group, consisting of Franz Marc, the Russian painter, Wassili Kandinsky, and Auguste Macke, followed in 1912–13. During the interwar years, Expressionism infiltrated other artistic media in Germany, including the theatre of Bertolt Brecht, Ernst Toller and Georg Kaiser, the poetry of Johannes R. Becher, and the prose of Kasimir

Edschmid. Paul Wegener's *The Golem* (1920), Robert Wiene's *The Cabinet of Dr Caligari* (1920) and Fritz Lang's *Metropolis* (1927) are important German Expressionist films. Expressionism significantly influenced the arts in other European countries, especially in France, Italy, Belgium, Spain and Czechoslovakia.

2   Raymond Williams, *Politics of Modernism: Against the New Conformists*, ed. Tony Pinkney, 2nd edn (London and New York: Verso, 2007), pp. 74–5.

3   Gwyn Thomas, 'The Central Wound', in *A Welsh Eye* (London: Hutchinson, 1964), pp. 9–24 (p. 18). As Glyn Jones notes, 'when short working and unemployment first began to be felt in the [South Wales] valleys in 1923, [Gwyn Thomas] was ten years of age; when prosperity was restored with the outbreak of the Second World War, he was twenty-six; so that part of his childhood and the whole of his young manhood were lived in a period of crippling poverty, emigration and unprecedented unemployment, and the widespread frustration, bitterness, suffering and despair that inevitably followed'; Glyn Jones, 'Gwyn Thomas', in *The Dragon has Two Tongues: Essays on Anglo-Welsh Writers and Writing*, ed. Tony Brown, 2nd edn (Cardiff: University of Wales Press, 2001), pp. 100–16 (p. 101).

4   György M. Vajda, 'Outline of the Philosophic Backgrounds of Expressionism', in *Expressionism as an International Literary Phenomenon*, ed. Ulrich Weistein, translated from the German by Linda Brust (Paris: Librairie Marcel Didier, 1973), pp. 45–58 (p. 48).

5   *Ibid.*, p. 58.

6   Jean Paul Sartre, *Being and Nothingness: An Essay on Phenomenological Ontology*, translated by Hazel E. Barnes (London and New York: Routledge, 1957), p. 56.

7   Georg Lukács, 'The Ideology of Modernism', in *The Lukács Reader*, ed. Arpad Kadarkay (Oxford: Blackwell, 1995), pp. 187–209 (p. 203).

8   M. Wynn Thomas, *Internal Difference: Literature in Twentieth-Century Wales* (Cardiff: University of Wales Press, 1992), p. 43.

9   Gwyn Thomas, *Oscar*, in *The Dark Philosophers* (Cardigan: Parthian, Library of Wales, 2006), pp. 3–101 (p. 3). All further references are to this edition and are given in the text.

10   Gwyn Thomas, *Simeon*, in *The Dark Philosophers* (Cardigan: Parthian, Library of Wales, 2006), pp. 243–95 (p. 251). All further references are to this edition and are given in the text.

11   Lynette Hunter, '*Animal Farm*: From Satire to Allegory', in *George Orwell: Contemporary Critical Essays*, ed. Graham Holderness, Bryan Loughrey and Nahem Yousaf (Basingstoke: Macmillan, 1998), pp. 31–46 (p. 34).

12   John Fordham, *Modernism and the Working Class* (Cardiff: University of Wales Press, 2002), p. 90.

13   José Ortega y Gasset, 'The Dehumanization of Art', in *'The Dehumanization of Art' and Other Essays on Art, Culture, and Literature*, translated from the Spanish by Helene Weyl (Princeton,NJ Princeton University Press, 1968), pp. 3–54 (p. 38).

14   Williams, p. 75.

15   Katherine Mansfield, 'Letter to J. M. Murry, 3 February 1918', in Vincent O'Sullivan and Margaret Scott, eds, *The Collected Letters of Katherine Mansfield: 1918–1919* (Oxford and New York: Oxford University Press, 1987), pp. 53–55 (p. 54). In this letter, Mansfield describes her writing as a '*cry against corruption.*'

16   Edvard Munch cited in Ulrich Bischoff, *Munch 1863–1944: Images of Life and Death* (Köln: Taschen, 2007), p. 53. Munch described his painting as 'an endless scream passing through nature'.

17   Thomas experiments with synaesthesia, or the mixing of the senses, in this way at several points in *The Dark Philosophers*. Synaesthesia fascinated many avant-garde and modernist artists, particularly the Italian Futurists. As John Willett explains, 'Expressionism made use of the visual discoveries of the ... Futurists, exploiting their ... simultaneity and sense of disintegration ... for expressive ends'; John Willett, *Expressionism* (London: Weidenfeld and Nicolson, 1970), p. 241.

18   John Davies, *A History of Wales* (London: Penguin, 1994), p. 580. According to Davies, 'a report in 1928 asserted that mothers of young children were suffering to an unusual extent from ... anaemia, and it was revealed in 1935 that 14.6 per cent of the children of the Rhondda were suffering from malnutrition. In the Rhondda there was [also] an

increase of 30 per cent in the proportion dying from tuberculosis between 1932 and 1937, a period when there was a marked decline in the incidence of the disease as a whole. Cases of mental illness also increased.'

19   T. S. Eliot, 'The Love Song of J. Alfred Prufrock', in *The Complete Poems and Plays of T. S. Eliot* (London: Faber and Faber, 1969), l. 3 (p. 13). All further references are to this edition and are given in the text.

20   Terence Brown, 'Introduction', in James Joyce, *Dubliners* (London: Penguin, 1992), pp. vii–xlviv (p. xv).

21   Gwyn Thomas *The Dark Philosophers*, in *The Dark Philosophers* (Cardigan: Parthian, Library of Wales, 2006), pp. 103–243 (p. 146). All further references are to this edition and are given in the text.

22   Stephen Knight suggests that *Oscar* is a 'modern version of a native unfriendly giant fable, with some resemblance to *Culhwch ac Olwen*'; Stephen Knight, *A Hundred Years of Fiction* (Cardiff: University of Wales Press, 2004), p. 99.

23   George Grosz cited in Norbert Wolf, *Expressionism*, ed. Uta Grosenick (Köln and London: Taschen, 2004), p. 42.

24   *Ibid.*

25   As Knight points out, Simeon, like the giant Ysbaddaden Bencawr in *Culwch ac Olwen*, is hostile to his daughter's suitor; Knight, p. 99.

26   Williams, p. 75.

27   This incestuous dimension was later omitted and Shelley's poem was renamed *The Revolt of Islam*; see Donald H. Reiman, ed., *Shelley's Poetry and Prose*, 2nd edn (New York and London: W. W. Norton and Company, 2002), p. 101.

28   Percy Bysshe Shelley, 'England in 1819', in Donald H. Reiman (ed.), *Shelley's Poetry and Prose*, 2nd edn (New York and London: W. W. Norton and Company, 2002), l. 14 (p. 327).

29   Willett, pp. 242–3.

30   Franz Kafka, 'In the Penal Colony', in *The Complete Short Stories of Franz Kafka*, ed. Nahum N. Glatzer, translated from the German by Willa and Edwin Muir (London: Vintage, 1999), pp. 140–67 (pp. 143–4).

31   David Smith, 'The Early Gwyn Thomas', *Transactions of the Honourable Society of Cymmrodorion* (1985), 71–89 (p. 74).

32   Susan Stewart, *On Looking: Narratives of the Miniature, the*

Gigantic, the Souvenir, the Collection (Durham, NC: and London: Duke University Press, 1993), p. 105.

33 Michael Parnell, *Laughter from the Dark: A Life of Gwyn Thomas* (London: John Murray, 1988), p. 23.

34 As John Lyon notes, the setting for *Bohemian Lights* is 'Madrid and Barcelona, between 1917 and 1922: the long smouldering industrial strife, the strikes and demonstrations, clashes with the police, political assassinations, the right-wing backlash in the form of vigilante groups like the Acción ciudadana, the impact of Lenin and the Bolshevik revolution, workers' meetings in the Casa del pueblo'; John Lyon, *The Theatre of Valle-Inclán* (Cambridge: Cambridge University Press, 1983), p. 107.

35 Ramón María del Valle-Inclán, *Bohemian Lights*, in *Valle-Inclán Plays: One*, translated from the Spanish by Maria M. Delgado (London: Methuen Drama, 1993), p. 160. All further references are to this edition and are given in the text.

36 *The Collins Spanish Dictionary Plus Grammar* (Glasgow: Harper Collins, 1998).

37 Maria M. Delgado, 'Introduction', in *Valle-Inclán Plays: One*, translated from the Spanish by Maria M. Delgado (London: Methuen Drama, 1993), pp. xiii–xlii (p. xxvii).

38 Friedrich Nietzsche, *Thus Spake Zarathustra: A Book for All and None*, translated from the German by Thomas Wayne (New York: Algora, 2003), p. 9.

39 Lyon, p. 109.

40 Gwyn Thomas cited in Jones, 'Gwyn Thomas', p. 103.

41 Victor Golightly, 'Gwyn Thomas's American "Oscar"', *New Welsh Review*, n.s. 22 (Autumn 1993), p. 27 (p. 30). Golightly argues that Lewis embodies 'two coincidental and antagonistic narrators'. One of these narrators, he suggests, appropriates 'the laconic style of the American detective hero that had been developed by [Dashiell] Hammett and [Raymond] Chandler', and the other is a 'buffoon [who also] has an American accent … and … is derived from the cinema and popular fiction', particularly the novels of Damon Runyon; Golightly, pp. 27–30.

42 *Ibid*, p. 30.

43 We might view the rural Welsh community of Manteg in Caradoc Evans's *My People* as 'a model of a real without origin or reality: a hyperreal'; Jean Baudrillard, *Simulacra*

and Simulation, translated from the French by Sheila Faria Glaser (Michigan: University of Michigan Press, 1994), p. 1.

44 Gwyn Thomas, 'The Central Wound', p. 21.

45 M. Wynn Thomas, Internal Difference, p. 32.

46 Tony Conran, Frontiers in Anglo-Welsh Poetry (Cardiff: University of Wales Press, 1997), p. 53.

47 Robert Hughes, The Shock of the New: Art and the Century of Change (London: British Broadcasting Company, 1980).

48 Peter Nicholls, Modernisms: A Literary Guide, 2nd edn (Basingstoke and New York: Palgrave Macmillan, 2009), p. viii.

49 T. S. Eliot, 'The Metaphysical Poets', in T. S. Eliot: Selected Essays, 2nd edn (London: Faber and Faber, 1934), pp. 281–91 (p. 289).

50 See Bertolt Brecht, 'A Short Organum for the Theatre', and 'Short Description of a New Technique of Acting which Produces an Alienation Effect' in Brecht on Theatre: The Development of an Aesthetic, translated from the German by John Willet (London: Methuen, 1964), pp. 179–205 and pp. 136–147.

51 M. Wynn Thomas, Corresponding Cultures: The Two Literatures of Wales (Cardiff: University of Wales Press, 1999), p. 61.

52 Willett, p. 241. Willett cites the work of the German writers, Hans Fallada, Kasimir Edschmid, Gustav Sack and Alfred Döblin as examples.

53 M. Wynn Thomas, Internal Difference, p. 29.

54 James Joyce, Ulysses (London: Minerva, 1992), p. 177.

55 Glyn Jones, 'Gwyn Thomas', p. 116.

56 Gilles Deleuze and Félix Guattari, Kafka: Toward a Minor Literature, translated from the French by Dana Polan (Minneapolis: University of Minnesota Press, 1986), p. 18. Ian Gregson also makes use of this theoretical model in his study of contemporary Anglophone Welsh poetry, The New Poetry in Wales (Cardiff: University of Wales Press, 2007).

57 Ibid, pp. 17–18.

58 Conran, p. 51.

59 Gwyn Thomas cited in Parnell, p. 9.

60 Chana Kronfeld, On the Margins of Modernism: Decentering Literary Dynamics (Berkeley, Los Angeles and London: University of California Press, 1996), p. 8. In this context, 'minor' obviously does not mean 'inferior' or 'unimportant',

but simply refers to Anglophone Welsh literature's minority-position within a dominant language.

61 Kronfeld, p. 8. Kronfeld notes that 'clearly, minor writing existed before modernism ... and will continue to exist after it', and therefore warns that 'to conflate the minor and the modernist without providing any historical criteria of contextualisation is to blur the temporality and cultural specificity of both'.

62 The term 'Anglo-Welsh' is used here simply to refer to Welsh writing in the English language.

63 Ezra Pound, *Make it New* (London: Faber and Faber, 1934). Thomas revealed his vision for Welsh fiction in English in 1971, when he stated that 'We [Welsh writers] should by now have created a body of intelligent fiction in English of unique, tempestuous quality, something that would have had the ... London weeklies trembling in admiration'; Gwyn Thomas, cited in Smith, pp. 71–2.

'Everything is Fluid in Me':

A Postcolonial[1] Approach to Alun Lewis's
In The Green Tree

Steve Hendon

In the Green Tree is a collection of letters and short stories
written by Alun Lewis while he was in India as an officer
in the South Wales Borderers. After much soul-searching
about the moral implications of fighting in the Second
World War, Lewis enlisted in the ranks in 1940. He
trained as an officer-cadet and, in late 1942, was posted
to India as a Second Lieutenant. He subsequently became
an Intelligence Officer and undertook reconnaissance
missions into the jungle. The experience of the sub-
continent was a significant dislocation from both Lewis's
Welsh roots and his position as an officer, a situation that
he found at once enlightening and disturbing. In early
1944, the Borderers were preparing for jungle warfare in
Burma. In February of that year they embarked for that
theatre of the war against the Japanese, but Lewis's
battalion were held in reserve about fifteen miles behind
the front line. On 5 March 1944 he was found with a
gunshot wound to the temple: his pistol was in his hand.
Lewis died that day, aged twenty-eight.

Alun Lewis was born in Cwmaman, in the south Wales
coalfield, in 1915.[2] His parents were teachers. He attained
a scholarship to Cowbridge Grammar School, and attended
Aberystwyth and Manchester Universities. Stephen Knight
describes Lewis's early career as a 'trajectory towards
colonial respectability', but notes that this path was
'disrupted by his strong literary instincts, [and] a sense of
social responsibility'.[3] Lewis's war time trajectory
accelerated his writing and led to his most significant
poems and stories. In 1943, *The Last Inspection*,[4] a

collection of stories that included the prize-winning 'They Came',[5] was published. The protagonist, the Welsh soldier, 'Taffy', senses a momentous movement into 'the world'; his future direction coincides with a 'violence growing in the sky ... a turbulent thunder of fire.'[6] The story's transitional theme anticipates Lewis's journey to India, the 'turbulence' of which was to be profound. That journey represents, in Homi Bhabha's terms, a 'moment of transit' towards a 'beyond', that produces

> complex figures of difference and identity ... For there is a sense of disorientation, a disturbance of direction, in the 'beyond', an exploratory, restless movement ... hither and thither, back and forth.[7]

Shortly before his death, Lewis reflected on just such a disturbance: he writes, 'everything is fluid in me, an undigested mass of experience, without shape'.[8] Fixed cultural reference points have disappeared, and are replaced by an ambivalent flux.

This essay examines the way in which three stories from *In the Green Tree*, 'The Raid', 'Ward 'O'3(b)' and 'The Orange Grove', represent sites of transitional identity and cultural production. The critical framework is that of Bhabha's postcolonial theory, as contained in *The Location of Culture* (1994): first, through his focus on the complex to-ing and fro-ing between multiple aspects of identity; and second, in respect of the hybridisation that occurs in the 'Third Space' between fixed cultural positions. These ideas will point towards the relevance of Lewis's texts to our modern world, and, particularly, for Wales as a country that is often seen as peripheral to the centre of British culture and perpetually subject to change and challenge. For instance, during Lewis's formative years, the 1920s and 1930s, industrialised south Wales moved from full employment, to the poverty of the Depression, and back towards productivity as re-armament for the Second World War began.[9] This underlying presence of cultural change suggests that the ideas of 'fluidity' which

Lewis expresses in India have a base in his Welsh upbringing. Thus, to examine his texts within a postcolonial framework that emphasises a divergence from 'singularities [as] organisational categories'[10] sheds light on both Lewis's positions: as a colonial Army officer and as a Welsh writer.

As a colonial officer from a marginalised Welsh background, Lewis was presented with complex issues of identity – those of the insider-outsider. 'The Raid' exemplifies the tense nature of such a position. The English officer, Selden, has the job of enforcing a collapsing colonial authority at the time of the burgeoning Indian independence movement. A terrorist has killed three British soldiers in a cinema bombing, and Selden is to lead a platoon into the jungle to capture him.

The story illuminates a key idea from Bhabha's theory: that of 'a double narrative movement' in which

> there is a split between the continuist, accumulative temporality of the pedagogical, and the repetitious, recursive strategy of the performative. It is through this process of splitting that the conceptual ambivalence of modern society becomes the site of *writing the nation*.[11]

In this passage, Bhabha sets out the manner in which ideas of national, cultural and, indeed, personal identity are 'narrated', or produced, in the real world. In the conventional terms of a written 'story' of identity in which we can all believe, facts are brought together in what might be called a timeline: they accumulate in a linear fashion to produce a deterministic end product. This product may then be used in a 'pedagogical' way; in other words, to teach or instruct people as to how they conduct themselves: the received wisdom of the imperialist discourse operated in such a governing manner. Bhabha suggests that the actuality is more that of a two-fold *process*. A dynamic 'performative' dimension affects the fixities of identity through the way in which people actually conduct their everyday lives in modern society. Elusive and challenging, it operates alongside, and against, the pedagogical in a 'recursive' or indefinite fashion. The two dimensions are interrelated, and, at their intersection, identity becomes the 'site' of continual change, of contradiction and ambivalence. The characters in the stories examined in this essay, such as Selden, undergo just such a dislocating experience.

Like Lewis, Selden does not fit into the pedagogical world of imperial authority. Previously a 'bank clerk in Civvy Street',[12] he tries to fashion a purposeful identity as he begins his first-person narrative – 'My platoon and I were on training that morning' – although his next sentence, 'We've been on training every morning for the last three years, for that matter' (95), mocks military strategy. As he meets the officers who will brief him on his mission, Selden 'brace[s]' himself: Self-defence is always the first instinct, self-suspicion the second' (ibid.), he thinks, as though about to be found out. The Commanding Officer gives Selden his orders:

> 'Here's your objective ... Route: track south of Morje ... and strike across the watershed on a fixed bearing. Work it out ... on the map ... Government has a paid agent in the village who will meet you ... at 06.00 hours.' (96)'

The C.O.'s instructions suggest the characteristics of an imperial adventure story. He adopts Boy's Own language when he encourages Selden: '"Stalk [the bomber] good and proper', and Selden's narrative displays a 'Sameness' through a complicity in the idiom: 'I'll give you a good show, sir' (97).

As Selden describes the platoon's march into the jungle, there is a change in narrative strategy. A different voice emerges, that of Selden's inner consciousness, and his register shifts from the colloquial 'I was a bit worked up' to convey a sense of moving to a different plane – '[I] began to enjoy the ... freedom and deep still peace that informs the night out in the tropics' (100).[13]

Selden's enjoyment of the 'Other' environment is problematic. As the platoon ascends a hill, he looks down on 'clusters of fires in the villages' below and comments:

> Either a festival or a funeral, obviously. I could hear the drums beating ... very clear and echoing, made my flesh creep. You feel so out of it in India ... very white and different. I don't know ... I'd have said that valley hated us that night ... Queer. (*Ibid.*)

Selden realises that the drumming which he hears has a profound ceremonial, cultural significance. The throwaway remark, 'obviously', undermines the insight: he assumes too much and, in doing so, recognises his own alterity.

Lewis was alert to ideas of difference. His own Commanding Officer noted his 'drawling Welsh accent,' and that he was 'alien to the refinements expected of an officer'.[14] Selden's narrative reflects an understanding that what might be 'expected' of a colonial situation – in other words, the received wisdom of the pedagogical – is distorted by a performative reality; the soldiers' difference, *their* white 'Otherness', generates 'hate' in a place where they represent a long-standing but imposed right to govern. The platoon's incursion into the Indian jungle exemplifies what Bhabha terms *'iteration'*.[15] It is a 'repetition' of colonialism; however, that very 'repetition of the same can in fact be its own displacement'.[16] In Selden's interior narrative, the deconstructing effect of this idea is suggested through extralinguistic means. Sound, for instance, is both 'clear' and 'echoing'; nothing in this in-between region has positive terms, since nothing in the performative realm may be repeated *ad infinitum* without change. Selden's 'obvious' readings of the situation now become redundant, as the confusing external environment forces itself on his inner consciousness – as he says, 'I don't know ... Queer.'

The platoon nears its objective, and Selden becomes increasingly anxious. This feeling is heightened when he meets the Indian informer who is to direct him to the terrorist. Remembering that Selden has spent years training for this operational moment, the dialogue between the two men confirms that the preparation represents only a token effort, at least in terms of efficient communication:

> 'Officer sahib huzzoor,' [the informer] said. 'Mai Sarkar ko dost hai,' or something. And he said the name of the man I was after, which was the password.
> 'Achiba,' I said, meaning jolly good show. 'Tairo a minute while I bolo my phaltan and then we'll jao jillo.'
> He got the idea. (101–2)[17]

Selden's face-to-face exchange with the informer transposes the iterative effect of the soldiers' position high above the jungle to the everyday arena. In Selden's 'show', the natives get only the generalised 'idea',[18] But, in its iteration, the idea fails.

The platoon reaches the village where the terrorist is hiding, but the Indian simply surrenders: 'I have nothing' (104) he pleads. That the terrorist speaks English improves, for obvious reasons, the clarity of Selden's approach: 'I'm taking you to Poona' he says. 'You killed three of our men'; the Indian's response, '[d]id I [do that]? ... It's dreadful' (105), sets up the story's deconstructive conclusion. Each side in the exchange has 'nothing' behind it in terms of guiding 'continuist' principles. Selden plays an inconsequential part in the procedure of British imperial enforcement, and the terrorist's bombing represents random disruption, rather than a concerted national campaign. As John Pikoulis observes, Selden is 'the bomber's "other" and exists with him in the same moment'; the Army officer's pedagogical world and the terrorist's performative realm are fused – both emerge 'as bundles of contradiction'.[19] Their narratives will repeat themselves in a degenerative political performance until something breaks the pattern. At this 'moment of transit', identity becomes increasingly indeterminate.

The narrative path in 'The Raid' tracks from the controlling world of the Army to the disrupting Indian jungle, and establishes the basis of a cultural movement that is extended in 'Ward "O" 3 (b)' and 'The Orange Grove'. Selden, however, completes his mission by returning to base with the terrorist, thus denoting a complicity with the dominant discourse. In 'Ward 'O'3(b),' that shaping influence is represented to be more disturbed and transitional. This story was written as Lewis was recovering in hospital in Poona following an operation to repair his jaw, broken while playing football. The soldiers in the Officers' Convalescent Ward of the story suffer from illnesses or injuries directly related to their mutilating war experiences. Part I begins with a distanced narrator's authority; he recalls the men who wait for the medical boards that will determine their future:

> At the time of which I am writing, autumn 1942, Ward 'O' 3 (b) ... was occupied by Captain A. G. Brownlow-Grace, Lieut.-Quartermaster Withers, Lieut. Giles Moncrieff and Lieut. Anthony Weston. (116)

Part II of the story assumes a performative aspect that undermines the authoritative opening. We are now with the men in the hospital in India, and the narrative flows in and out of Brownlow-Grace's free indirect discourse: 'Moncrieff [had] asked him questions [about] Burma ... if he'd been afraid to die. What a shocker, Brownlow-Grace thought ... He hadn't given death two thoughts' (118–9). He touches on his battle experience, in which he has lost an arm, and expresses a sense of abandonment: 'nobody came to see him ... He was the only officer to come out alive. He felt ashamed' (119).[20] In terms of his relationship with pedagogical principles, Brownlow-Grace goes some way towards accounting for the shifting narrative strategy in the three selected stories: '"I don't want to go back 'home',"' he says to a nurse, 'laying sardonic stress on the last word' (122). Brownlow-Grace's emphasis on 'home' as a place from which he desires detachment inverts 'normal' ideas of a stable environment to which one can return: for him, the received wisdom of the soldier's yearning for home no longer has meaning. The idea of detachment from fixed conditions of 'belonging' is a recurring feature of Lewis's writings and informs postcolonial readings of his texts.

Brownlow-Grace's provocative statement causes a narrative break. Part III follows a different strategy by slipping into a poetic voice which comes from Lieut. Weston's inner self. The effect is similar to that of the shift to Selden's interior narrative in 'The Raid', but is more disconcerting because its catalyst is the pathological detailing of Weston's bodily mutilation by a tank-mine: 'His jaw and shoulder-bone had been shattered, a great clod of flesh torn out of neck and thigh, baring his windpipe and epiglottis and exposing his lung and femoral artery' (123). The subsequent extended insight into Weston's near-death experience during an operation to repair his injuries, although mediated by the narrator, suggests that the trauma has also 'bared' his consciousness:

> although he had recovered rapidly, his living self seemed overshadowed by the death trauma ... There had been an annihilation, a complete obscuring; into which light had gradually dawned. And this light grew unbearably white, the glare of the sun on a vast expanse of snow, and in its unbounded voids he had moved without identity ... And then some mutation had taken place [in which] black eruptions disturbed the whiteness. (*Ibid.*)[21]

As Pikoulis observes, to 'one suffering all the tribulations of wartime life, the calm of the dark is a light that is deeply attractive'; 'hope' is thus set in a metaphysical context and comes 'with an annihilation of self'.[22]

Weston's experience makes a release desirable, but for this soldier's imperial self, it is significant that his move into a void-like state has 'obscured' his 'identity'. The form in which this condition is expressed – a dense stream of consciousness-like narrative – suggests that although Weston has been 'opened up', what is inside complicates the clear 'writing' of his identity. The nothingness that he senses, like Brownlow-Grace, leaves him in an indeterminacy, and this idea becomes more pointed since Weston has been mutilated in training: by the 'iterated' practices of his own imperial regime.

Weston's narrative expresses a paradoxical shifting from the pedagogical to the performative. White and light imagery that conventionally connotes positivity – colonialists as bearers of light to dark places, for instance – is inverted and becomes 'unbearable'.[23] Thoughts of escape are more painful than the indeterminacy. Yet the situation becomes more paradoxical: in the flux, the 'irresistible waves ... that surged up darkly through the interstices of life' (124),[24] Weston finds a double-voiced attraction. In this 'overlap and displacement of domains of difference',[25] the imperial regime that almost annihilated him offers a way forward.

Having established Weston's psychological anomalies, the narrator introduces him into the dialogue with the other soldiers. Their conversations suggest that all of their exchanges with 'narratives of originary'[26] at home have been terminated. Weston's 'recovery' is set within an inter-relational position with India, and, in response to Moncrieff's questioning about the possibilities for him at home, he answers,

> We're soldiers [and] I'm going in where you left off. I want to have a look at Burma. *And I don't want to see England.* (127; original emphasis)

For Weston, an epistemological journey is beginning.

Part IV moves on to the key dialogue between Weston and Brownlow-Grace. Weston now establishes his cultural difference by identifying his Welsh mining-community roots, and their significance for his colonial 'trajectory':

> Look. I didn't start with the same things as you. You had a pram and a private school .... My father was a collier ... He

> got rheumatism and nystagmus and then the dole and the
> parish relief ... I used to watch the wheel of the pit spin
> round ... and then from 1926 on I watched it not turning
> round at all, and I can't ever get that wheel out of my mind
> ... I just missed the wheel sucking me down the shaft. I got
> a scholarship to the county school. I don't know when I
> started rebelling. Against that wheel in my head. (131)[27]

In contrast to Brownlow-Grace, there are feelings of
competing cultural influences in Weston from a time
before he joined the Army. Like Lewis himself, Weston has
moved from his Welsh home, through the 'scholarship',
towards Brownlow-Grace's world – that of the 'train[ed]
... rigid' (129) imperialist. His compulsion, however, is to
reject the 'Sameness' of either position. This detachment
is re-affirmed in Part V of the story, which reveals the
decisions of the medical board for some of the soldiers.
Brownlow-Grace, for instance, is discharged, and he
simply fades out of the narrative. Weston's fate is not
revealed; Pikoulis suggests that this is because 'his is an
inner destiny', although it is apparent 'that he is heading
back to the war'.[28]

By the end of the story the narrator has all but
disappeared, and the final perspective is provided by
Weston, who is at once an 'R.A.C. man' (116)[29] and a
Welsh collier's son. By re-accessing Weston's consciousness
and updating his psychological condition, 'Ward "O" 3 (b)'
creates the freeing effect of an ongoing narrative. Moncrieff
and he

> sat on the circular ledge [of the garden pool] ... Circles of
> water lapped softly outwards, outwards, [and] lapped
> again inwards, inwards. [Weston] felt the ripples surging
> ... like a series of temptations in the wilderness. And he
> felt glad tonight, feeling some small salient gained when
> ... the men whom he was with were losing ground along
> the whole front to the darkness that there is. (139–40).

Brownlow-Grace is an example of the men who are 'losing

ground' to the iterative insistence of the 'wheel'; despite his protests, he is likely to return home. But Weston begins to progress. Remaining in India, he is at an imperial periphery: it is the kind of environment that encourages him to recall Wales in a similar peripheral context, having 'just missed' being drawn into a stable, albeit occupationally dangerous, working life in the pit. For Weston, a complicity with the governing regime still exists, but the pedagogical and the performative influences on him have become 'fluid'. An opportunity is suggested in the pool's displacing and doubling 'outwards, outwards ... inwards, inwards' motion. The 'ledges' that he and Moncrieff inhabit are insecure outposts that 'tempt' them towards the challenging 'hither and thither' of 'the beyond'.

Two aspects of Weston suit him to a position of flux. First, his imaginative capacity, demonstrated in the narrative of his near-death experience, facilitates a sense of the significance of the 'moment' at the pool. Second, his ambivalent social identity, located inside and outside both his Welsh and Army officer selves, furthers an inherent process of hybridisation. Although he commits himself to the almost-defunct governing regime, he realises that meaning is to be sought elsewhere – in the 'irresistible' turbulent 'interstices of life'. The irresistible nature of his uncertain and turbulent position suggests future potential and opportunity, an idea that is, of course, contrary to pedagogical notions of stable and secure identity. An understanding of Weston's position is assisted through Declan Kiberd's observations on national characteristics. Referring to Irish identity, Kiberd notes the presence of similarly turbulent cultural interactions, particularly those caused by colonisation, but that through the process an individual is instilled with 'the courage to become his or her full self'.[30] It is the act of *becoming*, of development, that is most relevant to Weston. His identity is 'a *project* ... unfinished, fragmenting';[31] as he says to Moncrieff, 'We'd better go now' (141).

'The Raid' and 'Ward "O" 3 (b)' concern fluctuating

identities that are developed on journeys which move from fixed bases increasingly towards indeterminate futures. Bhabha indicates the destabilising effect of such situations on narrative:

> The pact of interpretation is never simply an act of communication between the I and the You ... The production of meaning requires that these two places be mobilized [through a] Third Space [which] though unrepresentable in itself, ... constitutes the discursive conditions [that] ensure that the meaning and symbols of culture have no primordial unity or fixity; that even the same signs can be ... read anew.[32]

Bhabha remarks that individuals who 'initiate' such productive instability are 'bearers of a hybrid identity ... caught in the *discontinuous* time of translation and negotiation'.[33] However, hybridity is not always regarded so positively. Robert J. C. Young has suggested that such a condition marks 'a new stability', rather than 'social fluidity'; it emphasises 'Otherness' because 'Fixity' is sought in times of 'disruption'.[34] However, Bhabha concentrates on an organic process of 'revaluation',[35] and it is this notion that sheds light on Lewis's shifting narrative perspectives. The process 'displays the necessary deformation and displacement of all sites of discrimination and domination',[36] and Lewis's stories carry meaning through the idea of recursive disruption – something that displays the influence of his native Welsh cultural environment – rather than that of a 'new' stable condition.

'The Orange Grove', which is often regarded as Lewis's finest story, concerns ideas of 'revaluation'. The protagonist is a seemingly disciplined English officer, Staff-Captain Beale: his '*Pending* basket was always empty' (148), the narrator confirms. Beale enters a dangerously disorientating jungle on a reconnaissance mission amidst the nationalist unrest that is present in 'The Raid'; he undergoes a process of hybridisation that forcefully disrupts the fixities of his soldier's life.

As Beale and his driver, in their Army truck, arrive at a *dak* bungalow to rest, the narrator conveys a feeling of spatial dislocation:

> These bungalows are scattered all over India on the endless roads and travellers may sleep there, cook their food, and pass on ... they are quiet and remote, tended for the Government only by some old khansama or chowkey, usually a slippered and silent old Moslem. (143–4).

This space is, at once, 'scattered' and secure. What infrastructure there is, the 'endless' road system, emphasises discontinuity.

The narrator deploys two 'natural' figures to suggest an atmosphere of alienation. The first is the bungalow's caretaker; Beale discovers him

> squatting amongst the flies by the well. He was a wizened yellow-skinned old man in a soiled dhoti. Across his left breast was a plaster, loose and dripping with pus, a permanent discharge it seemed. (144)

The caretaker's T.B. disgusts the soldiers, and this part of the narrative instrumentally reveals the naïvety of colonial soldiers who are ill-prepared for such different cultural conditions.[37]

The second figure re-presents the caretaker's natural environment in a way which projects the old man's disease onto an approaching storm:

> [Beale] looked out at ... the fulgurous inflammation among the grey anchorages of cloud, the hot creeping prescience of the monsoon.
> 'I don't like it to-night,' he said. 'It's eerie; I can't breathe or think.' (*ibid.*)

The poetic language, 'fulgurous', introduces a 'third' voice that operates beyond the guiding narration and Beale's direct speech to begin a narrative hybridisation. The image of the caretaker's inflamed wound is associated with the sky to suggest a subversion of the stability implied in the 'anchorages of cloud'. The passage attributes the natural phenomenon of the monsoon with a knowledge of Beale's predicament that seeps back to the caretaker via the interchange between his 'dripping' wound and the 'creeping' storm.

The narrative hybridisation is continued as Beale settles himself for the night, and he recalls an earlier conversation with the unnamed, evidently Welsh, soldier who is his driver. The conversation is recalled through the driver's speech, and this introduces a competing voice to the story, but one that is mediated through Beale's consciousness. He recalls the driver to be full of the meanness of his working-class existence, which, presumably, is alien to Beale's class background:

> ... tried to emigrate first of all, didn't want to stay anywhere ... I ran away from home [when I was fourteen but the] Police sent me back. So then I [joined] the Army ... I went to Palestine, against the Arabs; seen them collective farms the Jews got there, sir? Oranges ... (146)

The Palestinian collective farms represent an alternative community, something that the driver holds against a theme of Welsh insularity that is also present in his story:

> Then I come home ... We got a pub in our family ... for the colliers it is ... Well, my mother 'ad a barmaid, a flash dame ... My mother said for me to keep off her. My mother is a big Bible woman, though nacherly she couldn't go to chapel down our way being she kept a pub ... the Bute's Arms ... it was my pub by rights, *mine*. She was *my* barmaid ... Monica [wanted] the pub and the big double bed ... She took good care to get pregnant, Monica did, and my mother threw her out. But it was my baby, and I married her ... It was *my* affair, wasn't it? *Mine*. (146–7; original emphasis)[38]

The narrative facilitates the subaltern driver's voice: he speaks for his own political position. However, Beale's rhetorical stressing of his possessiveness re-presents an intentionally 'distasteful' (147) viewpoint: commerce and women are associated as objects of exchange that combine to produce a meaningful life for the driver. One might suppose that Beale would distance himself from the driver's views, but instead he empathises with him: 'there had been no hard luck story told, [but simply] a man ... explaining the twisted and evil curvature of his being' (147). The images of physical and social dysfunction associated with the driver strengthen Beale's appreciation that a dramatic change is imminent. His natural sense of stability, organisation and purpose is progressively disrupted.

Something positive emerges from Beale's displacement. The conversation about the collective farms recurs in his mind, and he recalls the driver telling of how the 'the doctor and the school teacher' shared what they had, 'the same as the labourer or the children' (149).[39] This recollection halts the linear narrative; it now enters deep into Beale's consciousness. He experiences

> one of those enlargements of the imagination that come once or perhaps twice to a man, and recreate him subtly and profoundly. And he was thinking [of] the quiet categories of the possible and the quieter frozen infinities of the impossible. And he must get back to those certainties ... (*Ibid.*)

The 'enlargement' suggests a capacity to understand meaning beyond fixed ideological confines in an ambivalent space between the 'possible' and the 'impossible'. Nevertheless, despite the attractive proposition of the collective farms, he wants to 'get back' to absolutes, to opposites, to iterate the kind of 'Sameness' that in Weston's story was a source of dread:

> There would be perhaps one woman out of many, one life

> out of many, two things possible – if life itself were
> possible, and if he had not debased himself among the
> impossibilities by then. The orange grove in Palestine ...
> (150–1).

Beale's disjointed narrative suggests that he is undergoing
an organic process of hybridisation. However, he expects
some end product to arise out of the experience of 'many'
existences through the notion of 'one woman' – an idealised
wifely figure, perhaps[40] – that he can now represent as the
social superior of the driver's barmaid. But, in the process,
he also acknowledges contingency and interchange in the
potential for 'debasement'.

The story returns from Beale's inner narrative and
brings into focus the political disturbances. The device of a
storm functions to create a crisis point on which Beale's
story turns. The caretaker has gone, roads are flooded,
lines are down. Beale discovers that the driver, who had
gone to search for food, has been murdered, presumably by
insurgents. Beale carries the driver to the truck, and
attributes the dead body with a particular significance. He
treats the 'kid' with feminine, nurse-like care; he does not
'feel any ease' (153) until he cleans and secures the body.
Pikoulis suggests that this moment is key in relation to
Beale's identity and Lewis's own 'colossal experience' of
the jungle:

> The driver ... is Beale's double come to forewarn him of
> his own end; he is his mortal self. At the same time, he
> allays fears about death, assuring him that ... it is a
> venture into a new life.[41]

Beale not only lowers himself to the driver's social level,
but also adopts the egalitarian notions that had so appealed
to the Welsh man. However, he quickly re-asserts his Army
self when he prepares to escape from danger: 'Maybe ... he
could dry out the map and work out the best route' (154)
back to base. Beale now drives for six hours into the jungle.

Exhausted, he stops and falls asleep.

On waking, Beale feels guilty about a neglect of duty, but his nervous, free, indirect discourse indicates a complex double-voicedness:

> The driver had been murdered. What did they expect him to do? Stay and give them a second treat? ... Why hadn't he reported it earlier? How could he? ... Yet the guilt complex persisted. (155)

In an act of 'iteration,' he begins to write an accident report. However, as Selden's experience demonstrates, in the alien jungle-environment, no repeated assertions of order and authority may take place without some change. Beale's pre-determined Army existence fails: the report paper is soaked and disintegrates.

The driver's body is now decomposing: in the sunken 'inanition' (156) of his face recurs the caretaker's 'wizened' image. It is as though Beale is carrying responsibility for the range of social and political decompositions that are threaded through the story. In a panic, he again drives aimlessly, finally admitting that he is lost. At this point, Beale's mediating narrative position turns to a merging with the driver's: 'he scarcely knew more than the man in the back of the truck' (157). He drives on, encountering a primitive gypsy tribe that, unbeknown to him, were watching him earlier. As Beale's journey proceeds, the political disturbances with which the story began will fade into the distance as the tribe becomes the most influential factor in his existence.

As if to acknowledge the subconscious influence of the gypsy tribe, the narrative now emphasises fluidity. The jungle is a space infused by 'brown streams:' Beale, in turn, drives 'till the land was green with evening' (*ibid.*). In this discursive environment, the story's poetic voice returns to mobilise two linguistic cultural positions: 'in the crepuscular uncertainty he halted and decided to kip down for the night' (157–8). The 'act of communication' between the high-flown 'crepuscular', and the ordinary soldiers' slang, 'kip',[42] could simply reveal a clash in the narrative – the 'impossible' with the 'possible', perhaps. Instead, it assists in conveying the idea that within Beale a new interpretative faculty is being created, through which he now revaluates the fixed 'symbols of culture' in the driver's working-class narrative.

Beale reconsiders the driver, now that the binary oppositions established by rank have been eroded. He needs to find the truck's petrol tins; reaching them entails disturbing the driver's body, but he

> did all he had to do with a humility that was alien to him. Respect he knew; but this was more than respect; obedience and necessity he knew, but this was more than either of these. It was somehow an admission of the integrity of the man, a new interest in what he was. (158)

This passage espouses qualities of 'social responsibility' to which Lewis aspired in his own conduct: as he wrote to Robert Graves, the '*Humility* ... integrity and willingness to endure'[43] that he had witnessed in 'the people', especially the ordinary Welsh soldiers in his regiment.[44] The 'new interest' which Beale has in the driver is his ideological 'enlargement'. His thought processes have been facilitated, perhaps, by his allowing of the driver's story into his own narrative. The new position that Beale adopts is 'more than' the sum of two polarised narratives. It is the interchange of 'respect' and 'necessity' that is found in discontinuity, and this idea suggests that the mobilising, poetic voice in the story belongs, in fact, to Beale.

Beale washes himself and, in a seemingly unnecessary act, dignifies the driver by also washing his body. The two men are made to look the same, and Beale glances 'covertly' at this secret 'Other', 'satisfied that he had done something for him' (*ibid.*). He experiences a moment of optimism: the sun comes out and turns the sky to 'a young summer blue' (159). Beale anticipates that he can use the sun to navigate to a military base and report back. Thus, he would complete the process of hybridisation: still an Army officer, he would then be equipped with egalitarian ideals.

The events which follow confound Beale's expectations. The navigational aid of the sun takes him further towards the primitive. Human figures, confusingly, reinstate his feeling of displacement: 'lithe men like fauns' appear as both earthly – visible while they 'stand a moment' – and amorphous – they quickly 'glide away back into the bush' (*ibid.*). At the moment when the road ends in a river, the gypsies return as a recursive enticement.[45] As a community, they are fording the river: 'little mules, demure as mice, kicked up against the current … camels followed the halter, stately as bishops, picking their calm way' (160). The gypsies' procession is dignified, and this quality matches the condition that Beale has achieved for the driver. He attempts to join them by fording the river in the truck. Feelings of discontinuity prevail: the road has ended, and a different path has opened up, but the vehicle is swamped. His 'whole concern' is for 'the boy inside': the two men are joined, 'naturally'; he calls out to the tribesmen, but his language is useless. Something more basic is required, and Beale resorts to showing and pointing; these gestures turn into an act of negotiation with the gypsies. They

> helped him intelligently to hoist the body out. They contrived to get it on to their heads, ducking down under the tailboard till their faces were submerged. (160)

The figures of Beale, the driver, and the gypsies are bodily merged in the brown water, denoting a process of hybridisation in which cultural opposites join in a fluid 'Third Space'.

The process that is suggested in the immersion is, in Kirsti Bohata's terms, 'perhaps significant for a Welsh reading of [the] story', in that 'Nationality, history (with its linear temporality and written form, its maps and dates) and language [are] washed away.'[46] In respect of modern Welsh identity, Bohata has noted that 'hybridity is often viewed in terms [of] annihilation of identity'.[47] This idea recalls Weston's complex thoughts of the 'annihilation' that has occurred because of the persistent disturbances in his life, both in Wales and in India. However, in 'The Orange Grove', something that has been annihilated, the driver's body, is brought ashore; Beale follows with the trappings of his Army-self, 'his revolver and webbing' (161). The gypsies agree to carry the driver's body, in effect also to carry Beale, on their nomadic journey. Rather than a washing away, the hybridising immersion suggests a re-birthing commenced by Beale's earlier washing of himself and the driver. The water, at once fertile and polluted, denotes a recursive future – a fluid and ongoing process in the 'hither and thither' of the 'beyond'.

In the part of Beale that thinks in a conventional 'discriminatory' way, his position in the jungle entails a descent. Beale has 'debased' his officer-self through two connected acts: first, the social levelling with the Welsh driver; and second, his developing association with the primitive gypsies. Lewis's experience of the primitive produced complex feelings. His letters suggest him to be both the high-handed colonialist who, like Selden perhaps, enjoys 'boyish' pursuits in 'the wilds',[48] and someone who is capable of understanding an existence that renders his 'hyper-civilised world' redundant in the face of 'a rhythm of many universes and real truths'.[49] The last poem that Lewis wrote, 'The Jungle' (1945), traces an enlargement through descent similar to that which Beale experiences, and sheds light on Lewis's own positioning. In the poem, soldiers come to a jungle pool,

> To quench more than our thirst – our selves –
> Beneath this bamboo bridge, this mantled pool
> Where sleep exudes a sinister content
> As though all strength of mind and limb must pass
> And all fidelities and doubts dissolve ...[50]

The poem's water imagery, as in 'The Orange Grove', and

'Ward "O" 3 (b)', functions to create an ambivalent space. These colonial soldiers, who, like Beale's driver, are ordinary men from the 'sidestreets',[51] drink from the pool, but they know that the source of this sustenance, deep within the Indian landscape, is 'mantled' – covered by rotting matter.[52] They recall a corresponding descent in their industrialised homeland, presumably Wales, in the poem's allusion to coal mining – the 'day shift sinking from the sun'.[53] The association of the two national spaces implies that colonialism, or, in Wales perhaps, 'internal colonialism'.[54] is the cause of degradation, as is suggested in 'Ward "O" 3 (b)' through Weston's fear of being 'sucked down the shaft'. But, like Weston's hospital pool, the jungle pool dissolves any form of 'certain' interpretation. In 'The Jungle', the soldiers experience a replenishing sleep that is tainted by 'sinister' contentment: they participate, perhaps willingly, in something that is self-destructive.

In dissolution of 'fidelities and doubts' alike, the soldiers in 'The Jungle' become 'anonymous, unknown'.[55] Similarly, as Beale follows the tribe towards an uncertain destination, he loses his colonial officer's 'stiff self-consciousness'; A further 'enlargement' occurs:

> He was thinking [about] the barbarian migrations in pre-history; the Celts and the Iberians, Goths and Vandals and Huns. Once Life had been nothing worth recording beyond the movements of people like these ... with the poor property of their days. (162)

Pikoulis suggests that it is 'to this ancient sense of [community] that [Beale] returns, bare, humbled, driven'.[56] The tribespeople are opposed to all interpretable life: the Army, colonialism, the collective farms, and the driver's decomposed Welsh community. Nevertheless, in their 'intelligent' behaviour in rescuing the driver's body, they value human qualities, such as dignity, to which Beale now aspires.

The theme of a 'return' to ancient values is significant for

Lewis's writing. As M. Wynn Thomas argues, a hankering after the primordial unity of, say, the Celts of Lewis's Welsh homeland, may well be 'condescendingly romantic';[57] Beale's 'going native' could then be said to represent something that exists only in contemplation. However, Beale demonstrates a capacity to gain entry to the alternative culture that Lewis himself sought. Two months before his death, Lewis writes of a 'communion' with the 'simple and natural' life of the jungle villagers that he encountered on his reconnaissance missions; they are at once 'complete and uninhibited'.[58] To recall Kiberd's terms, they have the 'courage to become' their full selves, but instinctively understand that this idea is characteristically multiple.

In considering the villagers' life, Lewis realises that for him a 'climacteric is near'.[59] At a similar point, Beale 'reads anew' the conventional perception of a primitive jungle existence, and the fixed ideas of the colonial soldier that have governed his life thus far. The decomposing state of the driver's body means that the gypsies will have to 'burn him' (163) to protect their community from disease: the primordial tribe thus shows itself capable of self-management. Beale comforts himself with the signs of an organising discourse – he keeps hold of the driver's 'identity discs and paybook' (*ibid.*) – but a process of hybridisation continues: he may join the tribe, or his life may end. 'The Jungle' ends in equally ambiguous fashion. The soldiers imagine 'Annihilating paws' striking them, an understandable fear for the colonial soldier in the tropics, but this conventional narrative device merely prompts questioning:

> Then would some unimportant death resound
> With the imprisoned music of the soul?
> And we become the world we could not change?[60]

This one 'unimportant' soldier fears that he has become what he represents: like Beale and his driver, an unwelcome, iterative presence in India. However, the poem's concluding question suggests, as Bhabha puts it, the 'unrepresentable':

Or does the will's long struggle end
With the last kindness of a foe or friend?[61]

In the supposed finality of 'death' there is revealed a discursive 'Third Space' in which meaning 'resounds'' foe and friend, primitive and soldier, interchange.

There is an inter-textual connection between 'The Jungle' and 'The Orange Grove': in both, a concluding descent is performative and enabling. Beale ends his story wondering about his future direction: 'Maybe they weren't going anywhere much, except perhaps to some pasture, to some well' (163). This end does not suggest an intentional regression to any ancient or 'recordable' life. It also evades a resolving state of hybridity that 'annihilates' one's origins. The 'double narrative movement' is potentially more productive. On the one hand, the merged English-Welsh Beale-driver secures a sense of identity; on the other, he 'initiates' his own cultural instability,[62] and *continues* towards the fertile and fluid ideas of a 'pasture' and a 'well'.

The well symbolises organised community, but one which, at the start of the story, was contaminated: at the bungalow, it is where the caretaker 'squat[s] amongst the flies' (144). The driver's community in Wales is also portrayed as corrupted,[63] echoing the feelings of the soldiers in 'Ward "O" 3 (b)' who fear a return home to their ordered existence. Beale now re-assesses the idea of community. However, no simple 'act of communication' occurs between first and last positions. The exchange between Beale and the gypsies creates an end that subverts the notion of endings, as does the concluding questioning in 'The Jungle': there is left an ambivalent transition in which the idea of identity becomes an unfinished 'project'.

* * *

Towards the end of his life, Lewis wrote home with a 'clear' message: he was 'at the end of something and the beginning of something else'.[64] This way of thinking illuminates the three selected stories: they are stories of ideas, of ideas about increasingly 'exploratory' identities that are in the act of *becoming*. Selden and Weston are neither wholly colonial soldiers, nor what they were in their previous lives. Beale, like Lewis, is neither wholly the 'fussy' English officer,[65] nor a working-class Welsh driver, nor a gypsy tribesman. Elusive and challengingly performative, at the moment of their stories these characters exist within a multiplicity of identities. This positioning represents the texts' relevance to the 'writing' of modern identity, especially to a complex, changing Welsh culture. They suggest something that is imprinted in Lewis's writing because of his nationality: to be peripheral and to experience recursive change is invigorating. It forces enticing yet potentially irresolvable views of the future. For twenty-first century readers, Lewis's texts suggest the idea that even the most fixed point, 'annihilation of identity', may be read anew.

NOTES

1   The term 'postcolonial' is used in this essay to denote the analytical method that reads across supposedly fixed boundaries of culture, identity, and literary form. This is distinct from the hyphenated term, 'post-colonial', which is often used to indicate a historical period following colonisation. The two are, nevertheless, closely associated. For further reading regarding these issues in a Welsh context, see Kirsti Bohata, *Postcolonialism Revisited* (Cardiff: University of Wales Press, 2004), and *Postcolonial Wales*, ed. Jane Aaron and Chris Williams (Cardiff: University of Wales Press, 2005).

2   See John Pikoulis's *Alun Lewis, A Life* ([1984] Bridgend:

Seren Books, 1991), for an authoritative critical biography.

3   Stephen Knight, *A Hundred Years of Fiction* (Cardiff: University of Wales Press, 2004), p. 125.

4   *The Last Inspection* (London: Allen & Unwin Ltd, 1942) is out of print. Alun Lewis's stories are now available in *Collected Stories*, ed. Cary Archard (Bridgend: Seren Books, 1990).

5   'They Came' won the Edward J. O'Brien Short Story Prize for 1941.

6   Alun Lewis, 'They Came', in *Collected Stories*, p. 176.

7   Homi K. Bhabha, *The Location of Culture* ([1994] Abingdon: Routledge Classics, 2004), p. 2.

8   Alun Lewis, *In the Green Tree: The Letters and Short Stories of Alun Lewis* ([1948] Cardigan: Parthian, 2006), letter 41, p. 67.

9   In *The Dragon Has Two Tongues*, Glyn Jones discusses the paradoxical situation of 1939 in which long-unemployed miners had welcomed work in arms factories. Relative prosperity had been created by war, 'which was [likely] to destroy them and their community'; see Glyn Jones, *The Dragon Has Two Tongues* (London: J. M. Dent & Sons Ltd, 1968), pp. 32–33. In more recent times, and in a more positive context of change, the Government of Wales Acts 1998 and 2006 present Wales with the challenge of increasing degrees of self-government, but with a continuing reference to the UK Parliament.

10   Homi K. Bhabha, *The Location of Culture*, p. 2.

11   *Ibid.*, pp. 208–9; (original emphasis). In *Homi K. Bhabha* (Abingdon: Routledge, 2006), David Huddart comments that in the 'narration' of national identity 'there is a pedagogical dimension that foregrounds total sociological facts'; see p. 121. The *OED* defines a pedagogue as a 'schoolmaster, a teacher; *esp.* a strict, dogmatic, or pedantic one'; and 'Something that serves to teach; a source of instruction or guidance (Chiefly with reference to St Paul's use [of the term in] Galatians 3:24.' Galatians 3:24 reads: 'Wherefore the law was our schoolmaster to bring us unto Christ, that we might be justified by faith.' Imperialism, for instance, was fashioned as a discourse in which one could have faith: in such a discourse, national stereotypes convey fixed notions of identity. Huddart, of course, notes Bhabha's identification

of the more elusive 'performative' dimension which complicates the 'pedagogical'; each influences the other.

12 Alun Lewis, *In the Green Tree*, p. 99. All further references to the selected stories are from this edition and are given in the text.

13 Tony Brown has examined the shifting registers in Selden's narrative; see M. Wynn Thomas and Tony Brown, 'Colonial Wales and Fractured Language', in *Nations and Relations: Writing Across the British Isles*, ed. Tony Brown and Russell Stephens (Cardiff: New Welsh Review, 2000), pp. 71–88.

14 These remarks are included in a letter from Captain O. A. Evans, Lewis's Company Commander, to John Pikoulis, and quoted in *A Life*; Lewis's colleague, Alun Gwynne Jones (later Lord Chalfont), recalls him as 'the Englishman's idea of a Welshman, small, lean and dark'; see *A Life*, p. 117.

15 Bhabha, *The Location of Culture*, p. 38 (original emphasis). Bhabha notes the tendency for political movements to 'iterate' their principles so as to 'articulate antagonistic and oppositional elements'.

16 *Ibid.*, p. 195.

17 See letter 9 of *In the Green Tree* for an instance of Lewis recalling himself speaking in a similar fashion – 'proper Indian', as an Indian sergeant suggests (p. 24).

18 The idea of information as an imperial management 'tool', so to speak, is ironised by Selden's inability to communicate.

19 John Pikoulis, 'Alun Lewis and the Politics of Empire', *Welsh Writing in English*, No. 8, 2003, p. 164.

20 Brownlow-Grace's psychological condition typically represents the guilt experienced by survivors of tragic events.

21 John Pikoulis has examined Lewis's response to his period in the hospital at Poona, including the 'In Hospital: Poona' poems, and Lewis's own 'anaesthetic vision' of light and darkness during the operation to repair his broken jaw, from which Weston's narrative derives; see *A Life*, pp. 149–52.

22 Pikoulis, *A Life*, p. 154.

23 In Lewis's poem 'The Mahratta Ghats' (1945), the speaker surveys an Indian landscape in which 'Dark peasants drag the sun upon their backs': the deadening effect of a sun that never sets has 'exhausted' the environment; see Alun Lewis, *Collected Poems*, ed. Cary Archard (Bridgend: Seren, 1994), p. 131, ll. 1–6. Equally burdened, soldiers are 'landless' and

'lost in war'; (*ibid.*, l. 25).

24 The inverted imagery and themes of voiding in Weston's narrative are echoed in Lewis's poem 'In Hospital: Poona (2)' (1945): 'The sun has sucked and beat the encircling hills / Into gaunt skeletons'; and 'from the polished ward where men lie ill/ Thought rubs clean through the frayed cloth of the will, / Piercing the slow estrangement of disease, / And breaks into a state of blinding light / Where Now is a salt pillar, still and white, / And there are no familiar words or features;' see *Collected Poems*, p. 141, ll. 1–2 and 12–7.

25 Bhabha, *The Location of Culture*, p. 2.

26 *Ibid*.

27 Brownlow-Grace's and Weston's biographical details are interchangeable with Lewis's, in some respects. Brownlow-Grace's 'private school' background echoes Lewis's circumstances, as does the experience of Weston's scholarship. The collier father and experience of the Depression are more generalised representations of a culture to which Lewis was both attached, and from which he was separate. The reference in the passage to '1926' is significant since it was the date of the General Strike; for Lewis, it coincidentally marked the year that he started his grammar school scholarship. As John Pikoulis notes, the juxtaposition of the two events created a crisis of conscience: Lewis 'was ashamed to go round Cwmaman in his Cowbridge blazer, though in later years liked to savour the prestige of being a public school boy'; see *A Life*, pp. 27–8.

28 Pikoulis, *A Life*, pp. 154–5.

29 Weston serves in The Royal Armoured Corps.

30 Declan Kiberd, *Inventing Ireland: The Literature of the Modern Nation* ([1995] London: Vintage, 1996), p. 119.

31 *Ibid.*, p. 120 (original emphasis).

32 Bhabha, *The Location of Culture*, pp. 53–5. Bhabha discusses the 'Third Space' in an interview with Jonathan Rutherford, published in 1990. He comments: 'for me the importance of hybridity is not to be able to trace two original moments from which a third emerges, rather [it is] the "third space" which enables other positions to emerge. This third space displaces the histories that constitute it, and sets up new structures of authority, new political initiatives, which are inadequately understood through received wisdom'; see 'The

Third Space: Interview with Homi Bhabha', in *Identity: Community, Culture, Difference*, ed. Jonathan Rutherford (London: Lawrence & Wishart, 1990), p. 211.

33 *Ibid.*, p. 55 (my emphasis).

34 Robert Young, *Colonial Desire: Hybridity in Theory, Culture and Race* (Abingdon: Routledge, 2006) p. 4.

35 Bhabha, *The Location of Culture*, p. 159.

36 *Ibid.*, p. 160.

37 Beale's lack of preparation is suggested by his carrying of tokens of Western orderliness: for instance, a 'leather writing-pad', and 'all the letters he'd received from home'; (p. 144). In letter 8 of *In the Green Tree*, Lewis describes himself as 'a fussy little officer sahib'; (p. 20).

38 The driver's register, 'I come home', is typical of the everyday speech of south-east Walians, and his references to 'colliers' and the local chapel signify that his home is in Wales. The name of the pub, the Bute's Arms, denotes a connection to the Marquis of Bute who had, in the nineteenth century, turned Cardiff into a prosperous port. The theme of Welsh social restrictiveness in the driver's experience is also present in some of Lewis's earlier stories: see 'The Housekeeper' and 'They Came' (both 1942), for instance.

39 In letter 4 of *In the Green Tree*, Lewis recalls a soldier, 'little George', giving the 'loveliest talk ... in his singsong illiterate unaspirated Welsh voice, about the Jewish collective farms of Palestine which he'd seen when he was shooting Arabs out there'; (p. 12).

40 This 'one' woman recalls the 'pure' female figure, 'The Angel in the House', who sacrifices herself daily to family life; see 'Professions for Women', in Virginia Woolf, *The Death of the Moth and other Essays* (London: The Hogarth Press, 1942, pp. 150–1). Lewis's stories offer opportunities for gender-based readings, although that is not the purpose of this essay.

41 Pikoulis, *A Life*, pp. 168–9. Letter 21 of *In the Green Tree* refers to Lewis's 'colossal experience' of a journey into the jungle; 'I feel I could go on travelling like that for years', he comments (pp. 42–3).

42 Colloquial words like 'kip' appear in Lewis's everyday language. Letter 4 of *In the Green Tree*, for instance: 'I ... nip up in my shorts and lie on deck' (p. 11).

43 Lewis wrote to Graves on 4 November 1941; see *Alun*

Lewis: A Miscellany of His Writings, ed. John Pikoulis (Bridgend: Poetry Wales Press, 1982), p. 134 (original emphasis).

44 In letter 32 of *In the Green Tree*, Lewis writes of the 'emotional tug' that he experienced while away from his regiment on his jungle missions, 'a crying loyalty to the Welsh soldiers'; and 'yet I want to be away, too', he remarks (pp. 52–3).

45 Letter 21 of *In the Green Tree* refers to Lewis's own encounter with just such a tribe of gypsies (pp. 42–3).

46 Kirsti Bohata, 'Beyond Authenticity? Hybridity and Assimilation in Welsh Writing in English', in *Nations and Relations*,'p. 105.

47 *Ibid.*, p. 89.

48 See letters 39 and 40 of *In the Green Tree* (pp. 63–4).

49 See letter 40 of *ibid.* (p. 65).

50 Alun Lewis, 'The Jungle', in *Collected Poems*, p. 155, ll. 9-13. See also John Pikoulis's essay, '"Inwards where all the battle is": Alun Lewis's 'The Jungle', in *Moment of Earth: Poems and Essays in Honour of Jeremy Hooker*, ed. Christopher Meredith (Aberystwyth: Celtic Studies Publications, 2007), pp. 84–100. Pikoulis notes the 'personal confession' that the poem represents. He also identifies the ambiguities in the poem: in the passage cited, the word 'quench', for instance, suggests 'termination as well as satisfaction'; (see pp. 84–6).

51 Lewis, 'The Jungle', p. 155, l. 21.

52 The term 'mantled pool' is intriguing since it echoes Ariel's speech to Prospero in Act 4.1 of *The Tempest*: Ariel refers to two drunken conspirators who plan to usurp Prospero's power: 'At last I left them / I' th' filthy-mantled pool beyond your cell, / There dancing up to th' chins, that the foul lake / O'er-stunk their feet'; see William Shakespeare, *The Tempest*, 4.1, 171–84 (Oxford: Oxford University Press, 2008). *The Tempest* has been read increasingly in a postcolonial context, and Prospero discussed in terms of a colonising ruler of the island on which the play is set. The 'mantled pool' is close to Prospero's quarters, and the play sets up complex considerations relating to the complicity of colonisers and aspiring colonisers in their own downfall, as does 'The Jungle'. Pikoulis notes Shakespeare as one of

Lewis's 'literary predecessors', although more in the context
of 'Hamlet's soliloquy'; see 'Inwards where all the battle is',
pp. 84, 87.

53 Lewis, 'The Jungle', p. 155, l. 29.

54 Michael Hechter, in *Internal Colonialism: The Celtic Fringe in
British National Development, 1536–1966* (London:
Routledge & Kegan Paul, 1975), sets out a social 'model'
which he terms '*internal colonialism*', and relates it to Wales.
In this model, the 'core ... dominate[s] the periphery [and]
exploit[s] it materially', resulting in inequities of 'resources
and power'; see pp. 8–10. Wales, as peripheral to the
imperial 'core' in London, may thus be regarded as an
example of the model in that its natural resources, coal, for
instance, were so exploited. As Chris Williams notes, 'Welsh
economists, historians and sociologists have found Hechter's
analysis unconvincing': alternative terms, such as
'dependent periphery', have been suggested as more relevant
to Wales (see Chris Williams, 'Problematizing Wales: An
Exploration in Historiography and Postcoloniality', in
Postcolonial Wales, ed. Aaron and Williams, p. 8). However,
as Daniel Williams has recently suggested, a re-assessment is
now required in respect of the way in which the model of the
'internal colony' is reflected in Welsh writing in English.
(This suggestion was made by Daniel Williams as part of his
paper, 'Back to the Internal Colony', at the Ireland and
Wales: Correspondences Symposium in September 2009).

55 Lewis, 'The Jungle', p. 157, l. 72.

56 Pikoulis, *A Life*, p. 169.

57 M. Wynn Thomas and Tony Brown, 'Colonial Wales and
Fractured Language', p. 78.

58 Lewis, *In the Green Tree*, letter 40, pp. 65–6.

59 *Ibid.*, p. 66.

60 Lewis, 'The Jungle,' p. 157, ll. 94–7.

61 *Ibid.*, ll. 98–9.

62 This position develops the thoughts espoused in Lewis's
story 'Lance-Jack' (1942). In the Army, soldiers are part of a
structured regime, but everyone has to 'begin again. All you
were seems to have vanished.' Their situation forces them to
realise 'the possibility of change'. The soldiers' life, to Lewis,
is gypsy-like: 'He is a migrant ... needing surprisingly little of
the world's goods'; see *Collected Stories*, p. 64.

63 In Lewis's poem, 'The Mountain over Aberdare' (1942), the speaker deploys a similar image of 'squatting' in degradation. The poem expresses, in a Welsh context, strong feelings of communal culpability: 'The colliers squatting on the ashtip / Listen to one who holds them still with tales, / While that white frock that floats down the dark alley / Looks just like Christ; and in the lane / The clink of coins among the gamblers / Suggests the thirty pieces of silver'; see *Collected Poems*, p. 87, ll. 29–34.

64 Lewis, *In the Green Tree*, letter 45, p. 72.

65 See note 37.

In and Beyond the City:

The Places of Dannie Abse's
Ash on a Young Man's Sleeve

Matthew Jarvis

In an essay which was published in *New Welsh Review* in
2002, the critic James A. Davies makes an interesting claim:
that Dannie Abse's autobiographical novels – by which he
means 1954's *Ash on a Young Man's Sleeve* and 1991's
There Was a Young Man from Cardiff – sit at an awkward
angle to much twentieth-century fiction from Wales. The
reason, he suggests, is the fact that Abse's novels are set
within the physical and cultural geography of 'middle-class
suburban life' in a large urban area.[1] Rather than rooting
themselves in locations from the 'South Wales valleys, or [in]
small, mid- or west Wales places, or in the countryside',
these two volumes are, says Davies, novels of 'the urban,
English-speaking, middle or lower-middle class' – 'an area of
Welsh society', he claims, 'that receives little fictional (or any
other) attention' in writing from Wales.[2] Indeed, Davies even
implies that the middle-class urban environments of *Ash on
a Young Man's Sleeve* and *There Was a Young Man from
Cardiff* may be responsible for the 'almost complete silence'
with which these particular volumes have been greeted by
literary critics.[3] In effect, he is saying that these two novels
simply come from the wrong sort of Welsh place to fit
comfortably with prevailing literary patterns – emerging, so
he indicates, from an urban environment of relative comfort,
rather than from the remote spaces of Welsh rural life or
from the ravaged industrial locations of the Valleys. Whether
or not Davies is right about the environmental oddity of
Abse's autobiographical fiction within a Welsh context, he
does raise an important issue by drawing attention to the
significance of place within Welsh writing in general. On the

broadest literary level, of course, place is fundamental. As the environmentalist literary critic Lawrence Buell has succinctly put it, 'There never was an is without a where.'[4] In this sense, the worlds of literature happen *somewhere* – and it is thus vital to understand that the various *wheres* within which such worlds take place are freighted with meaning. In a specifically Welsh context, moreover, the poet R. S. Thomas catches something of the importance of place within the literary imagination when he writes that 'the true Wales is still to be found *in the country*';[5] in other words, for Thomas, Wales is most truly Wales in its rural spaces. Moreover, as Jason Walford Davies explains, the poet 'criticizes the Anglo-Welsh for conveying an imbalanced view of Wales as an industrial land, and stresses that the rural tradition reaches back through the centuries to a more essential Wales'.[6] Indeed, it is fear for the loss of precisely such a rural tradition which drives the concerns of R. S. Thomas's early essay 'The Depopulation of the Welsh Hill Country' (1945), when he observes how 'the hilly district of central Montgomeryshire' – which he offers as 'the prototype for the greater part of the Welsh uplands' – was then in danger of losing 'the true Welsh peasantry' who were, he claims, still clinging to a living there, producing 'poets, musicians, penillion singers, and men possessed of a rare personality, who will pass into local tradition as *hen gymeriadau*, old characters.'[7] In other words, for R. S. Thomas, the 'more essential Wales' was to be found in this particular sort of upland place and in the way of life associated with it – not in the lowlands, and certainly not in Dannie Abse's urban south, places where the hill folk would find 'no life at all, for they would be deracinés'.[18]

*   *   *

What, then, are the spaces, places, and environments which are important to the South Wales of Dannie Abse's fictional reminiscences in the pseudo-autobiography of *Ash on a Young Man's Sleeve?* What meanings do such places carry in the novel? Do the various environments of the narrative serve any particular purpose? And what, if anything, do they contribute to notions of what constitutes Welsh space? Or to put this latter question a different way: what sort of response might they offer to R. S. Thomas's constructions of Wales as essentially a place of remote uplands and his consequent rejection of life in the towns?

In the novel's opening paragraph, Abse's narrator offers up the Cardiff location of his upbringing as a place of 'tennis-players', of 'yellow seasick trams grinding down Cathedral Road', of 'windows open' and of hearing 'the neighbours' radio'.[9] The whole scene is, moreover, suffused with light in 'that year with all sunshine'.[10] As James A. Davies's comments should lead us to expect, this is a place that is immediately marked as urban (those trams, which were 'the foundation of Cardiff's transport system until 1950' after their initial introduction in 1902)[11] and as the arena of the middle classes (through the suggestion of people who have sufficient time to engage in polite leisure activities). Furthermore, the bright colour and the generous sunlight give the opening image of the city a distinctly positive glow, suggesting a place that is recalled with significant pleasure. But perhaps more importantly, these opening lines also hint at a place of lives lived in close proximity to the noise of other people – albeit at a respectable distance, as the chatter of someone else's radio filters through the open windows of summer time. A few paragraphs into the story, however, when we first enter the narrator's home, that respectable distance is gone:

> Near the White Wall, I was born in a smoky house, boasting. I knew the paper flowers, the Sunday suits, the stuffed animals, the brass, the clocks, and the ferns. Always there was too much furniture in the room. Always there was too much noise and familiarity. Always there were visitors. Lovely it was. (2–3)[12]

Here, then, Abse ties his narrative base clearly to Cardiff – the reference to the 'White Wall' indicating the eastern end of Albany Road in the Roath area of the city.[13] But just as important as precise physical location is the sense in these lines that place is *the location of social interaction*, with noise, familiarity, and visitors being fundamental keynotes of the Abse family house. And although there is 'too much' of these things, this sort of socially busy space is simultaneously 'Lovely'. Home, it seems, is where the company is.

The geographer Yi-Fu Tuan writes about how we get to know places by identifying significant markers within them, out of which we then build an image of the place in question.[14] The novel's opening pages offer up a number of such landmarks, plotting the world of its young narrator, Dannie (who is only ten as the volume begins), between the various locations of school, the house of his enemy Keith Thomas, home, 'the chapels and the pubs and the billiard halls' (2), Porthcawl, the street, the pub – and a place which is interestingly out of bounds (the Docks). Like the narrator's home, the places which we are offered as navigation points – what Tuan calls 'significant localities' – are crucially places of company.[15] Keith Thomas's house is a case in point, and indeed it is the physical environment of the place which perhaps particularly emphasises this. Here, though, it is not the *noise* of other people's lives which drives the sense of Abse's places as meeting places, but the *smell*. 'Other people's houses have a strange smell', the narrator tells us; 'Keith Thomas's home was no exception and I was sniffing' (2). The physical qualities of a particular place, in other words, are bringing the narrator nose-to-nose with other lives. It is important, moreover, that this initial visit to Keith Thomas's house is substantially about the problems of social interaction, as the narrator seeks to negotiate the minor social niceties of taking tea with the family of one of his peers. His sniffing having soon caused comment, the narrator is quickly in social difficulties: 'I went very red when the others sniffed.

... I tipped the tea over the tablecloth and grew redder' (2). Places, the novel seems to suggest at its opening, are present insofar as they are the stages on which we are offered the small dramas of social life. Thus, to choose another example, although the early recollection of childhood visits to Porthcawl begins with a sketch of the town's raw physical character ('Porthcawl was the place with the long wind and the terror of the sea coming over the promenade with sloppy white paws'), Abse's narrative gears soon shift:

> On Sundays, father would drive us down, plush and proud, scrubbed and avid, dodging in and out amongst the procession of cars that the seaside attracted like a magnet. (3)

The seaside may well be constituted by its physical attractions; indeed, the narrator goes on specifically to celebrate some of Porthcawl's amusements ('The Figure of Eight and the Ghost Train. The slowest Speedboats in the world and the thinnest Fat Lady'). But Porthcawl is also significantly figured through the minor drama of the family car dodging through crowds of traffic, weaving through the busyness of the place as a social arena. So it is entirely apposite that the Porthcawl episode ends with the vignette of 'Sandy Beach' where we are shown 'the parents shouting at the deaf children: "Don't' swim out too far." "Stop that!" "Dai, you'll get sick eating sand"' (3).[16] 'Always', as the narrator has said in describing his home, 'there was too much noise and familiarity. Always there were visitors.' In the book's opening pages, even the rain, it seems, creates places where lives resonate together, with Wales's 'lovely folk' sent 'scooting for the public shelters' by a downpour – only for them to 'sing whilst they waited' for the sun, for a bus, or for opening time (3–4). Admittedly, this rather syrupy reference to Wales's 'lovely folk' may be precisely what James A. Davies is talking about when he notes that *Ash on a Young Man's Sleeve* 'lightly but firmly satirise[s]' the 'excesses' of Valley writing – 'mainly', he suggests, 'the sentimentalised Welshiosity of Richard Llewellyn's *How Green Was My Valley* (1939)'.[17] But nonetheless, it is clear that the vitality of Welsh space is, at the start of the novel, very much to do with its social energy:

> This was all a long time ago: I was ten years high and I lived in South Wales. There everything was different, more alive somehow. The landscape and the voices were dramatic and argumentative. Already I knew the chapels and the pubs and the billiard halls and the singing. (2)

Voices, drama, and argument, rooted in the collective spaces of chapel, pub, and the billiard hall – all of that, perhaps, condensed into the symbolism of song. In short, as the novel opens, Welsh space in Abse's urban south is unequivocally social space.

*　　*　　*

The Cardiff locale in which the majority of *Ash on a Young Man's Sleeve* is set is the novel's geographical base, and although various incidents take the narrative beyond Cardiff itself – in moments to which I shall turn in the penultimate section of this essay – the city is the foremost place of the text. But what sort of a place is it? At one interesting point, Abse's Cardiff is an environment crucially defined by technology. As the narrator and his friends have been waiting to catch a glimpse of the beautiful Lydia Pike near her house in the Cyncoed area of the city – significantly a location in which the novel suggests there is 'the feeling ... of almost being in the country' (84) – dusk falls, and the narrator observes:

> Suddenly, some anonymous futuristic man, a long way away in the power house, touched some gigantic switch and the lamp-posts jerked to life; and, though it was not dark, the electricity demarcated the country from the

town more absolutely than any fumbling sunshine of a
windy summer afternoon. (85–6)[18]

Here, the electricity grid is the basis of the city; and this
product of some dimly realised technological centre –
figured in the near mythical figure of that 'anonymous
futuristic man' who flips 'some gigantic switch' –
apparently does a far better job of suggesting the limits of
the urban than anything which the natural world might
offer up.[19] The non-human world is all very well and good,
such a moment might suggest (there is a quiet lament, a
few paragraphs earlier, about new house building
destroying the sense of being close to the rural in Cyncoed);
but when it comes to the city itself, the natural is
subordinate to technology.

What makes this moment of technologically defined
cityspace especially interesting is that it sits in an
intriguing dialogue with one of the novel's significantly
returning locales: Cardiff's green spaces.[20] The city's
parkland is a recurrent environment (albeit sometimes
fleetingly so) within the narrative.[21] We initially find
ourselves confronted with it among the book's opening
stories of 1934, as the ten-year-old Dannie runs 'out of
school ... into the summer evening' of the park and offers
a mild attack on the authority structures of public property
by kicking over the notices which read 'PLEASE KEEP OFF
THE GRASS and DOGS ALLOWED ONLY ON A LEASH'
(8). However, in reality, the authority figure of the park
keeper is as removed from immediate experience as the
mysterious 'futuristic man' of the electricity grid ('*In the
distance*, the park-keeper stabbed with his little iron spear,
cigarette cartons, pieces of newspaper and other rubbish';
emphasis added). The park is not really to do with
confronting authority, whatever Dannie's initial response
to it here may be. Far more important is its function as a
locus for the revelation of the town's broad social life – and
for the narrator's own immediate social interactions. Thus,

in this initial parkland episode, we are shown 'Old men ... playing bowls' and 'Young men' in 'tigerish blazers' who are getting ready to 'play tennis on the red gravel court'. The park is, in other words, a place of leisure, apparently far removed from the economic troubles of Cardiff in the mid-1930s. Indeed, in this context, it is perhaps significant that the Docks are declared out of bounds to the young Dannie: in terms of its dealings with Cardiff itself, the novel typically keeps the sites of labour at a distance (even if labour issues make their way into the discourse of the Abse family).[22] As such, parkland is logically a presence in the text in a way that the Docks are not; the spaces of polite leisure are thus highly visible, whilst the economic sufferings of a city in which 'Unemployment ... rose to 25% in 1930 and, until the Second World War, ... rarely fell below 20%' are pretty much absent.[23] However, alongside this display of urban green space as leisure made manifest, the park also offers Dannie comparable social challenges to those which he faced in the house of Keith Thomas. In this initial park vignette, then, Dannie again finds himself confronted by Keith and is given a beating by his enemy – who is, significantly, not alone ('all the other boys who had come to watch exhorted him to further savagery': 8); in other words, the fight is very much a social affair. Moreover, although the narrator claims that 'Nobody was in earshot', the aftermath of the fight is punctuated by the shouting of a tennis score and by 'the wooden click as the bowls cannoned off each other'. Just as it was at home, the noise of other lives is never far away in the supremely social space of the park. Similarly, in a later parkland moment, Dannie has to negotiate dealing with Lol (initially called 'the idiot boy': 8), who demands Dannie's services for assistance with writing a letter to Lydia Pike (the focus of Dannie's own affections, of course). This incident is all to do with Dannie having to deal successfully with the demands of this large and sometimes aggressive boy ('"If you 'ave me, I'll get you," [Lol] warned': 99), having been taken by him into the relative seclusion of the park's summer-house. The park, in this sense, is about the challenges of youthful socialisation. Moreover, once inside the summer-house, the boys disturb 'a couple of lovers' (98), whose own use of the park for a romantic and/or sexual assignation again catches the novel's approach to the city as, in its green spaces at least, the location of socialised leisure and pleasure.

Indeed, it is only at the novel's very end that the park becomes a place for solitary reflection when the narrator – now in his late teens and crucially alone in the aftermath of Keith's death – considers the leaves falling from the park's trees in 'that late autumn afternoon' (207). 'Their falling was their dying', the narrator declares – the park, at this point, seemingly giving Dannie a way of revisiting the death of the young man who had become his best friend, as the association between falling and death sharply recalls the air-raid in which Keith died. (In this context, it also seems significant to note that the natural phenomena of the park are all effectively in a shattered state too: 'Near the air-raid shelters I heard, also, the waterfall crashing down into its distance and saw, in the harp of wind, pools of rain-water trembling on the gravel pathway, reflecting shuddering fragments of sky. Pieces of sky, water, leaves, hands all fallen, falling in the convalescent sunlight': 207–8). More important than this, however, the concluding shift to the park as solitary space crucially signifies the end of youth:

> I stood up and walked out of the park, crossing the brook over the toy bridge, only stopping when I reached the street to gaze back at the distant summer-house ... – and I heard not one lingering cry of a child playing in that park which was made for children. I lit a cigarette, turned up the collar of my mackintosh, and strolled home that was never to be home again. (208)

Paralleled by the final overturning of the park as social space, the novel concludes with a sense of rupture in the narrator's larger social structure that constitutes the final transition into adulthood (the realisation of the now un-homely parental home). Shattered in its physical forms – 'Pieces of sky' (208); leaves in their 'death agony' (207); tree branches 'lean[ing] nakedly into the scant oxygen' (207) – and thus abruptly recalling the novel's earlier suggestion of nature's urban insufficiency, the socialising function of city parkland similarly seems to collapse at the novel's conclusion. And in that collapse is childhood's end.

*   *   *

Parkland, of course, is clearly not the whole city and the Cardiff of *Ash on a Young Man's Sleeve* is also significantly characterised by a network of buildings and streets – those navigation points by which Yi-Fu Tuan suggests we begin to learn our neighbourhood. The importance of streets, for example, becomes clear in the opening lines of the novel, with the reference to Cathedral Road. The narrator's Jewish identity is abundantly clear at numerous points throughout the novel, but here – right at the start of the book – it is written into the very geography of the text. As the historian John Davies explains, 'Jews began settling in Cardiff in 1813, and the first synagogue was built in 1858 at East Terrace – now the bottom end of Churchill Way. Further synagogues would be built in Edwards Terrace, Windsor Place *and Cathedral Road*.'[24] The synagogue in Cathedral Road – 'a spacious, elegant' building – had been opened in 1897, and was a response to Cardiff's rising Jewish population at the time.[25] The text's very first specific geographical reference is thus fundamentally important for establishing a particular cultural awareness of Cardiff's cityscape: the geography of the text's opening is, in part, a response to Jewish history within South Wales. Of course, the synagogue which the narrator attends[26] and the house of the rabbi, Rev. Aaronowich, both function as part of this same particular cultural geography within the novel. For the by-now eleven-year-old narrator (31), the synagogue is a place for meeting friends and thus, functionally, shares important qualities with the park:

> I used to sit next to Bernard and Simon. We would wear our skull caps and whisper to each other beneath the chant of the Hebrew prayer. (28)

However, it is also a space where the Jewish community can confirm its identity in shared knowledge, and take pleasure in that fact:

> Every New Year, Rosh Hashana, [Rev. Aaronowich] would begin his speech, raising his hands, eyes round, mournfully direct, 'Another year has passed ... another nail ... in the coffin.' The congregation knew this preface to his sermon by heart. They could have joined in, if they so wished, in some sorrowful chant; instead ... each would nudge and pinch his neighbour. (29)

Interestingly, it is only when the young narrator goes into the empty synagogue on a weekday that the place becomes threatening. In its stillness, the synagogue is transformed into a distinctly alien space, where Dannie becomes conscious of the potential proximity of God ('Supposing God rose out from one of the corners, from the stillness, from the silence, from the dark?': 31). According to the religious historian Mircea Eliade, such 'breaks' in space – places which are 'qualitatively different from others' – are what mark out sacred spaces as distinct locations.[27] The narrator's response is to flee such a place and to return to the noise of the street ('I ran out from the silence, from the dark, into the glittering sunshine and the loud street, not even daring to glance over my shoulder. I didn't want to see the face of God': 31). In the terms of the novel, it seems that social space is infinitely preferable to sacred space. Indeed, when the police at Cardiff Arms Park remove the 'intense spectators from the holy pitch', they are greeted with boos and cries of 'Shame' (12). Here, of course, the aim of the spectators is to get *into* sacred space. But the point is ultimately the same as it was with the synagogue: that places, for Abse, seemingly need to contain people. They should be full of folk.

It is this issue which, seemingly, constitutes in large part the tragedy of Keith Thomas's house after the death of his mother: that it is far emptier than it should be. As Dannie's mother puts it, when discussing who to invite to a party:

> 'Let's ask Mr Thomas,' mother implored. Tears came to her eyes. 'Think of it. A poor widower living in a big house with a boy only as big as our youngest son.' (66)

The sadness of Mr Thomas's life is, for Dannie's mother, explicitly expressed in relation to *place*: the Thomas house is no longer full, and this is seen as a particular focus for the grief of that family. Moreover, the point is emphasised by contrast with the Abse house in the aftermath of this moment. The narrator, having echoed his mother by proclaiming that 'It must be awful for Keith ... I mean not to have a mother or brothers' (70), recounts how his own brothers returned home:

> Father put some more coal on the fire and my brothers came in hungry, whistling, talking, making all the house alive. (70–1)

Place, in short, is 'alive' insofar as it is thoroughly peopled. Indeed, the novel's seeming horror of emptiness or the solitary within the city is perhaps most sharply captured in the final events of the Thomas house. Moments before his death in the air-raid, Keith has seemingly taken upon himself a solitary existence: rather than joining Phyllis the maid in the slightly safer space under the stairs, Keith explicitly rejects her company and stays alone, playing the piano, in one of the rooms. The oddity of being by oneself in a place is emphasised by the maid's sense that she 'felt foolish, sitting alone under the staircase' (202). But it is Keith's rejection of the remaining social life of the house – he seems determinedly deaf when Phyllis tries to persuade him to join her ('Phyllis came into the room and stood there watching Keith playing the piano. She called his name but he just went on playing': 201) – which ultimately results in his death, as the narrative's delivery of a bomb in the air-raid abruptly destroys the location and life of one who chooses to be alone. Abse's Cardiff, it seems, abhors a social vacuum.

None of which is to say, however, that the character-istically socialised spaces of Abse's cityscape are necessarily comfortable ones. I have already suggested that a number of locations function as arenas of social challenge for the young Dannie. Moreover, even in the heady pleasures of the early rugby match at Cardiff Arms Park – which is presented as a place of communality perhaps above all ('The kind Welsh crowd would pass us down over their heads, hand by hand, laugh by laugh, right to the front': 12) – even here there is danger, for among the crowd of fifty thousand spectators Keith happens to see the 'Black Curse man' (12), thus moving the narrative into the sequence of events which leads to the death of his mother. Sharper still is the meeting in memory of Jimmy Ford, a young man who has been killed in the Spanish Civil War. The location for the memorial is 'the October Hall' (72), a 'bare Hall' somewhere in the city, lit harshly by a 'naked electric bulb' and distinguished by a 'cracked ceiling' (71).[28] The meeting simply parallels the desolation of the building itself: it is punctuated by awkward silences; Jimmy Ford's mother cannot console the crowd when she gets up to speak; his widow sits sobbing for much of the event; and the closing scenes of social interaction quickly turn to argument. But however physically bleak it may be, and however much it may offer up a scene riven by emotional awkwardness and devastation, in its housing of a meeting in which so many griefs and angers are played out in public, 'that dry, cold Hall' (75) is emphatically a place in which a community comes together, albeit in brokenness. Here, to put it another way, the novel presents Cardiff space as the location of collective memorial, grief, and anger – and it is that note of the *collective* which is crucial.

* * *

But what lies beyond the city? In 1934, the narrative tells us, there are the Valleys, 'thirty miles from Cardiff, [where] the rain fell absently across the town square and the queue at the bus stop suddenly started singing into the rain ... – the chapel of voices *together*, ever rising higher into the thin rain' (25–6; emphasis in original). This sounds like the communal space of the city itself, especially with the text's emphasis on the word '*together*'. But Abse quickly undercuts the pattern by shifting this italicised word to another one. Recounting how one of the singers suddenly has a 'fit of coughing', the story tells how:

> All the people in the queue watched his convulsion of coughing, and like prisoners they filed through the pin-striped rain into the red-coloured bus, terribly mute, wet, *lonely*. (26; emphasis in original)

What seemingly shifts the Valleys here from sung communality to silent loneliness is the coughing man, who 'spat from his mouth a yellow viscid fluid, mixed with coal and blood'. This suggestion of mining-related lung disease follows on swiftly from the image of 'the Rhondda Valley naked, bony, the green dress pulled off it', and the two together point directly to the area's industrial character. More particularly, in the illness of the man and the stark suggestion of a violated landscape, we are given a striking sense of what Lawrence Buell has called a 'poisoned community' – a place where both the environment and the people who are part of it have been devastated by industry.[29] Indeed, the narrative of Gwennie and Alun (which concludes the Valleys episode) merely emphasises Abse's apparent sense of the failure of togetherness under the degradations of industry. Although Alun initially bows to notions of communality ('A man has to keep his roots or he's lost. Alun's father had been a miner. The family always had been miners': 26), the explosion in the mine, and the consequent disfigurement of many of the men who were trapped below, help Gwennie resolve that the two of them should depart to London. For Gwennie at least, the dangers of a 'poisoned community' are too great; or, to put it another way, roots and singing are, seemingly, not enough. Such presentations of industrialised space, moreover, also emphasise the way in which, in these narratives, the Valleys are very much figured as the location of labour. As Dolores Hayden has observed, 'Space is shaped for both economic production – barns, or mine shafts, or piers, or a factory – as well as for social reproduction – housing for the workers, managers, and owners, a store, a school, a church.'[30] Whereas much of what we have seen in relation to Cardiff could be defined in terms of Hayden's 'social reproduction' (the generation of community in and through places such as the park and the synagogue), with the economic life of the city remaining relatively unseen, Abse's Rhondda is emphatically a space shaped for economic production. Confronted with both the consequences of labour (the sick man; the injured miners) and the site of labour itself (the stripped land; the mine), Abse's vision of the Valleys brings us face to face with the economic landscape of 1930s south Wales. As such, it makes considerable sense that, in place of Wales's 'lovely folk' (3), here we find a people 'smelling of wet mackintoshes, listless, *dull with unemployment*' (26; emphasis added).

The shift from *'together'* to *'lonely'* which the opening of the Valleys vignette articulates is also precisely figured in another moment beyond Cardiff – the story of Jimmy Ford's death in Spain (which is ostensibly told by Leo, at the memorial meeting). Spain has, in this tale, initially constituted togetherness, with 'the drinks, the earnest conversations' (73) of the International Brigade. Indeed, recounting the day before Jimmy's death, the text observes how:

> Yesterday each [man] had mingled through the lines looking for someone from his home town. And when they found a compatriot from a town away, or a street away, they would talk avidly, their location of birth giving them some kinship. Names of streets, pubs, dance halls were swapped as if they were names of exotic treasures. To be born in Cardiff and to meet a man from Newport was not to be solitary. (74)

However, it is precisely solitariness which triumphs as dawn breaks, for 'now everybody stood unspeakably alone'. Jimmy, we are told, is unable to keep in his mind anything which reminds him of home: as both Cardiff and his wife slip through the net of recollection, even the memory of being in community, of being in relationship with another human being, has been lost. It is, perhaps, no surprise that, rather than dying in the arms of concerned comrades, Abse has Jimmy Ford die utterly alone, as the man closest to him has no idea that his comrade has been shot down and thus 'marche[s] on oblivious of Jimmy's fate' (75). In places beyond Cardiff, it seems, solitariness is as crucial a keynote as conviviality is to the city itself.

Indeed, in what Tony Curtis has pertinently called 'the nightmare transformation at Cardiff station',[31] the novel offers up one of its most terrifying renditions of such solitariness. Waiting for the return of his parents from London, the narrator experiences a species of vision in which Cardiff station morphs into another place entirely – and into the very centre of the Holocaust itself:

> The voice over the crackling loudspeaker shouted, 'All change at Auschwitz-Dachau.' The engine gave a shriek

> of pain and the dogs would not look. Near the
> Refreshment Room stood a hygienic-looking shed
> containing a few gas chambers. (155)

On the train, the Jewish passengers sit in silence, with all interaction utterly stopped. There is no eye contact; there is no conversation; there is no movement. In a moment of devastating imagery, the functions of community have categorically and finally ceased. As in Spain, here too, in the fused locale of Auschwitz-Dachau,[32] the links from one human being to another have been devastatingly severed. The social hum of so many of the novel's Cardiff locations seems to belong to another world entirely. As Tony Curtis observes about the novel, 'Recollections of an essentially happy childhood are counterpointed by [geographically] wider references.'[33] And it is, I would suggest, in the strikingly differing presentations of place as social space that such counterpointing becomes most sharply focused.

Indeed, even in Ogmore-by-Sea, in the novel's longest sojourn beyond its home city, Keith and Dannie's initially convivial camping trip turns to loneliness for Dannie as Keith spends increasing amounts of time with Henrietta Gregory. Interestingly, however, Dannie's human loneliness results in a kind of Romantic communion with the non-human world. Ogmore has, from the beginning of the episode, been presented as a place utterly outside the urban, and is characterised by a range of resolutely non-human environmental identifiers ('Ogmore covered by light green turf and dark green ferns. Ogmore by the sand by the river by the sea': 157). However, when Dannie goes for his solitary swim in Hardy's Bay – again, determinedly figured by rural qualities (boulders, sheep, a 'narrow path' (172), green ferns, butterflies, rabbit-holes) – Ogmore's non-human world seemingly overruns him:

> I shook my head to get water out of my ear and lay down
> on the sand in the sun. Gradually everything grew calm and
> there was nothing at all but the sound of the sea. All the

> noise in my head fell away, crumbled to nothingness, and I
> lost my identity. I was as much part of the beach as the
> mustard-tainted rock on which earlier I had piled my
> clothes. I felt clean inside and strangely elated. (173–4)

At this moment of 'benediction', of 'great exultation and ...
holiness,' Dannie's human solitude is effectively
transformed as he is 'integrated with the landscape' (174).
In the aftermath of this incident, Dannie considers that it
has made him 'older and more lonely' (175) – the novel's
familiar motif of loneliness in places beyond the city again
being made explicit. But loneliness here must be set against
an astonishing, if temporary, sense of new communion: not
with human community but with the physical world itself.

*   *   *

It would be easy, I think, to conclude that, in *Ash on a
Young Man's Sleeve*, places in Cardiff tend towards a
vibrant and noisy social energy while those outside it
ultimately tend towards loneliness. However, while there is
clearly a strong degree of truth in this – and while it does,
I think, reflect the primary geographical division of the text
(between Cardiff and everywhere else) – the Ogmore
incident, in its suggestion of Dannie's visionary fellowship
with the non-human world, indicates that the issue is
ultimately more complex than a simple binary division.
Moreover, in the social devastation of the Auschwitz-
Dachau vision, in the scene of 'Oswald Mosley posing on a
lonely platform in London' (39; emphasis added) and
vilifying Jews, and in the narrative of Grynszpan (pp.
104–10) – significantly a young man very much *on his own*
– one might also argue that, in these scenes beyond Cardiff,
Abse is effectively building a Europe-wide geography of
Jewish community and politics. These are, in other words,
navigation points around which a geography of collective
Jewish experience can be triangulated. To put it another
way, that which lies outside the narrative's home city does

not *necessarily* correspond to the demise of communality. Moreover, one might also point to the fact that the early vignette of Porthcawl offers up a vibrantly peopled place, while the closing pages of the novel see solitariness take root in Cardiff itself (however much the city may abhor it). Thus, rather than simply dividing the world of *Ash on a Young Man's Sleeve* between two different sorts of space – the socially vibrant and the lonely – I think it is more appropriate to see the novel as articulating a journey away from the former and towards the latter. The narrative's engagement with the variant social character of different places ultimately stands as a way for Abse to prepare for the transition of his narrator away from home – in other words, to make the shift from the 'smoky house' of his birth (2), always full of noise and visitors, to the novel's very final words, in which the late-teenage Dannie leaves the deserted, broken park and strolls away to a 'home that was never to be home again' (208). To put it another way, Abse's primary Welsh space – the urban communality of Cardiff – is what the novel ultimately grows beyond. Which is not to say that Abse follows R. S. Thomas in rejecting Welsh cityspace. Rather, as a drama of place, what the novel crucially achieves is a movement beyond the static, singular sense of Welsh space suggested by Thomas, as Abse's Cardiff enters into a dynamic process of exchange with those locations in the wider world – both within Wales and further afield – which intrude upon it.

NOTES
1   James A. Davies, 'Dannie Abse's Autobiographical Fiction', *New Welsh Review*, 56 (Summer 2002), pp. 14–20 (16).
2   Davies, 'Abse's Autobiographical Fiction', pp. 16 and 17.
3   Davies, 'Abse's Autobiographical Fiction', p. 14. Davies is, here, somewhat unfair to Tony Curtis whose Writers of Wales volume on Abse offers a useful analysis of *Ash on a Young Man's Sleeve*: see Tony Curtis, *Dannie Abse* (Cardiff: University of Wales Press, 1985), pp. 7–18. Davies's

assessment, however, reduces this to a 'a few pages ... emphasising the moral force' of the novel ('Abse's Autobiographical Fiction', p. 14).

4   Lawrence Buell, *Writing for an Endangered World: Literature, Culture, and Environment in the U.S. and Beyond* (Cambridge, MA: Belknap, 2001), p. 55.

5   Translation provided in Jason Walford Davies, '"Thick Ambush of Shadows": Allusions to Welsh Literature in the Work of R. S. Thomas', *Welsh Writing in English: A Yearbook of Critical Essays*, 1 (1995), pp. 75–127 (99–100); emphasis added.

6   Walford Davies, '"Thick Ambush of Shadows"', p. 100.

7   Sandra Anstey, ed., *R. S. Thomas: Selected Prose* (Bridgend: Poetry Wales Press, 1983), pp. 19–25 (19, 21, and 23).

8   Anstey, *R. S. Thomas*, p. 24.

9   Dannie Abse, *Ash on a Young Man's Sleeve*, Library of Wales (Cardigan: Parthian, 2006), p. 1. Subsequent references to this volume are given in the text.

10   In his autobiography, Abse notes the early memory of these yellow trams and, alongside 'coal-black horses', Cardiff City as the Bluebirds, and 'The Red Sea of Bolshevism', observes how his early years were 'colour, colour all the way': see Dannie Abse, *A Poet in the Family* (London: Robson, 1984; orig. Hutchinson, 1974), p. 5.

11   Dennis Morgan, *The Illustrated History of Cardiff's Suburbs* (Derby: Breedon, 2003), p. 130.

12   The 'smoky house' of the narrator's birth draws directly from Abse's own beginnings. As he explains in *A Poet in the Family*, referring to the period around 1940, 'We lived in a rented, semidetached house in Windermere Avenue, a few doors away from the allotments. Over a period of sixteen years my family had moved from "the smoky house" in Whitchurch Road where I was born to 298 Albany Road near the White Wall, to 237 Albany Road, to 66 Albany Road, to 66 Sandringham Road near Waterloo Gardens, to the house in Windermere Avenue' (pp. 22–3). The novel, however, gives no indication of such moves; moreover, it places the 'smoky house' near the 'White Wall' (which Whitchurch Road is not). So the narrator's home should not be tied to any one particular house from Abse's own youth.

13   The so-called 'White Wall' runs partially around what is now

a funeral home, but which was, at the time of the novel, 'Roath Court, a handsome early nineteenth-century villa ... The house was the seat of the Crofts Williams family, whose members provided Cardiff with several of its mayors': see John Davies, *Cardiff: A Pocket Guide* (Cardiff: University of Wales Press; Western Mail, 2002), p. 89. According to Davies, Albany Road is the 'boundary between the community of Roath and that of Plasnewydd' (p. 88).

14 Yi-Fu Tuan, *Space and Place: The Perspective of Experience* (Minneapolis: University of Minnesota Press, 1977), pp. 17–18.

15 Tuan, *Space and Place*, pp. 17–18.

16 Abse presumably means Sandy Bay: see Ordnance Survey National Grid Reference (NGR) SS 824 776.

17 Davies, 'Abse's Autobiographical Fiction', p. 16.

18 Although Abse here refers to 'the town', Cardiff had been a city since 1905: see John Davies, Nigel Jenkins, Menna Baines, and Peredur I. Lynch, eds, *The Welsh Academy Encyclopaedia of Wales* (Cardiff: University of Wales Press, 2008), p. 117.

19 Such a technological centre had been close by for the young Abse, so perhaps it is no surprise that the city should be figured in this fashion. As Dennis Morgan explains, 'The Roath Power Station in Newport Road [had begun] supplying electricity in 1902' (*Cardiff's Suburbs*, p. 130).

20 For a brief but useful history of Cardiff's parks, see Dennis Morgan, *The Cardiff Story: A History of the City from Its Earliest Times to the Present* (Cowbridge: Brown, 1991), pp. 196–9.

21 The park of *Ash on a Young Man's Sleeve* is seemingly rooted in Waterloo Gardens, an Edwardian park near Albany Road. (My thanks are due to Gwyneth Lewis for discussion on this point.) However, the novel typically leaves the park unnamed, so its real-world basis is perhaps less important than its status as a kind of mythical or generic green space within the city environment of the fiction. (For a brief description of Waterloo Gardens, see the leaflet 'Roath Mill Gardens & Waterloo Gardens', Cardiff Council, 14 October. 2009 <http://www.cardiff.gov.uk/objview.asp?object_id=3618>.)

22 See, for example, the words of the song 'I'm the man, the very fat man' (81–2).

23 Morgan, *Cardiff Story*, p. 222. The Docks were, perhaps, a particular focus for the city's economic tribulations in this period; as Morgan explains, 'by 1935 nearly half the registered dockers were unemployed'.

24 Davies, *Cardiff*, p. 88; emphasis added.

25 Morgan, *Cardiff Story*, p. 195. The Cathedral Road synagogue closed in 1989: see 'Cardiff United Synagogue', *JRC-UK: Jewish Communities & Records*, 9 October 2009 <http://www.jewishgen.org/jcr-uk/Community/card/index.htm>.

26 As *A Poet in the Family* makes clear (p. 16), the young Abse attended the synagogue in Windsor Place; the synagogue in *Ash on a Young Man's Sleeve* is, however, unnamed.

27 Mircea Eliade, *The Sacred and the Profane: The Nature of Religion*, tr. Willard R. Trask (London: Harcourt Brace Jovanovich, 1987), p. 20.

28 In *A Poet in the Family*, Abse recalls the memorial for 'One of Leo's friends, Sid Hamm' (p. 7), who had been killed in Spain: 'I remember the memorial meeting for Sid Hamm at a dolorous little hall in Cardiff, misnamed Sunshine Hall' (p. 8).

29 Buell, *Writing for an Endangered World*, p. 35.

30 Dolores Hayden, *The Power of Place: Urban Landscapes as Public History* (Cambridge, MA: MIT Press, 1995), p. 20.

31 Curtis, *Abse*, p. 14.

32 Abse here draws together locations in southern Poland (Auschwitz) and southern Germany (Dachau). For the Nazi camps in these places see 'Auschwitz', *Encyclopædia Britannica*, 2009, Encyclopædia Britannica Online, 15 October 2009 <http://search.eb.com/eb/article-9011296> and 'Dachau', *Encyclopædia Britannica*, 2009, Encyclopædia Britannica Online, 15 October 2009 <http://search.eb.com/ eb/article-9028484>.

33 Curtis, *Abse*, p. 14.

A Huge Assembling of Unease:

Readings in A Man's Estate

M. Wynn Thomas

A vengeful wife murders her unfaithful husband with the tacit complicity of her secret admirer. That gaunt suitor, a cousin of the deceased, subsequently marries her. Their sin is visited upon the children of both her marriages. The son born to the grim pair, indulged by his mother, proves wilful and dies in war; his life is a 'judgement' on his parents, his story makes for 'a puny provincial tragedy'.[1] The brother of the original union is separated from his sister at birth. Growing up scarcely aware of each other's existence, the siblings are nevertheless eventually united. This marks the fateful culmination of the sister's long-cherished dream of the arrival of a saviour who will release her from the house and family that have long held her spirit captive. Reluctantly returning to claim his 'estate', her impecunious brother finds himself nightmarishly entangled in a past about which he knows nothing. And when the gruesome truth about the family history finally surfaces, their ageing mother escapes incontinently into madness, while their stepfather commits suicide. The atmosphere throughout is doom-laden; a judgemental God hovers ominously over the scene; gloom seems to pervade every corner of the action.

Reduced to the bare essentials of its plot, *A Man's Estate* (1955) proves to be massively built on an ancient substratum of legend – the primal stuff of which Greek tragedy was made, and Shakespearean and Jacobean drama likewise. The dominant stories of the Old Testament – so relevant to this novel about a 'biblical' society – are also of the same 'archetypal' character. During the period he was writing the novel, Emyr Humphreys was in the grip of a fascination with myth, with classical tragedy, and with plays such as *Hamlet*.[2] 'A huge assembling of unease' (*ME* 84) – a phrase used by the sentimental young minister, Idris Powell, bewildered by the dark complexities of love – is a fair description of *A Man's Estate* as a whole, with its labyrinthine rootedness in human passions. There is something repellent about even the most marginal characters:

> Katie is thin and rodent: she scuttles about the house, always too fast to do anything properly, her small head carrying a flopping flappy cap, and when she speaks, her teeth seem very sharp as she makes her indistinct squeaks and noises. (*ME* 155)

Not only does this highlight unsavoury physical signs of Katie's spiritual deformity, it reflects the sour, twisted soul of the neurotic and 'barren spinster' who is here viewing the maid through jealous, jaundiced eyes.

Much that was best in modern Welsh literature, Emyr Humphreys's great friend and exemplar Saunders Lewis once observed, derived from the Calvinist strain in nineteenth-century Nonconformity. Through its insistent recognition of the evil ingrained in human nature, Calvinism nurtured an unillusioned consciousness creatively alive to the moral ugliness of the human condition. War experience refocused attention on the lurking presence of evil within the human soul – William Golding's *Lord of the Flies* (1954) was a memorable fifties fable emphasising this. Likewise indirectly a product of Emyr Humphreys's wartime experience, *A Man's Estate* is a classical Welsh Calvinist tragedy (even a kind of 'revenger's tragedy') in two senses. It deals with the morbid, decaying Calvinist culture of the chapels midway through the first half of the twentieth century; and it views that culture from the standpoint of an author capable of empathising with the tough realism of Calvinist belief in original sin. As such, the novel is the radical Welsh Nonconformist complement to the Catholic novels of sin and guilt written by

Humphreys's early friend and mentor, Graham Greene.[3] It may also be revealingly juxtaposed with another important 'Calvinist' novel of the fifties, Robin Jenkins's *The Corn-Gatherers* (1955), set in the Calvinistic society of Argyllshire.

One possible consequence of the replacement of a Calvinist vision by a more tolerant post-Calvinist theological outlook is explored in *A Man's Estate* through the character of the young idealistic minister, Idris Powell. Devotee of a facile liberal theology of universal love, he crushingly discovers that he lacks the moral, psychological and spiritual resources to deal with the harsh realities of devious human existence. Like the spiritually lightweight Morton Densher in Henry James's great novel *The Wings of the Dove*, Powell is judged in the sombre light of human tragedy and found wanting. 'Murderer' and hypocrite though the morally weathered and withered Vavasor Elis may be, in his daily implicit recognition of the severe Puritan values by which he will eventually be implacably judged, he possesses a compelling moral weight; a monstrous integrity.

The very title of the novel bears the heavy burden of its central preoccupations. As the epigraph makes clear, the phrase 'A Man's Estate' alludes to the opening lines of a familiar Welsh Calvinist hymn by Dafydd Jones of Caio: 'Plant ydym eto dan ein hoed / Yn disgwyl am ystad ...' The translation provided in the novel reads: 'We are all still children / waiting for an inheritance ...' As modified in Humphreys's title, the theological meaning is double. *A Man's Estate* alludes to the state of sin that is the inheritance of all the sons and daughters of Adam. But the reference is also to that other 'state', of Divine Grace, to which spiritually infantile mankind as a whole should aspire, but which can be entered only by the elect; by the few mysteriously chosen as sole beneficiaries of Christ's self-immolation. In some important respects, the action of the novel oscillates between these two meanings. If the 'barren spinster' Hannah, daughter to Mrs Elis and her first (murdered) husband, is in one sense manifestly an innocent victim of her mother's tyrannical grip on life, she is also (as she recognises) 'bound' to her mother and step-father 'in the blood-cement of likeness. I have their coldness, their calculation, their trained hypocrisy, their perpetual misery, their unexpiated guilt' (*ME* 156). Recognising her own 'sinfulness', Hannah's dreams euphorically of a salvatory act of secular grace in the form of the return of her long-lost brother. But in its vengeful aspects, such a Messianic expectation in turn evokes uneasy memories of the strong leader cult of the thirties. To the domestic fascism of her everyday life on the family farm, 'Y Glyn', she secretly opposes her own fascist fantasy of supreme personal empowerment. Finally, having begun as a victim of her circumstances, Hannah ends up guilty of perpetuating the status quo; a 'feudal' biblical order grown rotten to its core.

*   *   *

If, then, *A Man's Estate* is modelled on classical tragedy, it is set not in ancient Greece but in the morally decadent chapel culture of rural Wales during the first half of the twentieth century. In this society, relationships involve the kind of ruthless power-struggles so nakedly and memorably illustrated in some of the primal stories of the Old Testament. And just as, for all its roots in 'universal' human legends, Greek tragedy is actually woven out of the conflicting values of ancient Greek society at a particular historical juncture, so Humphreys's novel specifically addresses the tensions within the dying 'Nonconformist nation', a century after its mid-nineteenth-century prime. In this connection, it is useful to register the pivotal place *A Man's Estate* occupies in the development of Emyr Humphreys as a novelist.

The novel was written some three years after Humphreys's return from London to teach at Pwllheli, on the Lleyn peninsula. A teacher in Wimbledon, but living in Chelsea, and a coming young writer with three novels already to his name, he had spent four years mixing with aspiring, talented young writers, artists and actors in a metropolitan, cosmopolitan, atmosphere heady with the excitement of new beginnings after an exhausting war and the establishing of a Welfare State. The return of this native to Wales was prompted by a commitment to the Welsh language and the values it had nurtured. This was the result of the schoolboy Humphreys's 'conversion' to cultural and political nationalism in the thirties. But his move 'home' was at a considerable price – Graham Greene strongly advised against it, forecasting the miscarriage in the 'provinces' of Humphreys's talents as a novelist. The resulting tensions within the ambitious young author found expression in *A Man's Estate*, a novel that subjects the concept of 'rootedness' (to which Humphreys nevertheless remained tenaciously faithful) to sceptical scrutiny. Cross-examined about his 'pietas' by his prospective father-in-law, the odious Master of an Oxford college, the scientifically-minded Philip dismisses all discussion of family (as opposed to property) inheritance as nonsensical superstition, 'unscientific neo-fascism'. (*ME* 19–20). He acknowledges blood groups but not blood lines. The novel, however, calls Philip's supposedly objective, 'scientific', outlook into doubt, exposing it as simplistic by indicating its compromised origins in family and society. Meanwhile his sister, the claustrophobically cloistered Hannah, is aware of how the Elis family farm has remained in stubborn, decaying stasis while life in the surrounding Welsh countryside has been undergoing revolutionary change. Although resentful of her parents' glowering dominance, she is nevertheless a willing prisoner of 'the old dispensation'. In its apparent immunity to springtime's infectious revivifications, the rural scene almost completely filling her window, and blocking her 'view', resembles a consolingly timeless frieze:

> I sit watching through my square bedroom window a man
> ploughing a field that slopes upwards. If I lean back this
> field fills all the window space except the top right which
> gives me a further horizon and a small view of the bay.
> The white gulls wheel perpetually around the tractor and
> the plough. (*ME* 27)

'Rootedness' here appears in the form of the arrested development of a personality fearful of facing up to the challenges of life.

Life at 'Y Glyn' acts as a corrective to the younger Humphreys's weakness for rural idyll. In his teens, he had embraced the conservative social ideology of Plaid Cymru under Saunders Lewis's leadership, with its anti-industrial bias and alternative valorisation of rural, 'yeoman' life. While wartime work on the land, as a conscientious objector, had modified his ideal, it had been reaffirmed by the happy experience of working on the Llanfaglan estate, near Caernarfon (1941–3). Memories of that period were, no doubt, gilded by recollections of his courtship there of his wife-to-be, Elinor Jones. But the family's return from London to Pwllheli, a small seaside town on the Lleyn peninsula, prompted a more mature, and nuanced, estimate of rural, traditional Welsh society. *A Man's Estate* is therefore, for Humphreys, what *The Return of the Native* was for Thomas Hardy: an ambivalent affirmation of 'roots', of 'origins', of 'belonging'. This takes the form of a fictional balance-sheet scrupulously weighing the advantages of staying against those of leaving; of social memory against forgetting.

Humphreys's ambivalent meditation on people's stubborn, complex, compromised, and often problematic allegiance to place was no doubt also informed by his experience, as charity worker, of administering a 'transit camp' for displaced peoples in Italy at the close of the war. These were vast encampments – temporary cities of transients housing not just individuals but virtual populations, some desperate to return to (frequently

obliterated or forcibly appropriated) 'homes', others
equally anxious to start anew by making a 'home' in any
welcoming country. Humphreys's sensitivity to their
refugee condition may have been all the more acute given
his own angry discovery, as a sixth-former, that he had
hitherto been living as a 'displaced' person in his own
country. That unwitting displacement had been cultural
rather than geographical in character. Humphreys's
exposure to the 'colonial' reading of Wales offered by
Saunders Lewis and Plaid Cymru had opened his eyes to
his own 'disinherited' condition as a monoglot English
'Welshman', He suddenly saw himself as a subaltern
colonial subject, effectively prevented from 'reading' the
history of his own country inscribed in its (Welsh-language)
place-names, instanced by its distinctive (Welsh-language)
religious history, and tenaciously recorded in its (Welsh-
language) literary culture. By setting-to and learning Welsh,
Humphreys further felt he was equipping himself to
counter the enormous centrifugal forces generated by the
wartime British state. Even while serving as a Save the
Children Fund officer first in Egypt and then in Italy, he
was able to continue reading Saunders Lewis's weekly,
Welsh-orientated, commentary on political events in *Y
Faner*. But if Humphreys thus became, as he has remained,
a committed nationalist, *A Man's Estate* is his dark fifties
reflection on a Welsh nation whose future existence was in
real jeopardy, because its only potent sustaining image of
its own modern identity (the seminal nineteenth-century
concept of 'the Nonconformist nation') was in monstrous
terminal decline.[4] As Humphreys was to make clear in his
later fictions, the image of its 'proletarian', industrial self
adopted by early twentieth-century Wales in preference to
its outmoded nineteenth-century religious self-image was,
in his view, a destructively Anglocentric one, spuriously
masquerading as 'internationalist' in character.

But nationalism is not given an easy ride in *A Man's
Estate*. Mrs Elis's version of that ideology is fanatical,

chauvinistic and paranoid, a grotesquely pathetic echo of the brutally swaggering thirties nationalism of Germany, Italy and Spain. Not so that of Humphreys. As developed through his exposure to wartime European conditions, his nationalism became internationalist in its implications. The transit camps helped him realise the universality of the 'Welsh condition' – of a small national culture's struggle to retain a separate identity in the face of (linguistic, cultural, economic and political) powers 'innocently' intent on its obliteration. To members of a dominant, seemingly omnipotent, Anglophone culture immeasurably reinforced, in the aftermath of victory, by the world dominance of the USA, such a struggle might seem to be the product of an outmoded and futile kind of petty, 'provincial' self-preoccupation. But the transit-camp experience had taught Humphreys that such an endangered condition was in fact the post-war European norm. And soon it would become the common fate of nations worldwide vulnerable to the culturally corrosive processes of 'globalisation' and its attendant Anglicisation.

Nor is this the only 'international' dimension of the novel's concerns. In *A Man's Estate*, Humphreys fashions a Welsh 'family saga' suitable for obliquely exploring a Europe-wide post-war crisis: how to deal with a 'guilty', humanly destructive past; but also how to apportion 'guilt' in such morally opaque circumstances. There is a striking resemblance between the terms in which Humphreys recalled the experience of serving in Italy in the immediate aftermath of war and those used in his novel by a Hannah bewildered by her family situation. Her problem is that

> I must somehow, out of myself like an industrious silk-worm produce the thread that will bind the fragments together, or lead me back through the labyrinthine wood of incidents behind whose apparently solid trunks sinister outlines seem to move in the dark. (*ME* 48)

Speaking in interview about post-war Italy, Humphreys uses a similar image: 'in the terrible situation Europe was in at the time, we were moving around like children in the forest to a great extent'.[5]

Like the characters in some Ibsen play, the Elises are so obsessed with their terrible secrets they seem little more than pallid ghosts, helplessly haunting the site of a violently vivid family crime. And in their gloomy moral paralysis, Humphreys seems to see, more locally, the state of a Welsh nation unable either to connect with its past in a way that would guarantee its future, or to break with it in ways that could offer a way forward. The other side of the coin represented by the monstrously deformed chapel 'morality' of the Elises is the vigorous self-interested resourcefulness of predatory 'survivors' like the scornfully anti-chapel Wally Francis and Winnie Cwm. Ada is a much more complex character – sympathetic, attractive, even heroic perhaps, but with her tragic aspects. She pays the price for being both genetically and socially a product of both the world of the chapel and the world of her mother. Thus internally torn, she is only imperfectly able to turn her moral instincts into an opportunistic amorality. Willing herself to be manipulative, she struggles to get the better of the born, and therefore instinctive, manipulators (including Dick) by whom she is surrounded. To her irritation, she senses that compared to them she remains little more than a sheep in wolf's clothing.

The novel is thus coolly open-eyed in what is its (nevertheless guarded) advocacy of a committed concern with 'belonging' and with the difficulty of establishing an honest, appropriate, responsible, creative connection with the past. This becomes apparent if one considers its treatment of the alternative – an opting for a 'rootless', culturally amnesiac existence. Such is the life of the ambitious young Liberal politician, Elis Felix Elis, loosely modelled on the morally and physically footloose career of the brilliant opportunist, Lloyd George. Greedily allured by London's promise of office and power, Elis maintains the merest cynical token of a connection with his Welsh home and family, just sufficient to allow him to continue to be the darling of the chapels. Such a metropolitan path had, in Humphreys's opinion, proved the headlong highway to national destruction for the Welsh and their country ever since the assimilationist Act of Union. During the first half of the twentieth century, this well-trodden route had been enthusiastically followed not only by ambitious Liberal and Labour politicians but by the professional classes, including generations of Welsh teachers like Gwendoline Esmor (who has discreetly jettisoned that shameful brand of Welsh identity, the vulgar surname 'Jones'). Miss Esmore and her secret lover Elis Felix Elis MP are well matched in lamenting 'the misfortune of being Welsh' (*ME* 215), in their desperate attempt to escape 'that octopus country, that cannibal mother country' (*ME* 216). The MP's middle name, 'Felix,' nicely conveys his conscienceless and insouciant blitheness ('felix' being Latin for 'happy'), while the repeating of 'Elis' perfectly captures his ruthless narcissism. Nurtured in the outlook of this pair, Philip views his journey to the family 'estate' as a descent into a pit of 'Calvinistic sadists and hypocrites' (*ME* 231). Nor is he far wide of the mark.

*   *   *

Like Philip, when Emyr Humphreys returned to Wales he was brought into intimately close contact with Welsh Nonconformity. His wife, Elinor, was the daughter of a highly respected minister with the Annibynwyr (Welsh Independents), and, although Humphreys had been raised an Anglican – he had even considered taking holy orders as a teenager – on his marriage he was accepted into membership by his wife's denomination. As her father grew older, Elinor assumed responsibility for his care, and this culminated with the Reverend Jones spending his declining years with the Humphreys family. This afforded his son-in-law an opportunity to acquaint himself thoroughly with the richness and complexity of Welsh Nonconformist culture. As a respected liberal, the Reverend Jones provided Humphreys with an excellent example of the effort made by the chapels after the First World War to remedy the damage that had been done by the publicly vociferous, jingoistic support for wartime recruitment of some of the more prominent conservative ministers. Partly in response to this, and to the perceived indifference of the denominations to the condition of the industrial working class, disillusionment and disaffection gripped chapel members during the post-war period, and mass defections followed. A generation of young, progressive ministers, sympathetic to liberal theology, reacted by attempting to reconnect Nonconformity to the political radicalism that had characterised it during the later nineteenth century. While Humphreys greatly respected his father-in-law as embodying the impressive qualities of this generation, in Idris Powell he examines not only the challenges faced by any young minister who commits himself totally to a humanly unexamined and untested gospel of love but also the challenge such a Christian idealist represents for the majority of us who settle for a much more pragmatic approach to life. Is Powell disastrously naïve, or is he spiritually pure? Does he mistake *eros* for *caritas*? Is he a danger not only to himself but to others? What are we to make of a 'holy fool'? Urgent questions of this kind have continued to trouble Humphreys throughout his long writing career, and the enigma represented by Powell has been re-presented time after time in his fiction by similarly puzzling, morally indecipherable characters.[6]

A related issue explored through the character of Powell, and one that would again continue to haunt Humphreys for half a century thereafter, is whether a resolutely pacific approach to life is a sign of weakness, in a world so evidently governed by power and violence, or a sign of spiritual strength. This issue had presented itself in particularly anguished form in Humphreys's own life when he had to choose whether or not to stand by his pacifist beliefs during the Second World War. And, having done so, he was faced with a related dilemma as a committed Welsh nationalist. Determinedly opposed to any kind of resort to force, he nevertheless had to admit that history seemed to offer no reassuring example anywhere of national liberty won without the shedding of blood. These moral dilemmas are clearly focused in *A Man's Estate* by the placing of Idris Powell in a society entirely at the mercy of the fierce struggle for power within the Elis family and between it and the community it dominates. Puzzled, moved, attracted and irritated in equal measure by the singular, stubbornly non-violent character of the young minister of Bethania, Ada intuits that his gospel of love represents a serious threat to her. Briefly infatuated by his sweet difference, she comes to regard him impatiently as an ineffectual naïf, a dangerous succubus likely to compromise her independence and liable to leech away her precious power of survival. She particularly resents, and fears, his attempt to treat her as an adored, redemptive figure at the centre of a new religion of romantic love. Ada's reaction is, of course, significantly shaped by the feeling that she has twice previously fallen victim to her own dreamer's weakness for ideals. Viewed in this light, Idris Powell is only the latest instance of this recurrent inner temptation she has previously failed to resist.

*   *   *

Although the action of *A Man's Estate* covers more than thirty years, the novel was published in 1955 and can therefore usefully be viewed in the wider context of fiction's response to British society during that decade. Long regarded as a pallid period in the history of a British novel exhausted by the exhilarating modernist experimentations of earlier decades and resorting to drearily familiar and superannuated realist conventions, the fifties has recently undergone substantial revaluation and rebranding.[7] The decade's literary culture is now styled 'late modernist', or 'intermodernist', and emphasis has shifted to an appreciation of how the post-war generation of novelists can best be understood as engaged in a range of textual conversations with their celebrated modernist predecessors. For instance, as was noted by William Cooper, one of the significant writers of the decade, some of this new fiction was concerned to recognise the claims of its society upon it. Whereas the modernist 'Experimental Novel', Cooper later observed, 'was about Man-Alone ... we meant to write novels about Man-in-Society as well'.[8]

This was a distinction with which Emyr Humphreys strongly identified. Just two years before the publication of *A Man's Estate* he published a seminal essay in *The Listener*, one of the leading periodicals of the age. Entitled 'A Protestant View of the Modern Novel', it began by recognising that all fifties novelists were working in 'a post-Joyce era of English fiction'.[9] Acknowledging Joyce's genius, Humphreys proceeded to criticise the Irishman as a driven aesthete, intent on maintaining an 'extraordinarily detached' attitude towards life. Such an attitude, Humphreys argued, was no longer possible after 1945, because Joyce was a man of the 'pre-atomic-age' who had also antedated the rise to power of the working class. The latter 'have become a key factor in the technique of political power: monstrously large, frighteningly gullible, defenceless as a jelly fish – the raw material of the dictator's or the advertiser's art' (*CR* 70). The urgent function of the contemporary novel, the essay implies, is to educate this new mass society by providing it with a moral compass. Otherwise, the impressionable population will continue, as during the thirties, to fall victim to unscrupulous demagogues and populist manipulators of public opinion. The danger of a socially empowered but morally directionless working population is indicated in *A Man's Estate* by Humphreys's treatment of the amiably exploitative garage-owner Wally Francis and his family and cronies. Raised in the chapel, Francis has long abandoned it, recognising that its moral, as well as its social, authority has crumbled away, not least through inner corruption. His alternative gospel, like that of all those who lie within the orbit of his petty dictatorship, is one of shrewd opportunism.

In adopting his formalist attitude to human experience, Joyce was, Humphreys further argues in his essay, wholly at odds with the great tradition of the European novel as instanced by Dostoevsky, Tolstoy and others. For them, 'human life was not [as it was for Joyce] the raw material of art; it was a strange sea in which humanity thrashed about like a powerful, bewildered whale, harpooned by death, and still consumed with a desire for immortality' (CR 70-71). This vision of mankind finds expression in the tragic action of A Man's Estate. In any tragedy, Humphreys observes in his 1953 essay, 'a lifetime leads to a meaningful crisis of disaster' (CR 71) – a comment that brings the Elises immediately to mind.

Both Vavasor and Mary live out their lives to their tragic conclusion with a conscious sense of living under divine judgement. Theirs is a religious tragedy, as well as a personal and social one. And, like many another writer and intellectual of the fifties, Humphreys attributed the dangerous moral disorientation of his society to the decline of religion. Unlike his contemporaries, however, he refused to indulge in fantasies of 'restoring the myth', of defying science in order to reinstitute an 'organic society' of faith. 'Religion', he roundly insisted, 'must embrace what is true in science' (CR 74). The dangers of divorcing the one from the other had been manifest in the terrible uses to which scientific knowledge had been put during the Second World War, culminating in Hiroshima and Nagasaki.

And the issue of how to handle scientific understanding – in particular of how to deal with a human mind irreversibly refashioned in the image of science – is a very live one in A Man's Estate. Could Vavasor have so arranged the scientifically undetectable murder of Felix Elis had he not possessed a chemist's understanding of the exact consequences of ceasing medication and withholding water? Isn't Hannah Elis's wish to become a chemist an expression of her wish to evade responsibility for confronting the complex mess of human motives and actions? Doesn't the coolly cynical Dr Pritchard afford an excellent example of a medical man's untroubled adoption of a materialist and hedonistic philosophy, on the questionable assumption that science has demonstrated there is no more to life than such pleasures and satisfactions as can be wrung from one's moral span? And isn't Philip's claiming of the scientist's prerogative of 'objectivity' and 'dispassionateness' likewise clearly revealed, by the end of the novel, to be an abrogation of moral duty, a failure of imagination, conscience and nerve, and a refusal to face up to the bewildering claims upon him of the human condition? These instances of science's failure to recognise key constitutive features of human existence are, of course, complemented in the novel by the failure of the chapel faithful to recognise science as religion's challenging partner in humankind's endless pursuit of truth. As is noted in 'A Protestant View of the Modern Novel', 'Religion cannot ignore science on the so-called spiritual plane any more than science can ignore religion on the material' (*CR* 74).

Central to Humphreys's important essay is his plea for the reinstatement of the 'Protestant principle of personal responsibility' (*CR* 74). His is partly a reaction to the subordination of the individual to the mass will, evidenced so appallingly by both fascist and communist regimes. Humphreys's concern was not, however, primarily with these vestiges of past ideology; rather he shared the worry famously articulated by George Orwell in *Animal Farm* (1945) and *Nineteen Eighty-Four* (1949), that democratic states, too, were liable to turn authoritarian, even totalitarian, as they grew more dominantly systematised and centralist. Although in sympathy with that child of the fifties, the Welfare State, Humphreys saw both in it and in the state rhetoric of a society fearful of the communist threat, the seeds of a totalitarian democracy. It is worth bearing in mind that *A Man's Estate* is roughly contemporary with the McCarthy witch-hunt of 'Reds' in a United States hysterically convinced it was at risk from communist fifth-columnists.

'The artist', Humphreys observed in his 1953 essay, 'has shied away from the crude strength of the Protestant conscience – that constant, hoarse, dynamic whisper. But it possesses an exciting paradoxical combination of simplicity and complexity: an awareness of the great mystery, the infinite unconditional nature of God, and the egocentric solitude and sin of man in his trap of time' (*CR* 74). The core subject of *A Man's Estate* is the Protestant conscience, that stern guardian of a sense of personal responsibility. Many of the main characters are urgently aware of being finally answerable for their own lives and actions. The novel is a sustained study of the history of the Protestant conscience in a period of moral confusion and uncertainty. Those consequences are various, ranging from the case of Vavasor and his wife who finally fall tragic victim to the moral conscience that has worn their minds to tatters and their bodies to the bone, to that of Wally Francis, in whose comfortably corpulent case moral self-scrutiny has metamorphosed into wily self-interest. Ada's tragedy, of course, is that she is internally divided, trapped between the one principle and the other. As for Idris Powell, sexual passion and an attractive human compunction threaten to soften the iron backbone of his spiritually progressive principles.

*   *   *

Revisiting 'A Protestant View of the Novel' some fifty years after its publication, Emyr Humphreys concluded he would still stand by the insights and commitments in that text but would now prefer to substitute the term 'Dissident' for 'Protestant'. It is an interesting substitution because when writing during the 1950s about the contemporary novel Kenneth Allsop suggested that, whereas it had become common practice to speak of the fiction of 'angry young men' as a phenomenon of the period, 'a more accurate word for this new spirit that has surged in during the fifties is dissentience'.[10] *Room at the Top* (1957), *Saturday Night and Sunday Morning* (1958) and even *Lucky Jim* (1954) – all feature rebellious young male characters. These novels remain familiar landmarks of the period, and continue to be accepted as symptomatic of the social revolution afoot in Britain at the time. It was the coming of age of the social outsider. The war had effectively marked the end of Imperial Britain, and some of the scarce resources and energies of a weakened and exhausted country had to be devoted to the (frequently bloody) dismantling of Empire from India to Africa. Along with the implementing of the Welfare State and the social impact of the grammar schools, decolonisation accelerated the erosion of traditional respect for the authority of the middle class.

During the fifties, the novels of Braine, Sillitoe and Barstow were primarily (and rightly) understood as demonstrating the right of the largely neglected English working class to serious social and fictional attention. But in retrospect, they may also be regarded as instances of a new decentralising process at work within a post-war British state that, under the pressures of wartime, had reverted to its authoritarian centralist instincts. These 'working-class' novels were unmistakeably 'regional' in character, and as such they may now be usefully re-viewed in the light of other fiction of this period. The two decades immediately following the war saw the appearance of such classic texts as Chinua Achebe's *Things Fall Apart* (1958), V. S. Naipaul's *A House for Mr Biswas* (1961) and Jean Rhys's *Wide Sargasso Sea* (1966). Emanating from Africa and the Caribbean they were the forerunners of what later, following the landmark publication of Salman Rushdie's *Midnight's Children* (1981), came to be classed as post-colonial fiction. This was the exhilarating result of the appropriation of the English-language novel by natives of the erstwhile 'colonies' who thus gave expression to their own, distinctively non-English, experiences and concerns. English backlash took the form of the 'Little Englandism' exemplified in the fiction and poetry of Kingsley Amis and John Wain and in the 'Movement' poetry most powerfully instanced by Philip Larkin.

Given Emyr Humphreys's early tutelage under Saunders Lewis, and his resultant sensitivity to the colonial aspects of the Welsh condition, *A Man's Estate* may also reasonably be regarded as broadly anticipating the Welsh 'postcolonial' fiction Humphreys went on to write. It was an early product of his identification (implicit in his turning of his back on the metropolis) with a Welsh nation acquiring a consciousness in English, during a decade of rapid decolonisation, of its long cultural and political subordination by England. In looking to Philip for salvation, Hannah is also looking to England, as the servile Welsh had repeatedly done ever since the Act of Union. She busily weaves her self-protective fantasies out of materials from the Bible and from fairy-tales:

> In my thirty-sixth year I wait and I am skilled in waiting. But it is dangerous. It is easy to confuse the coming of a knight errant with the coming of the Saviour, and I sometimes see myself among the idolators throwing palms before the short nervous steps of the frightened ass. (*ME* 54)

Needless to say, her callow dreams of rescue are rudely dashed, and at the end she is left to her own resources, however impoverished and dubious they may be. Recognising himself to be an outsider, disqualified on many different grounds from intervening, her anglicised and alienated brother returns 'Y Glyn' to Hannah's care. She is left to make what she can of her personal and cultural inheritance. The idiom of the novel likewise refuses to compromise with any respected English discourse of its day. *A Man's Estate* respects the rural religious society with which it is dealing sufficiently to judge it by its own best light and not by those of any supposedly more advanced cultural 'centre'.

*   *   *

One significant sign of Humphreys's mental orientation at this time was his adoption as role model not of any of the leading fiction writers of the British and Irish modernist tradition but of a confirmed American decentralist: William Faulkner, the great novelist of the defeated, subordinated culture of the southern states of the USA.[11] Cleanth Brooks opens his classic study, *William Faulkner: the Yoknatawpha Country*, with the following paragraph:

> Most writers associate William Faulkner with the South quite as automatically as they associate Thomas Hardy with Wessex, Robert Frost with northern New England, and William Butler Yeats with Ireland, and perhaps more naturally than they associate Dylan Thomas with Wales. The regions and cultures to which these writers are linked differ in character, but they all stand in sharp contrast to the culture of the great world cities of the twentieth century. They have in common a basically agricultural economy, a life of farms, villages, and small towns, an old-fashioned set of values, and a still vital religion with its cult, creed, and basic norms ... for all their differences, each provides its author with a vantage point from which to criticize, directly or perhaps merely by implication, the powerful metropolitan culture.[12]

Replace the name of Dylan Thomas with that of Emyr Humphreys in this paragraph and one begins to understand why he was so powerfully impressed during the fifties by the fiction of the great southerner.

Faulkner was first fully 'discovered' in his own country with the publication in 1949 of Malcolm Cowley's anthology, *The Portable Faulkner*, but he came to worldwide attention the following year when he was awarded the Nobel Prize for literature. Exactly when Humphreys became aware of his work cannot be established, but he has testified to an intensification of his appreciation of Faulkner's work during the period he spent in Salzburg in 1954 in the company of the great American critic, Edmund Wilson. A recent recipient of the Somerset Maugham Prize, Humphreys had repaired to Austria with his family to spend a year there working on what was to become *A Man's Estate*. But a number of factors – including serious concern about the condition of his eldest son who developed peritonitis during this period – meant he was unable to embark on the novel until he had returned to Wales. Nevertheless, the work had been incubating throughout his stay in Austria and therefore his discussions with Wilson about Faulkner's novels must have been directly influencing the development of his ideas.

Humphreys seems in part to have encountered in Faulkner a like-minded writer whose singular, and signature, modernist innovations of style and expression were driven, like Humphreys's own much more modest experimentations in *A Man's Estate*, by a compulsion to access the deep truths of his own culture. Robert Penn Warren, another great critic of southern literature like Cleanth Brooks, feelingfully noted: 'as a technician, Faulkner, except for his peers, Melville and James, is the most profound experimenter in the novel that America has produced. But the experiments were developed out of – that is, were not merely applied to – an anguishing research into the Southern past and the continuing implications of that past.'[13] For instance, the stylised, poeticised, internal monologues that characterise such classic novels as *The Sound and the Fury* (1929) and *As I Lay Dying* (1930) convey the weight, complexity and intensity of the characters' embeddedness in a stiflingly conservative society. In *A Man's Estate* Humphreys uses a similar device, most conspicuously when probing the state of mind of Hannah. By such means he is able to resolve one of the most pressing difficulties facing a writer seeking to fashion a modern tragedy out of lives lived in a democratic, egalitarian, levelling society – how to imbue the characters with the density, gravity, and high seriousness that would effectively heighten the tone of their lives in the manner necessary for producing the rich, resonant tragic effect. Conscious of this problem, the great American dramatist Arthur Miller first attempted to solve it in *Death of a Salesman* (1949) by staying faithful to a naturalist, demotic style, but went on to draw memorably on Scriptural speech when writing *The Crucible* (1953), which appeared just two years before *A Man's Estate*. Both Faulkner and Humphreys similarly drew extensively in their fiction on the cadences of the Bible – the sacred 'founding' text of their respective, originally biblical, societies. And in the cases of both writers, accessing this resource helped make possible their central achievement – what André Malraux described, with reference to Faulkner, as 'the renewal of tragedy' (*F* 205–6).

Critics likewise spoke approvingly of the 'primal' quality of Faulkner's writing and, as has already been noted, this is a feature of *A Man's Estate*. The novel is concerned to demonstrate that human life tends to approximate to 'archetypal' patterns, a characteristic underlined by the way we make our lives intelligible both to ourselves and to others by shaping them into the form of familiar narratives. So Idris Powell images the abortive relationship between himself and Enid, his friend Lambert's wife, in terms of a Medieval chivalric romance:

> Like legendary lovers, woven on the edge of a medieval wood, too poor to trouble about time or place, we walked in the garden of the hotel at night as if it were a rich man's castle that would admit only our most innocent dreams. (*ME* 89)

And when the virtuous Powell begins to consort oddly with the far-from-virtuous Frankie (Ada's brother), village tongues begin to wag: 'Housewives wondered to see Frankie's turned out steps alongside my untidy strides, their myth-making minds having more to make of so untoward an alliance' (*ME* 95).

Humphreys actually causes his novel to reflect on this storytelling and myth-making propensity of the human mind, and in the process causes it to reflect on its own narrative strategies, by including a story within his story. Owen Owens is a traditional Welsh *cyfarwydd*, an enthralling rural storyteller who acts as communal remembrancer. He holds his audience spellbound as he weaves his narrative, while 'The wind rushed through the cobbled yard outside the long window and the flames of the wide fire stretched into the cavernous mouth of the chimney' (*ME* 65). Owen's story feeds the mind of his listeners as surely as the table laid for the morning's breakfast promises to satisfy their stomachs. He tells of a treacherous young farmer's wife whose unfaithfulness drives her innocent husband to suicide but who lives on to enjoy a prosperous life with her lover, a cowman. The tale has been repeated by him many times, and honed to a gratifyingly familiar shape. The episode ends with a comic reprise of Owen's story when Dick, Hannah's unruly brother, and his friend Willie, frighten Hannah by persuading her that, like the cowman, Dick has hanged himself from a beam in the barn. But then Owen Owens' story is later reprised in an entirely different key. His tale echoes that of Vavasor and Mary Elis, while the cowman's suicide foreshadows that of Vavasor, who poisons himself. He is discovered by Hannah collapsed over the sink he had been struggling to reach in an effort to alleviate his pain with a drink of the water he had, of course, murderously denied Elis Felix Elis. Story, like history, has an uncanny, unnerving, habit of repeating itself in human experience.

Also significant for Humphreys was Faulkner's genius

for devising stylistic means of conveying the omnipresent, suffocating pressure of the past – felt too in the oppressive heat of the South – on the lives of his characters. Such a sense of the inescapable burden of cultural history corresponded to Humphreys's ambivalent sense of the significance for Wales of its inheritance: its Nonconformist 'estate'. Faulkner's achievement is of course very appreciably greater than that of Humphreys, and as the past of Southern history is immeasurably more terrible than that of Wales so is its sinfulness and guilt proportionately more massive. But the felt parallels between Humphreys and his Wales and Faulkner and his South are nevertheless an important strand in the dense weave of *A Man's Estate*.

Humphreys attributed his recognition of himself in Faulkner to the fact that both the Southern states and Wales were defeated 'nations', subsequently incorporated into the victorious alien state (*DPR* 85–6). The values and practices of that nation-state were fundamentally different from, and inimical to, those of the cultures it had so comprehensively defeated. It was natural for the victorious to espouse a confident ideology of progress and of self-fulfilment that it was difficult for the defeated to share.

The consequences of the defeat of the Confederate cause are everywhere, and obsessively, explored by Faulkner. One recurrent structural feature of his fiction is the contrast between relics of the 'old order' – the impoverished, socially disempowered, and impressively flawed members of the cultivated classes that had traditionally sustained the ethos, the elaborate courtesies and the ethical codes of the antebellum South – and the creatures of the new order. The latter consisted not only of those carriers of Northern commercial values, the original 'carpetbaggers' who entered the former Confederacy as entrepreneurial interlopers to dismantle a semi-feudal society and to open the South up to the modern, thrusting world of capitalist competition, but also of their native allies, the lower-class Southerners who profited by allying themselves with this new 'foreign' culture of enterprise. Prominent instances of such creatures of the new post-bellum South in Faulkner's fiction are the semi-literate and nakedly opportunistic members of the large Snopes family. They roughly correspond to the members of Wally Francis's clan and their associates who occupy a not dissimilar position within the structure of *A Man's Estate*. Their relationship to those decadent representatives of the old Nonconformist 'aristocracy', the Elis family, is broadly similar to that of the grossly fecund Snopes family to the decaying leadership of the old antebellum South. Hannah Elis disdainfully dismisses Winnie Cwm, Wally Francis, and their promiscuously intertwined families as 'a low family scheming to rise' (*ME* 196). How, she asks herself, can she 'allow our family pride to be fouled by gutter people like Winnie Cwm and Frankie Cwm?' (*ME* 197). She consequently refuses to acknowledge Ada as her sister, and so fails to grasp the social implications of the fact that they both actually have the same father.

* * *

These, then, are some of the matters with which Emyr Humphreys was concerned when writing *A Man's Estate*. But they can matter to us as readers, of course, only if they are fully grounded in the fiction; in other words, if they are fully inscribed in the text, are discursively constructed, and are thus rendered convincing in fictional terms. Take the dominant figure of Vavasor Elis, a candidate for tragic stature. That there are repellent aspects to his character is evident enough. Yet he remains a compelling, if forbidding, figure because virtually alone among the main characters he is afforded the dignity of reticence. Whereas we are made privy to the inner feelings of Hannah, Philip, and Ada, any insight into Vavasor Elis's state of mind is denied us until the late, and therefore memorable, scene when he voices his inner torment through the heightened, measured, biblical rhetoric of public confessional prayer:

> Elis' lips trembled as they always did before he began. His eyebrows twitched rapidly. But tonight I noticed his head moving slowly from side to side as if he were rocking some crying sleepless grief within himself.
>
> 'Almighty and ... Almighty ... O Lord in the words of Cain, my punishment is greater than I can bear ... year after year ... from the day my eyes grew dim to this thou hast visited me with these afflictions ... Must I speak O Lord ... Must I confess as a criminal still when I have accepted each affliction as a just punishment?' (*ME* 393)

Even this climactic scene is carefully counterbalanced by an emphasis on the bathos of Vavasor's punctilious observation of the rituals of the prayer-meeting and on his affectingly uncoordinated, ungainly physical presence: 'He pushed open the door and sat down on the nearest seat exhausted, slowly removing the black hat he always wore to come to chapel. It was too big for him and almost rested on his large ears' (*ME* 391). And in his electrifying confession before the Lord, Vavasor demonstrates an impressive indifference to any effect he may have on the solitary adult listener, Idris Powell: 'I was an aider and abettor in his untimely death: the waters of succour trickled away between my opening fingers as they approached his mouth' (*ME* 393). The weighty authority of the judgement he unsentimentally passes on himself is palpable: he is speaking not just of 'murder' but of mortal sin. There is a terrible fatalistic composure about him to the end. 'He hurried off towards the door as he always did as if he had endless business affairs waiting for his attention. "Good night now then," he said, as he always did leaving chapel' (*ME* 396).

That obliviousness to the impression he is making is, in fact, one of Vavasor's most impressive characteristics. His semi-blindness emphasises his unconcern with social interaction, and, in its way, figures his bleak self-arraignment. There is a permanent unconscious helplessness about him, and he is unnerving because his obliviousness to anyone's gaze seems to prompt the observer (and thus vicariously the reader) to subject him to bold, guilty scrutiny. Yet for all this Vavasor baffles one's understanding. This is evident in Hannah's obsessively focused evocation of his gawky, helpless appearance:

> He is very thin, but the tweed suits he wears are so thick that you do not at first notice this, until you observe the loose skin of his neck is untouched by the stiff white wing-tipped collar that encircles it. His head is large and bald enough to appear flat along the top. The eyebrows above his deep-set staring blue eyes are thick and red, and seem to blink themselves when he exposes his old false teeth – beneath a broad moustache that my mother trims, after shaving him – in a constant nervous smile that is meant to disguise the hopeless intensity of his stare. (*ME* 32–3)

Vavasor's old-fashionedness is here painfully obvious and embarrassing, yet his complete indifference to it bespeaks an implicit moral judgement on all those who follow the prevailing currents.

Vavasor remains a lonely enigma. In taking his own life he leaves no note – that would have been totally out of character. He is answerable only to God. Implicit in everything he is and does is an acceptance that he alone must take responsibility for what he has done and therefore is. His wife breaks down: he does not, not because of any psychological robustness but because of a stubborn moral strength. He is even more isolated in the terrible sanity of his unsparing self-indictment than she in her wild madness. Unlike him, she can take a kind of crazy comfort in the fantasy that hers had been an act of moral retribution, that she had sent her baby son away to protect him from knowing (what? about his father's sinful adulteries or about her own guilt?), and that she had similarly shielded her daughter by effectively imprisoning her. In killing the chickens that are her favourite 'children' she finds symbolic expression for her guilt, and so finds a kind of irrational relief. There is for her a kind of relief in the bloodiness of it – it contrasts with the bloodlessness of her silent, secret murder, just as her melodramatic voicing of the act contrasts with the muteness of that murder. And her killing of the chickens combines a re-enactment of her murder of her husband with a ritualistic punishing of herself for that crime. It is also her symbolic admission that with the killing of Felix she had effectively killed her capacity to love the children born of their union. They had become the innocent scapegoats for her husband's infidelities. In turn, of course, her frustrated need to love had found an outlet in her doting indulgence of Dick, with eventually disastrous effects.

Philip, a man who preens himself on his scrupulously 'scientific' objectivity, is naively disturbed to realise how slippery a concept 'truth' is outside the confines of the laboratory:

> I was thinking about truth. ... And how maddening to realise the difficulties when by instinct you felt that somewhere absolute truth existed, waiting for your arrival however long you delayed on the journey. There lie waiting your life's meaning and the secret of your unrest. (*ME* 338)

If only it were as simple as that. While, in detective-story fashion, the novel maintains suspense for much of its course by prolonging uncertainty about whether or not Felix Elis was actually murdered by his wife and her admirer, as local rumour supposed, this 'mystery' is, of course, solved well before the end. That is because *A Man's Estate* is not centrally interested in soluble mysteries. It is concerned not with the issue of (theoretically) ascertainable 'facts' but with the wholly insoluble enigma of judgements – with the enigma, in other words, of any life's 'meaning'. Vavasor Elis may, in his prayer and suicide, pass 'definitive' judgement on the meaning of his own life, but the novel refuses to pass final judgement on him: it cannot second guess the verdict of the God in whom Vavasor believes with such terrible, fervent, devotion. Perhaps all tragedy is rooted in enigma; that is, it may be a terrible manifestation of the unfathomable character of human beings and the incalculable implications of their actions.

Compared with Vavasor and, to a lesser extent, his wife, Hannah Elis and Idris Powell are diminished characters. Their inner tensions and torments may generate pathos, but lack the dignity of tragedy. Ada, however, commands much greater respect, and if the tragedy of Vavasor and Mary Elis is an old-fashioned religious tragedy, hers may be a secular tragedy after the modern fashion. In several important ways she is the mirror image of that of the murderous couple. It is partly because their language of self-understanding is religious that hers is secular. It is in part their hypocritical ethics that fires her ambition to be amorally selfish and opportunistic. Of their self-deception and deceptions are born her own ruthless honesty. But beyond these superficial divergences between her life and theirs lie much deeper convergences. It is from the lives of the Elises quite as much as from the example provided by her mother, Winnie Cwm, that Ada learns the lesson that life is all about survival, and is therefore no more than one long unremitting struggle for power. No wonder that when she breaks the news to Hannah that her mother and step-father are murderers, she seems to be acting the role of one of the avenging Furies of ancient Greek tragedy. Her wailing 'coiled itself as smoothly as a trained snake into the empty spaces in my knowledge of the past', admits Hannah. 'It was familiar as soon as I heard it in the way that only Truth can be' (*ME* 206).

Ada enters her half-sister's world like the Reality Principle itself, exposing not only the 'Truth' about Vavasor and his wife, but also Hannah's long, wilful suppression of any sense of misgiving about her family. In a sense, Ada thus reveals Hannah's tacit complicity in the concealment of her father's murder. And if the 'barrenness' of which Hannah, the self-styled spinster, bitterly accuses herself is a metaphor for the desiccated moral and emotional state in which she has chosen to live, then Ada's 'promiscuity' is its complement, as well as its opposite, because it, also, is a defence against being trapped in any complex relationships of committed attachment. And in mourning Dick, Ada is harbouring her own fantasy and lie, refusing to acknowledge his chronic selfishness and unreliability.

It is by rebelling against the patriarchal character of the Elises' religion that Ada takes on the role of the New Woman. This figure had fascinated Emyr Humphreys ever since childhood. He had grown up in the years immediately following the First World War, a period that saw a dramatic extension of the freedoms, rights and opportunities that women had been granted during wartime when they were allowed into the workforce as replacements for the men who had marched away, never to return. Although the social and political liberation of women had been a subject of fiction ever since the concluding decades of the nineteenth century, Humphreys became fascinated with the figure's increasing prominence during the period between the two world wars and beyond. A great admirer of independent women, he nevertheless struggled in his fiction to come to terms with them and to calibrate the implications of their growing social power. Time after time, a female figure of this powerful kind is uneasily twinned in his novels with that of a seemingly ineffectual, 'emasculated' man. Such, of course, is Idris Powell in part in *A Man's Estate*. It is the ambivalence of feeling manifest in such twinning that makes the portrayal of Ada so complex, and therefore so compelling.

As for Hannah, she takes refuge throughout the novel in loving her 'place'. She knows her very character has been formed in its image. Of herself and her mother she reflects that 'Out of our basic landscape our figures lost their recognisable shape and we became foreign to one another'.

(*ME* 185). Others may treat 'Y Glyn' and its acres merely as property, but for her it constitutes identity. It exists sensuously – a displacement of her frustrated sexuality:

> A good year for blackberries. With the aid of a walking stick a quart gathered in a few minutes. The horses free of work galloped around the salt pools in the rough fields near the shore. Smoke from the chimney of Miss Aster's cottage blown about. Wet sheaves still out sticky to touch. A slow corn harvest. (*ME* 197)

Hers is the kind of passionate identification with territory ('estate') that is the product of the Nonconformist emphasis on place as the sacred locale of a people, a notion based on the biblical (and particularly Old Testament) notions of land. But hers is also a decadent and perverted version of that Nonconformist 'theology' of place and nation.[14]

So what are we to make of the conclusion of the novel, when Hannah inherits 'Y Glyn' and 'A Man's Estate' thus becomes 'A Woman's Estate' instead? Does this bode well? Does it indicate that evil has been purged through the storm of tragedy? Does it signify that restoration of sound order that allowed Shakespeare to end his tragedies reassuringly with such firm, quiet conviction? That is difficult to believe. Hannah may have been released from enthralment to her parents, but she remains the prisoner of their world – the only world she has known or has ever wished to know. In the end, she can offer only a more humane continuation of the old, exhausted, 'feudal' dispensation. As the new mistress of the Glyn, she resumes the ritual of greeting the faithful retainers: 'My response echoes my uncle's. The voice is different but the formula must be the same' (*ME* 410). Her earlier comment proves prophetic: 'Spinsters, it is their function and their fate, are custodians of family history. They knit the temporal net with ropes of their heart's blood' (*ME* 195). And so the novel seems unable to imagine through Hannah a substantial, vibrant, living new future for the moribund, not to say morbid, Welsh

Nonconformist world of which she is the belated
representative. For any hint that such might be possible, one
must turn instead to Idris Powell and his faithful pursuit of
Ada. Such an unconventional pairing might yet augur hope
for the future of the chapels. But whereas the minister very
evidently needs her, it is far from clear that she needs him
– nor is it clear that, even should she accept him, such a
union could possibly work and endure.[15] In being entirely
open-ended, or noncommittal, about the prospects of this
relationship, the novel also concludes without resolving the
question of whether there can be a future for Nonconformity
or not. And so, *A Man's Estate* offers us no confident
reassurance that its Wales has come to terms with its past
and is thus well 'placed' to face its future.

NOTES

1   Emyr Humphreys, *A Man's Estate* (London: Eyre &
     Spottiswoode, 1955; reprinted Cardigan: Parthian, Library
     of Wales, 2006), p. 162. References hereafter (*ME*) are to
     the latter edition.

2   In an interview about his fiction, Humphreys noted that
     during his London period he was reading Robert Graves' *The
     White Goddess*, and that he even took a copy of F. L. Lucas's
     study of *Greek Drama* as 'light reading' for his wife who was
     in hospital preparing for the birth of their child! He also
     mentions attending Shakespeare productions at the Old Vic
     featuring Olivier and Richardson: R. Arwel Jones, gol., *Dal
     Pen Rheswm: Cyfweliadau gydag Emyr Humphreys*
     (Caerdydd: Prifysgol Cymru, 1999), pp. 68–71. Hereafter
     referred to as *DPR*.

3   See in particular *The Heart of the Matter* (1948) and *The End
     of the Affair* (1951).

4   For the contribution of literary texts to the construction, and
     eventual deconstruction, of the 'Nonconformist nation' see M.
     Wynn Thomas, *In the Shadow of the Pulpit: Literature and the
     Nonconformist nation* (Cardiff: University of Wales Press, 2009).

5   My translation of comments made in DPR, p. 64.

6   The great example is that of the minister J. T. Miles in

Outside the House of Baal (London: Eyre & Spottiswoode, 1965; revised and reprinted, Bridgend: Seren, 1996).

7   See the following: D. J. Taylor, *After the War: The Novel and England since 1945* (London: Flamingo, 1994); Brian W. Shaffer, ed., *A Companion to the British and Irish Novel, 1945–2000* (London: Blackwell, 2005); and Marina MacKay and Lyndsey Stonebridge, eds, *British Fiction After Modernism: The Novel at Mid-Century* (London: Palgrave Macmillan, 2007). None of these makes any mention of the novel in Wales. This is, however, given cursory attention in Dominic Head, *The Cambridge Introduction to Modern British Fiction, 1950–2000* (Cambridge: Cambridge University Press, 2002) in a chapter dealing with 'National Identity.'

8   Quoted in *British Fiction After Modernism*, p. 5.

9   M. Wynn Thomas, ed., *Emyr Humphreys: Conversations and Reflections* (Cardiff: University of Wales Press, 2002), pp. 67–76. Hereafter *CR*.

10   Quoted from Kenneth Allsop, *The Angry Decade*, in Gilbert Phelps, 'The Novel Today', Boris Ford, ed., *The Pelican Guide to English Literature 7; The Modern Age* (Harmondsworth: Penguin, 1961), p. 485.

11   Humphreys acknowledges his debt to Faulkner in DPR, pp. 85–6.

12   Cleanth Brooks, *William Faulkner: the Yoknapatawpha Country* (New Haven: Yale University Press, 1966), p. 1.

13   'Introduction: Faulkner: Past and Present', in Robert Penn Warren, ed., *Faulkner: A Collection of Critical Essays* (Englewood Cliffs, NJ: Prentice-Hall, 1966), p. 5. Hereafter *F*.

14   Such ideas are discussed with subtlety and penetration in Dorian Llywelyn's important study, *Sacred Place, Chosen People* (Cardiff: University of Wales Press, 1999).

15   The not-too-dissimilar union between J. T. Miles and Lydia in *Outside the House of Baal* ends in sadness.

Writing Against the Grain:

Raymond Williams's *Border Country* and the Defence of Realism

Daniel G. Williams

I've been aware since *Border Country* that I've been ... writing against the grain of the forms. The 19th century forms of the novel were shaped within a bourgeois world. So the first modes of access to working-class experience in fiction were often those of some distanced observer. Then between the wars writers emerged who had grown up inside a working-class community and sought to re-create its world – typically the world of childhood or of the family, while cancelling their present selves from this original situation ... The early versions of *Border Country* were continuous with these kinds of writing. But I was dissatisfied with that form, initially without knowing why. Then I gradually realised that with the degree of change after 1945 the problem was to find a fictional form that would allow the description both of the internally seen working-class community and of a movement of people, still feeling their family and political connections, out of it. ... I found that what I was writing was an experience of uncertainty and contradiction, which was duplicated in the problem of discovering a form for it. So I learnt the hard way the theoretical lesson that if a writer in a certain mode does not have social forms available to him for development, then his writing experience is likely to be prolonged and difficult, and the work very much more problematic.[1]

In this account of the writing of *Border Country*, Raymond Williams foregrounds the extent to which the 'problematic novel' which he was continually drafting and re-drafting throughout the 1950s was self-consciously written against the grain of the genre's dominant forms.[2] Williams's argument that the novel form had been 'shaped within a bourgeois world' reflects a widespread consensus that the novel emerged concurrently with a newly dominant middle class within industrialising societies, and, according to Ian Watt's influential work, the new genre became characterised by a 'formal realism' which was 'typical of the novel genre as whole'.[3] It would seem from Williams's account that *Border Country* was an attempt at developing a new kind of writing which would allow for the novelistic exploration of his own journey from a valued working-class background in the Welsh border village of Pandy, to a career as a literary critic in English higher education. This would not be an account of working-class life from a middle-class perspective common in (what Williams influentially described as) 'the industrial novels' of the Victorian era, for the author was himself brought up in a working-class environment.[4] But neither would the novel be the narrative of a 'journey out' from the perspective of one who had transcended the 'provincialism' of a working-class background that he saw as characteristic of D. H. Lawrence's *Sons and Lovers* (1913).[5] Williams's novel would be closer in character to the Welsh industrial novels in that it aimed to describe an 'internally seen working-class community', but departed from that tradition in wishing to reflect the new generation's experience of 'movement' through education out of the native community, while 'still feeling their family and political connections'.[6] Williams's challenge was to avoid the dangers of nostalgia on the one hand, and the denigration of the working-class 'masses' on the other. He explains the novel's long gestation in relation to the lack of models for this kind of work. In order to give voice to his, and his generation's, experience, a new form would need to be forged.

Yet, students are often struck by the formal conservatism of Williams's first novel. At the most basic level, the novel represents a public and social world, using the convention of the third-person omniscient narrator. As Harry and Ellen Williams walk to their lodging in Glynmawr, for example, the narrative voice roams widely in its description of the semi-fictional landscape in which the novel takes place:

> To the east stood the Holy Mountain, the blue peak with the sudden rockfall on its western scarp. From the mountain to the north ran a ridge of high ground, and along it the grey Marcher castles. To the west, enclosing the valley, ran the Black Mountains: mile after mile of bracken and whin and heather, of stunted thorn and myrtle and bog-cotton, roamed by the mountain sheep and the wild ponies. Between the black ridges of Darren and Brynllwyd cut the narrow valley of Trawsfynydd, where the ruined abbey lay below the outcrop of rock marked by the great isolated boulder of the Kestrel.[7]

The knowledge of history, of flora and fauna and of place names suggests that this passage is spoken in the characteristic, all-knowing voice of the omniscient realist narrator, and, with the possible exception of the Welsh names, there is little here that is unusual or unconventional. Indeed, while he claims that there were no models for the kind of writing that he wanted to achieve, the extent to which Williams's observations on Thomas Hardy in *The English Novel from Dickens to Lawrence* and *The Country and the City* can be applied to his own creative writings is striking.[8] 'The real perception of tradition' he notes in a key passage on Hardy

> is available only to the man who has read about it, though what he then sees through it is his native country, to which he is already deeply bound by memory and experience of another kind: a family and a childhood; an intense association of people and places, which has been his own history. To see tradition in both ways is indeed Hardy's special gift: the native place and experience but also the education, the conscious inquiry. Yet then to see living people, within this complicated sense of past and present, is another problem again. He sees as a participant who is also an observer; this is the source of the strain.[9]

Williams's intensely autobiographical novel *Border Country* is informed, at the level of both content and form, by the backward gaze from his education at Cambridge to the 'intense association' of family and childhood in Pandy. When the fictional academic Matthew Price travels back from London to the bedside of his dying father in Glynmawr, he is following Raymond's own journey back to his father's bedside in 1958.[10] Matthew becomes known as Will, his childhood name, upon his return, just as Raymond was known as Jim in Pandy.[11] If Hardy's novels emanated from the 'crisis' faced by the returned native in Williams's account, then *Border Country* can be read as an updating of that familiar narrative which was continually to inform Williams's writings about his native Wales.[12] How, then, can *Border Country* be considered a novel written 'against the grain'?

Realism: from Method to Process

One way of beginning to answer this question is to register Raymond Williams's abiding preoccupation with the history, practice and future of realism in the novel. This concern does indeed seem to set him against the dominant values of literary criticism, for one of the characteristics of the poststructuralist criticism that emerged in the 1970s and has influenced much literary criticism since was an attack on the assumptions informing literary realism. Drawing on Roland Barthes's analysis of the 'reality effect', critics such as Catherine Belsey and Colin MacCabe sought to explore the ways in which realism was based on an outmoded 'reflectionist' view of language that assumed that the novel could hold a mirror to reality, simply describing what is 'out there' in the objective authoritative language of the third person narrator.[13] What they termed the 'classic realism' of the nineteenth century was unable to 'foreground contradiction', for where a diversity of view points coexisted in the text, this 'variety of points of view', between masters and workers, for example, was 'contained in a homogeneity.'[14] According to MacCabe, contradictions are overcome in the classic realist text by recourse to a 'hierarchy of discourse,' an argument that he illustrates by analysing the use of inverted commas in realist texts:

> The meta-language within [the classic realist text] refuses to acknowledge its own status as writing. The text outside the area of inverted commas claims to be the product of no articulation, it claims to be unwritten. This unwritten text can then attempt to staunch the haemorrhage of interpretations threatened by the material of language. Whereas other discourses within the text are considered as materials which are open to reinterpretation, the narrative discourse functions simply as a window on reality. This relationship between discourses can be taken as the defining feature of the classic realist text.[15]

In George Eliot's *Middlemarch*, for example, the narrative voice is the voice of truth. That voice is separated from the biased and partial views of the novel's characters by inverted commas. When Mr Brooke goes to visit Dagley's farm, the text introduces us to two discourses: 'the educated but not very intelligent discourse of Mr Brooke', and the 'violent and very nearly unintelligible discourse of the drunken Dagley'.[16] The whole dialogue between Brooke and Dagley is surrounded by a meta-language which exposes the truth of the scene. When Mr Brooke responds with surprise to Dagley's violent language, the narrator intervenes to tell us that his surprise is a form of self delusion:

> He [Mr Brooke] had never been insulted on his own land before, and had been inclined to regard himself as a general favourite (we are all apt to do so, when we think of our own amiability more than of what other people are likely to want of us).[17]

The narrative voice therefore interprets the other discourses within the classic realist text. It has an insight that is greater than that of any character, and is able to intervene to explain individual motivations to the reader. This meta-language has a twofold role for MacCabe: first, it presents itself as 'unwritten', as a window on the world which denies its own status as written discourse; second, it establishes its superiority as the interpreter of other discourses, thus controlling the various other 'object languages' within the text. In McCabe's discussion of *Middlemarch* and Belsey's discussion of Dickens's *Bleak House*, warring voices and incompatible points of view within these novels are in the final analysis controlled by the authoritative authorial standpoint and voice of the omniscient narrator – the voice of 'truth' in classic realism.

Belsey takes the analysis a step further by arguing that the realist author's claim to be engaged in a process of portraying reality dispassionately serves to hide the values and prejudices which inevitably colour any account of the real. Deconstructing the realist text thus involves unmasking the inevitable biases which inform any claim to represent the 'truth'. Literary realism is therefore seen to collaborate in the work of ideology, it plays a role in the naturalisation of the social, and imposes one version of reality as the 'real' that can be 'taken for granted'. Realistic writing, in its complicity with the ideological dominant, is unable to tolerate multiple versions of reality. The function of realism, then, is, according to Stephen Heath, 'the naturalization of that reality articulated by a society as the "reality" and its success is the degree to which it remains unknown as a form'.[13] 'Reality' as presented in the realist text is therefore a particular, usually privileged, version of what is 'out there' passing itself off as the way things really are. Realism, for the poststructuralists, functions as a method of maintaining the privileged position of those in power. Social structures are therefore sustained and defined by the written. Realism in their view is a conservative method of writing, based on a naïve and untenable view of language. It is a form that reinforces social structures, and should be abandoned in favour of more linguistically experimental methods of writing which, rather than merely reinforcing the ways in which we see the world, interrogate and challenge our conceptions of the real.

The poststructuralist critique of realism, and the ensuing debate, was most influentially centred on the innovative film and media journal, *Screen*.[19] Raymond Williams was thus stepping into the lion's den when he indirectly criticised those arguing for the rejection of realism in a lecture delivered at a *Screen* 'weekend school' in 1976. He began by making

> just one obvious general distinction between conceiving realism in terms of a particular artistic method and conceiving realism in terms of a particular attitude towards what is called 'reality'. Now if, taking the first definition, we concentrate on method, we put ourselves at once in a position in which the method can be seen as timeless: in which it is, so to say, a permanent possibility of choice for any particular artist. Certain things can be learned from this kind of emphasis, but once we become aware of the historical variations within this method, we find ourselves evidently dissatisfied with the abstraction of a method which overrides its relations with other methods within a work with other aims and intentions.[20]

Williams seems to be making a distinction between conceiving of realism as a 'method', defined by certain thematic and formal characteristics, and thinking of realism as an 'aim' or project which can take on and incorporate different forms and procedures in different periods. In 1979, writing in the shadow of the post-structuralist critique of realism, Williams accepted that the history, development and future of literary realism had been an abiding preoccupation of his work as critic and novelist, but wished to emphasise that

> I have never been concerned to defend realism in the historically reactionary sense that ... those who are now

> attacking realism limit it to. My argument for realism has
> always been that it is a certain perception of reality and
> a certain awareness of interrelationships, not that it
> carries a certain mode of composition with it, nor that it
> has a second-order relation to a pre-existing reality.[21]

The problem with the poststructuralist critique of realism
for Williams was that it was based on defining realism as a
'method' of writing, based on the 'historically reactionary'
bourgeois novel of the nineteenth century. Williams's own
writing on *The English Novel from Dickens to Lawrence*
(1970), and later on 'The Welsh Industrial Novel' (1979),
had traced the ways in which realism had changed in both
form and content as new voices and experiences – those of
the working class, peripheral nationalities and so on –
sought to express themselves within the novel. If the
poststructuralist critique of realism proved influential, and
was no doubt useful in drawing attention to the dimension
of language which was often downplayed in discussion of
nineteenth-century novels, it was based on a disablingly
narrow definition of the realist text. If some classic realist
texts of the nineteenth century could be proven to be
essentially reactionary in politics and conservative in form,
did it necessarily follow that realism was inherently
conservative? As Raymond Tallis memorably puts it, 'if a
monkey plays a violin badly it is hardly fair to condemn all
violin music or the instrument itself'.[22]

In challenging those who viewed realism as a form, or
method, of writing that could easily be dismissed, Williams
was in fact adapting for the 1970s an argument that he
had developed fifteen years earlier in *The Long Revolution*
(1961). In a chapter on 'Realism and the Contemporary
Novel', which can be read as a theorisation of his creative
practice in *Border Country*, Williams noted that:

> The old, naive realism is in any case dead, for it depended
> on a theory of natural seeing which is now impossible.
> When we thought we had only to open our eyes to see a

> common world, we could suppose that realism was a
> simple recording process, from which any deviation was
> voluntary. We now know that we literally create the world
> we see, and that this human creation – a discovery of how
> we can live in the material world we inhabit – is
> necessarily dynamic and active; the old static realism of
> the passive observer is merely a hardened convention.[23]

Realism, for Williams, is conceived as a process; an aim in
writing that calls for new forms and approaches as our
world, and our understanding of that world, changes. He
shares the poststructuralist awareness of the discursive
construction of the world that we inhabit, but sees this as a
reason to pursue and develop the realist project understood
as 'the interaction ... in the individual's effort to
communicate what he has learned, to match it with known
reality and by work and language to make a new reality'.[24]
Rejecting those voices in the late fifties who argued that 'the
realistic novel ... went out with the hansom cab', Williams
argued that realism was an 'intention' that did not require
an adherence to an already established form.[25] Williams
argues that there had been a 'polarisation of styles' in the
twentieth century, as the 'object realist' novel (such as that
of Arnold Bennett) tended to concentrate on the social world
to the exclusion of the individual, while the 'subject-
impressionist' novel (such as that of Virginia Woolf)
concentrated on 'voices and feelings', lacking any social
substance. 'Realism' is the form, for Williams, which can
potentially achieve a balance between these two distortions.
But 'realism' did not refer to the novel's nineteenth-century
form, for Williams insisted that new social realities would
require new realisms. His conclusion was that 'a new
realism is necessary, if we are to remain creative'.[26]

Border Country may therefore be read as Williams's
attempt at substantiating a new realism. He viewed himself
as writing against the grain of both the naturalist novel of
objective surfaces and the modernist novel of inner
subjectivity. The goal was to create a balance between these

modes. Read in the light of Williams's lifelong defence of the realist project, his first novel can be read as a self-conscious, creative meditation on the purpose, practice and possibilities of realism. In writing against the grain of the forms, Williams, as I shall seek to illustrate in the second half of this chapter, was engaging self-reflexively with the practices and conventions of realism itself.

Ways of Seeing and Speaking

We may begin to discuss Raymond Williams's engagement with the problems of realism in *Border Country* with the scene in which Will is encouraged to visit the vicar, Arthur Pugh, who has been asked to help the young boy to prepare for a University scholarship exam:

> Pattern was the word that Will grasped at, through the crowded impressions of these first weeks. There was never any talk of religion, and very little of books. But there were the stars, endlessly exciting, and when the sky was overcast there was the microscope, in the untidy study, with slides left haphazard on shelves and chairs and sills, and again there were shapes and patterns that had been closed to the eye. Arthur Pugh was a collector, rather than even an amateur scientist. But the different ways of seeing, whether from the tower or through the microscope in the study, had their deep effect. (276–7)

If the fields of astronomy and biology offer Will new 'ways of seeing', the problem of placing patterns on what's seen, of giving formal expression to human experience, preoccupies him for the rest of his life. Matthew (the adult Will) later describes the historical work that he's doing on 'population movements into the Welsh mining valleys in the middle decades of the nineteenth century' in scientific terms:

> The techniques I have learned have the solidity and precision of ice-cubes, while a given temperature is

maintained. But it is a temperature I can't really maintain;
the door of the box keeps flying open. (4)

If the empirical work of the historian is approximate to
scientific observation, the human experiences on which
that work is based force Matthew to consider other, less
easily measured, considerations: 'It wasn't a piece of
research, but an emotional pattern', he notes (353). *Border
Country* continually juxtaposes different ways of seeing
and knowing as, upon his return to Wales, Matthew feels a
growing sense of uncertainty about his work as a historian,
the trajectory of his life, and ultimately his own sense of
identity.

As the train from London crosses the border into Wales,
Matthew considers the map of 'pig-headed Wales', and
proceeds to observe the 'usual photographs' at 'the sides of
the map':

On the far side was the abbey, that he had always known:
the ruined abbey at Trawsfynydd that had not changed in
his lifetime. On the near side was the front at Tenby. (8)

Matthew is reminded of these images the following day when,
upon waking in his childhood bed in Glynmawr, he picks up
a county history describing the village church as
'distinguished by its relics', its 'Norman porch' and 'Saxon
tomb' located in a landscape where the 'bloodiest of border
castles' and the 'Stone of Treachery' are to be found.
'Yesterday the pictures in the train, and now this', muses
Matthew, 'the pieces of past and present that are safe to
handle. Here, in this living country' (81–2). Against the living
history of which, as both a historian and a native of this
place, he is all too aware, Matthew turns to those ways of
seeing that offer to fix that ever-changing experience, thus
making it 'safe to handle'. As a returning exile, Matthew
seems to find some solace in the fixed images of the train
carriage and the descriptive accounts of popular history.
These are ways of seeing that turn the fluidity of experience

back into ice cubes. At the novel's outset Matthew's past does seem 'another country', best imagined in static, unchanging ways closely related to his own childhood memories, as is suggested by his observation that the images in the train were 'more than thirty years old: nearly his own age' (8). As the narrative proceeds, Matthew begins to question the assumptions that he brings to bear on this landscape, questioning the values that inform his conception of reality:

> In Gwenton he had met nobody he knew, and the simple shopping had been difficult, after London: the conventions were different. He had felt empty and tired, but the familiar shape of the valley and the mountains held and replaced him. It was one thing to carry its image in his mind, as he did, everywhere, never a day passing but he closed his eyes and saw it again, his only landscape. But it was different to stand and look at the reality. It was not less beautiful; every detail of the land came up with its old excitement. But it was not still, as the image had been. It was no longer a landscape or a view, but a valley that people were using. He realised, as he watched, what had happened in going away. The valley as landscape had been taken, but its work forgotten. The visitor sees beauty; the inhabitant a place where he works and has his friends. Far away, closing his eyes, he had been seeing this valley, but as a visitor sees it, as the guide-book sees it: this valley, in which he had lived more than half his life. (89)

As he learns again to become an inhabitant within a living space as opposed to a visitor who sees only the image, Matthew comes to realise the extent to which he moulds the landscape and environment of the border country according to his own changing perspectives.

Matthew's shift in perspective from 'visitor' back to 'inhabitant' can be related to the novel's broader exploration of the position of exile. Contemporary discussions of the role of the social critic tend to emphasise, and generally to celebrate, the critic's role as an 'alienated intellectual', an 'outsider' or an 'exile'. The assumption is that marginality provides a stimulus for insight, that a sense of exclusion encourages an analytic detachment, that a sense of geographical and metaphorical 'exile' allows the critic to address and challenge 'the constituted and authorized power of one's own society'.[27] In Raymond Williams's writings, however, positions of exile and marginality are continually problematised. Eira, a childhood sweetheart who has remained in the border country, challenges Matthew's simplistic reasons for 'going out and living differently' (187). In a significant dialogue, her husband John notes that Gwenton 'is a nice place,' the 'sort of place I could grow old in':

> 'Yes' Matthew said. 'I feel it being away.'
> 'It's your own choice,' Eira said.
> 'It's my work.'
> 'I saw Morgan at lunchtime,' John said. 'He was telling me about your work.'
> 'He's studying Wales,' Eira said, 'and he goes to London to do it.' (337).

Eira notes that 'it hurts, now, when you come back as a stranger' (341). The 'crisis' of the 'return of the native' that Williams identified in Thomas Hardy's fiction manifests itself not only in terms of interpersonal relationships in *Border Country* but also as a crisis of language and representation. Matthew feels at times that he has been 'away too long ... I've forgotten it all, and can't bring myself back':

> As he looked away he heard the separate language in his mind, the words of his ordinary thinking. He was trained to detachment: the language itself, consistently abstracting and generalising, supported him in this. And the detachment was real in another way. He felt, in this house, both a child and a stranger. He could not speak as either; could not speak really as himself at all, but only in terms that this pattern offered. (98–9)

The initial stilted conversation with Morgan Rosser, who comes to pick Matthew up from the station, gradually gives way to humorous exchange that is 'easy at last', once 'enough had been re-established' (12). If Matthew arrives in Glynmawr speaking the 'different idiom' of academic life, when he phones home his wife notices that 'your voice is quite different already ... Changed back ... I prefer it' (346). This shift from the 'abstracting and generalising' language of academia to the 'quick Welsh accent', is reinforced in the shift from 'Matthew', a name he has used since his student days, to the 'Will' of his childhood in Glynmawr.

Indeed, the question of discourse, of the process by which ways of seeing are reflected, embodied and constructed in ways of speaking, is a central, reiterated, theme in the novel. Characters are consistently identified by their speech. Harry, from 'this side of the river', has 'the quick Welsh accent', while his wife Ellen speaks 'with the slow, rich, Herefordshire tongue' (35). Dr Evans's voice is a 'Welsh voice' but 'different from the Glynmawr accent: smoother with narrower vowels, and with the intonation of the mining valleys' (177). Language is also significant in that it can be a barrier to, as much as a mode of, understanding. Jack Price, for instance, teases his grandson with 'dialect words that he had known as a boy but that had gone out of use' (240), and, more seriously, when the policeman comes to tell Matthew and his mother that Harry has died, Ellen listens to the breaking news 'as if the men were speaking a language she did not understand' (400). The 'reflectionist aesthetic' that critics such as MacCabe and Belsey saw as characteristic of classic realism, and regarded as evidence for the realist's naïve understanding of language, is problematised in *Border Country*. The novel's omniscient narrator tends to sustain the abstracting language of the visitor, referring consistently to 'Matthew', for instance, when all the voices in the text refer to 'Will'. When Morgan Rosser states 'No,

Will, it's coming to a different thing. Take a look', for example, the narrator reports that 'Matthew did not answer' (359). The sustained distance of the narrative voice led James A. Davies to suggest that Williams's narrators often seem to 'occupy the vantage-point of a reserved English visitor', but that meta-language – the language of the omniscient narrator that is close in tone and feeling to the 'abstracting' language of Matthew's academic work – is consistently challenged by other viewpoints (such as those of Eira and Harry), and by other voices and languages in *Border Country*.

In his discussion of George Eliot's *Daniel Deronda*, Colin MacCabe seems briefly to acknowledge that his model of a rigid hierarchy of languages within the classic realist text enforces a structure on works of art that is difficult to justify:

> It would be a distortion to consider George Eliot's texts as totally determined by the discursive organisation that I have defined as the classic realist text. Within her novels there are always images which counter the flat and univocal process which is the showing forth of the real. ... perhaps most powerfully of all, the Hebrew language which rests uninvestigable at the centre of *Daniel Deronda*, question[s] and hold[s] in suspense the project of Eliot's text. ... Deronda's discovery of the Jewish language and the poems of Mordecai trouble the meta-language in so far as the Jewish language constitutes an area outside its control. Deronda hears the news that Mordecai's work is in Hebrew and untranslatable with 'anxiety'. Such a feeling is not surprising when we recognise that the poems constitute a fatal threat to the meta-language. Confronted with a discourse that it cannot transform into an object (that it cannot name) the meta-language forfeits control of the novel.[29]

In *Border Country* the question of language is most clearly articulated in relation to the submerged presence of the

Welsh language in the text. For the 'Baptist anniversary' at the chapel, the child Will is taught 'a little Welsh poem of two verses' by Harry, which the boy recites 'clearly' while standing 'nervously under the arch of the pulpit' (145). Will is given a book entitled *The Holy Child* for his efforts which he throws into the river, much to the embarrassment of his parents. In another scene Harry, who rarely expresses his emotions overtly, can't seem to control his anger when he hears the 'little minister', Joshua Watkins,

> rehearsing his prayers and sermon. It went on for more than an hour, in Welsh, although the eventual delivery would be in English. The practice, it seemed, was to get the first flow right. (219)

Harry's anger is primarily a response to Watkins's unwillingness to help with spreading ashes on the frozen lane, followed by the minister's impertinence in asking Harry to empty his lavatory bucket. But it is surely significant that the issue of language difference appears at those moments of heightened emotional pressure in the novel, where character motivations become difficult to fathom, and where the realist narrator's claim to 'know' the characters' thoughts and inner beings breaks down. In MacCabe's terms, it would seem that the Welsh language does represent a discourse that the narrative meta-language 'cannot transform into an object (that it cannot name)' resulting in the 'loss of control of the novel' at those very moments where Will and Harry lose control of their own contained emotions.

The role of Welsh in the novel reaches its climax in the section on the eisteddfod. Here, the boundaries between languages, between generations, and between Will and the culture which surrounds him, become dissolved in the performances of the choirs which are followed by the communal singing of the Welsh national anthem:

> It was time now for the choirs, and Will knew, looking up,

that it was no use at all even trying to stay separate. ...
The drop of the raised hand, and then not the explosion
of sound that you half expected, but a low, distant sound,
a sound like the sea yet insistently human; a long, deep,
caressing whisper, pointed suddenly and sharply broken
off, then repeated at a different level, still both harsh and
liquid; broken off again, cleanly; then irresistibly the
entry and rising of an extraordinary power, and everyone
singing; the faces straining and the voices rising around
them, holding, moving, in the hushed silence that held all
the potency of these sounds, until you listening were the
singing and the border had been crossed. When all the
choirs had sung, everyone stood and sang the anthem. It
was now no longer simply hearing, but a direct effect on
the body: on the skin, on the hair, on the hands. (258–9)

Will's desire to 'stand apart' is clear, but when the choirs
begin to sing, that position of detachment becomes
untenable. We're told that a 'border had been crossed' as
listener becomes singer in an act of empathy that again
seems to lie 'outside the control' of the narrator's meta-
language. Indeed, the eisteddfod in *Border Country* can
stand metonymically for Welsh culture itself; it is a
transformative space in which 'I. Morgan, Watch Repairer',
becomes 'Illtyd Morgan y Darren' (250), in which a border
is crossed as the power of the art produced by a community
has a 'direct effect on the body'.

If Wales, as Williams was to note later, tends to be
viewed as 'usually singular' from an English perspective, he
reverses the gaze in *Border Country*, where it is on the
Welsh side of the border that identities become unstable,
that variousness and openness replace an English reserve
and insularity.[30] On the novel's very first page Matthew
notes the 'contained indifference' of London, where 'you
don't speak to people', and goes on to generalise that 'in
fact you don't speak to people anywhere in England; there
is plenty of time for that sort of thing on the appointed
occasions' (3). England is seen later to be 'a great house
with every room partitioned by lath and plaster. ... If you

went out of your own cupboard, to see a man in another cupboard, still you must wait for the cupboard door to be opened, with proper ceremony, and by a proper attendant' (331–2). Wales, on the other hand, is a place of openness. The 'ease' of speech 'that had almost been lost' that Matthew encounters in the 'West Indian conductress' in the novel's opening scene is mirrored upon his return to Glynmawr when the tense and formal exchanges between Matthew Price and his father's friend, Morgan Rosser, give way to the native rhythms of the border as Price notes that 'it was easy at last, and enough had been re-established' (12). This ease of speech is mirrored in an openness observed at several points in the novel. In Glynmawr, the men

> walk slowly, showing all their layers. Mack open, jacket open, cardigan open, waistcoat open, collar-band open – nothing, you see, to hide. (368)

The binary terms of this distinction between English reserve and Welsh openness is surely too simplistic, but it can be seen to inform Williams's later engagements with his native country where he argued that 'the most valuable emphasis in Welsh culture is that everybody should speak and have the right to speak'.[31] While Christopher Prendergast is certainly right to note that Williams is similar to the Hungarian Marxist critic Georg Lukács in 'preferring to the art of dispersal and fragmentation promoted by the sanctioned versions of modernism an art that connects, especially ... forms that join, as mutually necessary for intelligibility, individual experience and social formation', matters are slightly different in relation to his evaluation of Welsh literature.[32] For, while championing the writings of the 1930s realists, Williams was primarily attracted to two non-representational narratives where the controlling voice of the omniscient realist narrator gives way to a chorus of competing voices, and where the view of the world is coloured by wild hyperbole and black comedy: Dylan Thomas's 'play for voices', *Under Milk Wood* (1954) and Gwyn Thomas's *All Things Betray Thee* (1949). Both works can be seen to illustrate Williams's notion that 'Welsh writers cannot accept the English pressure towards a fiction of private lives.'[33] In Williams's revealing readings, Dylan Thomas follows Joyce in discovering a 'living convention' that juxtaposes the 'language of dream' with the 'public language of chorus and rhetoric', while Gwyn Thomas creates a 'composition of voices' that will express a historical experience not confined to the 'flattened representations or the applied ideological phrases'.[34] This celebration of dialogue and plurality in the writings of Gwyn Thomas and Dylan Thomas reinforces Williams's emphasis that Wales 'has been a plurality of cultures', resulting in a situation in which 'any formulation becomes a challenge'.[35]

This presentation of the internal variedness and plurality of a Wales viewed from a dominating external perspective as singular and static is one of the key characteristics of *Border Country*. In this respect, Williams can be seen to be offering a fictional enactment of an argument developed in *The Long Revolution*. If Matthew's career in London has led him to view the Wales of his youth as a static, idealised, periphery in the novel's opening scenes, then his perspective is shared by many English novelists in their representations of other places. Williams revealingly selects E. M. Forster's *A Passage to India* (1924) as a 'good example' of a novel which romanticises the 'actual society to the needs of certain of the characters':

> This is quite common in this form: a society, a general way of living, is apparently there, but is in fact often a highly personalized landscape, to clarify or frame an individual portrait rather than a country within which the individuals are actually contained.[36]

This analysis echoes Matthew's realisation, quoted above, that 'the visitor sees beauty; the inhabitant a place where he works and has his friends' (89). Forster's India is a subjective projection rather than an actual society. We may begin to see here the influence of Williams's formative work on the emergence of postcolonial criticism. In *Orientalism*, Edward Said traced the tension between the tendencies to visualise and narrativise within descriptions of the colonial 'Other'. 'Against the static system of "synchronic essentialism" I have called vision', noted Said,

> there is a constant pressure. The source of pressure is narrative, in that if any Oriental detail can be shown to move, or to develop, diachrony is introduced into the system. What seemed stable – and the Orient is synonymous with stability and unchanging eternality – now appears unstable.[37]

Matthew's development in *Border Country* sees him rejecting the tendency to see Wales in static, visualised terms, as he becomes increasingly, and troublingly, aware of the inherent instability of his native country. The novel's contrapuntal movement back and forth between Matthew's experiences in the present and the longer historical sections centring on Harry Price and the General Strike of 1926 aims to allow for an emphasis on personal perception but always within a deep social contextualisation that foregrounds social and historical change.

This fusion of the personal and the social reaches a heightened intensity when, shortly before his departure for Cambridge, Will climbs the 'great isolated boulder of the Kestrel' and surveys the border landscape. It is one of the most sustained and remarkable passages in the canon of Welsh writing in English, but its broad trajectory can be indicated by selective quotation:

> He had come up past Parry's farm and the sheepfold, and over the long climbing ridge of Brynllwyd. At first the paths had been wide, through the dense bracken, past the last cottages and the occasional pool. Then, where the bracken dropped back, the wilder country of heather and whin stretched ahead. ...

There were the two chapels by the river, and then Daveys' cottage. There, up the line of the road, was the school, and the boys' playground, and the green rectangle of the bowling green. ... The station was out of sight, hidden in its cutting. Work went on there, in the ordinary routine, but from here it might not have existed, and the trains might have been moving themselves, with everyone gone from the valley.

He sat very still, preoccupied by this strange feeling of quiet. ...

Now it was not just the valley and the village, but the meeting of valleys, and England blue in the distance. In its history the country took on a different shape. On the high ground to the east the Norman castles stood at intervals of a few miles, facing across the wide valley to the mountains. Glynmawr, below them, was the disputed land, held by neither side, raided by both.[...] There on the upland had been the power of the Lords of the Marches, Fitz Osbern, Bernard of Newmarch, de Braose. Their towers now were decayed hollow teeth, facing the peaceful valleys into which their power had bitten. ...

Or look out, not east, but south and west, and there, visibly, was another history and another border. There was the limestone scarp where the hills were quarried and burrowed. There along the outcrop stood a frontier invisible on the surface, between the rich and the barren rocks. On the near side the valleys were green and wooded, but beyond that line they had blackened with pits and slagheaps and mean grey terraces. ...

He looked out in each direction in turn, his eyes narrowed against the keen wind, his mind excited as it had been when he stood with Pugh on the church tower, looking up at the shapes in the stars. The mountain had this power, to abstract and to clarify, but in the end he could not stay here; he must go back down where he lived.

On the way down the shapes faded and the ordinary identities returned. ... That was the sense of it: to watch, to interpret, to try to get clear. Only the wind narrowing your eyes, and so much living in you, deciding what you will see and how you will see it. Never above watching. You'll find what you're watching is yourself. (pp. 361–5)

The mountains, like Pugh's astronomy in an earlier scene, have the 'power to clarify', but also foreground the need to 'go back down to where he lived'. In this scene the novel's broader project of melting the ice cubes of observation, of dissolving images into experiences, of relating the personal at every key point to the social, of transforming 'vision' into 'narrative', is powerfully enacted through language. The passage is characterised by a tension in the narrator's desire, following Williams's discussion of Thomas Hardy, both to observe and to participate. Will, who is about to leave this place, responds to the landscape in a series of spatial and temporal juxtapositions; the duration of his walk up the mountain is juxtaposed against the broader awareness of his life experience (as represented by the school), which is itself juxtaposed to the much longer processes of social history (as embodied in the chapels and castles) and environmental change (as represented in the descriptions of nature and rock formations). The passage moves from the particular to the general, as Will begins by observing the 'bracken', the 'wilder country of heather and whin', before looking outwards towards 'the meeting of valleys and England blue in the distance'. This shift from the specific to the general in relation to nature is mirrored as Will's shifting gaze leads to a series of historical observations which begin with the particular experiences of his native village and its farms, moving to the Norman castles and the on to the experience of industrialism. The landscape, as Tony Pinkney has noted, 'abruptly seems to release the very history it has shaped through and through'.[38] In a deliberate rejection of the distanced omniscience that Catherine Belsey and Colin McCabe view as being characteristic of classic realist narration, Will's perspective and that of the narrator seem to merge in their turning away from the position of observer. 'What you will see and how you will see it' is a 'choice', and this key scene ends with Will deciding never to be 'above', merely 'watching'. In a gesture that mirrors the overall trajectory of the novel itself, he leaves the abstracted world of 'shapes' for the society where 'the ordinary identities returned'.

Conclusion

In engaging with the problems of 'vision' and of 'voice', *Border Country* is a novel in which the fundamental assumptions of literary realism are brought into question. The border is a place where

> you can talk as you like: like Pugh certainly; like Billy Devereux if you put your mind to it. Talking's no trouble, not from here. Just leave it to your voice.
> Aye ... but which voice? The voice on the mountain, a voice waiting to be learned. The voice here, querulous. (368)

What voice should be used in the process of novelistic representation is a question that *Border Country* seems to ask of itself. And if the confident, monologic, voice of the classic realist narrator is challenged by a multiplicity of voices, the narrator's confidence in accessing the minds and motivations of individual characters is also brought into question. John Evans expresses one of the novel's insights in relation to character:

> We live as a rule on about five or six types. We meet somebody and we just try them on quickly for size. Only sometimes you look and the type breaks up. (336)

The *Border Country* is a land of voices, where the types into which we organise the world begin to break up. While Williams has been accused of nostalgia in his representation of Wales, it is important to note that this plurality can be as unnerving as it is liberating.[39] Following Harry's death, Matthew feels 'a loss of identity, that grew steadily more frightening' (423). The border is a place where the 'ice cubes' – Matthew's empirical investigations, character types, personal identity, static visualisation, and established realist conventions – begin to melt.

The danger with the kind of analysis that I have developed in this reading of *Border County* is that Williams's realist practice is being valued because, in Andrzej Gasiorek's words, 'it too can be shown to be theoretically up-to-date' in being self-reflexively aware of its own conventions.[40] While Williams is meditating on the possibilities and pitfalls of realism in *Border Country*, he ultimately values realism because of its cognitive power, its ability to foreground contemporary assumptions about the nature of reality in order that we may understand, and potentially change, it. The postructuralist critique of realism relied on a view of realism as bourgeois and conservative; nineteenth-century realists were seen to lack the epistemological scepticism of contemporary critics, and failed to see the social contradictions informing their world views. Raymond Williams did not engage in such historical condescension, seeing in the realist tradition of the past the basis for innovative forms of realism in the present. In the quotation with which I began, he briefly reconstructs a narrative which informs much of his critical writing, describing realism's expansion from its bourgeois origins to include an increasing range of experiences. Realism in this sense is not a form or method of writing but an aim or a project. And Realism in this sense is always, inevitably, unaccomplished; it is an aim that is never realised, and its exclusions return to seek recognition and representation in a continual process of questioning and renegotiation. *Border Country* marks a significant chapter in that process.

NOTES

1   Raymond Williams, 'The Welsh Trilogy and *The Volunteers*' (1979), in D. Williams ed., *Who Speaks for Wales? Nation, Culture, Identity* (Cardiff: University of Wales Press, 2003), pp. 112–3. Subsequent references to this volume are given as *WSFW*.

2   For a detailed account of the composition of *Border Country*, see Dai Smith, *Raymond Williams: A Warrior's Tale* (Cardigan: Parthian, 2008).

3   Ian Watt, *The Rise of the Novel: Studies in Defoe, Richardson and Fielding* (Harmondsworth: Penguin, 1957), pp. 10, 294.

4   Raymond Williams, 'The Industrial Novels', in *Culture and Society* (London: Chatto and Windus, 1958), pp. 87–109.

5   See R. Williams, *Culture and Society*, pp. 199–215, *The English Novel from Dickens to Lawrence* (London: The Hogarth Press, 1984 [1970]), pp. 169 – 184, *The Country and the City* (London: Hogarth, 1985 [1973]), pp. 264–8.

6   R. Williams, 'The Welsh Industrial Novel' (1979), *WSFW*, pp. 95–111.

7   R. Williams, *Border Country* (1960; Cardigan: Parthian, 2006), p. 34. This is the Library of Wales edition. Further page references will appear in the text.

8   See R. Williams, *The English Novel from Dickens to Lawrence*, pp. 95–118, *The Country and the City*, pp. 197–214.

9   R. Williams, *The English Novel from Dickens to Lawrence*, p. 109.

10 See Smith, *Raymond Williams: A Warrior's Tale*, pp. 450–1.

11 See 'The Welsh Trilogy and *The Volunteers*' (1979), *WSFW*, p. 124.

12 Williams describes himself as a 'returning migrant with all his doubts, in 'The Practice of Possibility' (1987), *WSFW*, p. 218.

13 Roland Barthes, *S/Z*, tr. Richard Miller (London: Cape, 1975); Catherine Belsey, *Critical Practice* (London: Methuen, 1980); Colin MacCabe, *James Joyce and the Revolution of the Word* (London: Macmillan, 1978).

14 Belsey, p. 78.

15 MacCabe, p. 15.

16 MacCabe, p. 16.

17 George Eliot, *Middlemarch* (London: Penguin, 2003 [1871–2]), p. 396

18 Stephen Heath, *The Nouveau Roman: A Study in the Practice of Writing* (London: Elek, 1972), p. 20. Belsey develops this line of argument in Chapter 3 of *Critical Practice*, pp. 56–84.

19 A useful collection of the key articles can be found in Tony Bennett et al., eds., *Popular Television and Film* (London: BFI

Publishing / Open University Press, 1981).

20 Raymond Williams, 'A Defence of Realism' (1976), in F. Mulhern et al., eds., *What I Came to Say* (London: Hutchinson Radius, 1989), p. 226.

21 Williams, *Politics and Letters: Interviews with New Left Review* (London: Verso, 1979), p. 350.

22 Raymond Tallis, *In Defence of Realism* (Lincoln: University of Nebraska Press, 1988), p. 196.

23 Raymond Williams, *The Long Revolution* (London: Pelican, 1975 [1961]), p. 314.

24 Williams, *The Long Revolution*, p. 315.

25 Williams, *The Long Revolution*, p. 303.

26 The argument is developed in *The Long Revolution*, pp. 300–16, quotation from p. 316. Williams is drawing on two famous twentieth-century debates on the nature of realism. The first is Virginia Woolf's modernist attack on Arnold Bennett in 'Mr Bennett and Mrs Brown' (London: Hogarth Essays, 1924), which Williams discusses in *The English Novel from Dickens to Lawrence*, pp. 188–9. The second is the debate between Georg Lukács and Bertolt Brecht. The key documents in this debate are collected in Adorno, Benjamin et al., *Aesthetics and Politics*, tr. Ronald Taylor (London: Verso, 1977). Williams discusses Lukács in *Politics and Letters*, pp. 349–50, and *What I Came to Say*, pp. 267–74. On Brecht see R. Williams, *Modern Tragedy* (London: Hogarth Press, 1992 [1966]), pp. 190–204.

27 Peter Osborne, 'Introduction: Philosophy and the Role of Intellectuals', in Osborne, ed., *A Critical Sense: Interviews with Intellectuals* (London: Routledge, 1996), p. xv.

28 James A. Davies, '"Not going back, but … exile ending": Raymond Williams's Fictional Wales', in W. John Morgan and Peter Preston, eds., *Raymond Williams: Politics, Education, Letters* (London: St Martin's Press, 1993), p. 209. fn. 14.

29 MacCabe, *James Joyce and the Revolution of the Word*, p. 21.

30 Williams, 'Community' (1985), *WSFW*, p. 27.

31 Williams, 'Who Speaks for Wales?' (1971), *WSFW*, p. 3.

32 Christopher Prendergast, 'Introduction', in Prendergast, ed., *Cultural Materialism: On Raymond Williams* (Minneapolis: University of Minnesota Press, 1995), p. 18.

33 Williams, 'All Things Betray Thee' (1986), *WSFW*, p. 161.

34 Williams, 'Dylan Thomas's Play for Voices', in C. B. Cox, ed.,

Dylan Thomas: A Collection of Critical Essays (Englewood Cliffs, NJ: Prentice-Hall, 1966), p. 98. Williams, 'Working-Class, Proletarian, Socialist' (1982), *WSFW*, p. 155.

35 Williams, 'Remaking Welsh History' (1980), *WSFW*, p. 72. Williams, 'West of Offa's Dyke' (1986), *WSFW*, p. 34.

36 Williams, *The Long Revolution*, p. 308.

37 Edward Said, *Orientalism: Western Conceptions of the Orient* (London: Penguin, 1995 [1978]), p. 240. Said discusses Williams in *The World, The Text and the Critic* (Cambridge, MA: Harvard University Press, 1983), pp. 237–42. See also the dialogue between Said and Williams in R. Williams, *The Politics of Modernism* (London: Verso, 1989), pp. 177–97.

38 Tony Pinkney, *Raymond Williams* (Bridgend: Seren, 1991), p. 51.

39 See, for example, Patrick Parrinder, *The Failure of Theory* (Brighton: The Harvester Press, 1987), p. 78. Fred Inglis, *Raymond Williams* (London: Routledge, 1995).

40 Andrzej Gasiorek, *Post-War British Fiction: Realism and After* (London: Edward Arnold, 1995), p. 13.

Against 'Journalese':

Form and Style in Brenda Chamberlain's
A Rope of Vines

David Lloyd

While Brenda Chamberlain is generally acknowledged to be an important English-language writer of modern Wales, and one of a handful of Welsh women writers to achieve recognition during the 1940s and 1950s,[1] she has received remarkably little critical attention outside of her participation with Alun Lewis and John Petts in the Caseg Broadsheets project. Critical surveys of modern and contemporary Anglophone writing from Wales seldom devote more than a few pages – or a few sentences – to her five published books.[2] In addition, her writing in all genres is often broadly dismissed or disparaged for reasons that do not hold up under scrutiny, in part because they misunderstand or ignore Chamberlain's commitment to unconventional, and unconstrained, writing strategies.[3] In her radical stretching and blurring of traditional boundaries of genre and form, for example, she is far more daring, focused, and accomplished than most critics have allowed.

One could usefully view the subject of this essay, *A Rope of Vines: Journal from a Greek Island*,[4] through a variety of critical lenses. One might situate the book in terms of Chamberlain's development and achievements as a Welsh writer, investigating how this text relates to her other books, and to the English-language literary culture of Wales during the 1940s, 1950s, and 1960s. One could study *A Rope of Vines* within its immediate historical, cultural, and political contexts, exploring Chamberlain's apprehension of the distinctly 'other' world of the Greek island of Ydra in the years prior to the 1967 military coup that transformed Greek life until the restoration of democracy in 1974–5.[5] One might approach the book from a feminist critical perspective, focusing on issues of gender identity and formation – the radical act of a woman in her early 1950s, electing to live alone on a Greek island rooted in a traditional, patriarchal culture. Such an analysis would surely correct the characterisation of Chamberlain's 'fey nature'[6] and her 'Celtic fatalism'[7] in favour of more complex and accurate formulations of her life as a Welsh woman writer and artist, 'committed to the work of [her] mind and hands'[8] (*RV* 79).

While I draw upon several critical approaches here, my primary focus is on exploring the text's formal qualities, in particular Chamberlain's characterisation of *A Rope of Vines* in the subtitle as a 'journal' written out of and about a foreign culture and environment, investigating the ways the text is, or is not, a conventional journal.[9] In recounting a significant portion of a writer's life, a journal is a sub-genre of the memoir and distinct from an autobiography (which typically recounts an entire life). The most relevant definition of 'journal' provided by the *Oxford English Dictionary* is 'A daily record of events or occurrences kept for private or official use' (def. 4). The word, after all, derives from the Old French word for 'daily' (*journal*) and most journals – commercial, literary, or private – retain a component of daily record keeping.[10] Readers anticipate that a published journal will be less personal and private than a writer's diary, though the terms are often used interchangeably. Many will first come to *A Rope of Vines*, as did the painter Shani Rhys James, author of the Foreword to the Library of Wales edition, anticipating 'a rather light diary of the author's observations and an account of her time on the island' (x). But *A Rope of Vines* refuses to fulfil expectations that this journal will provide mere record keeping, or indeed any conventional account of Chamberlain's life on Ydra. It is anything but a 'light diary'.

In a 9 May 1941 letter to John Petts, Brenda Chamberlain criticises a story Alun Lewis published in *New Writing*, describing his style as 'pull the plug journalese'. 'I get so tired of Reportage', she writes. 'How Bill drinks off his beer, and Mary slams the lipstick on ... Creative truth is what is needed.'[11] After reading just a few pages of *A Rope of Vines*, one discovers how thoroughly Chamberlain's disdain for 'journalese' and 'reportage' – and her attraction to 'creative truth' – define the form and style of her journal. 'Journalese' suggests for Chamberlain uncomplicated, work-a-day prose, evident in the OED's definition of the word as 'The style of language supposed to be characteristic of public journals; "newspaper" or "penny-a-liner's" English.' 'Reportage' refers to 'reporting of events for the press or for broadcasting, esp. with reference to its style; an instance of this, a piece of journalistic or factual writing' (OED def. 4). As an examplar of Chamberlain's alternative mode of writing, *A Rope of Vines* extends the boundaries of an artist/writer's journal, building upon the innovations of her earlier memoir, *Tide-race*.[12] The primary ways in which Chamberlain challenges, subverts, and transcends readers' expectations of genre and style are by rejecting or minimising the conventions we might expect – doing away with 'journalese' – while adding significant elements we do not expect. Together, those elements create Chamberlain's 'rope of vines,' her own image for this unusual text, and its title.

I

The main facts of Brenda Chamberlain's life are relatively uncomplicated. She was born in Bangor, Wales, in 1912. She studied art at the Royal Academy Schools in London, where she met her future husband, the artist John Petts. She returned to Wales in 1936, living with Petts in Tŷ'r Mynydd, near Llanllechid in Caernarfonshire, where they collaborated with poet Alun Lewis on the Caseg Broadsheets.[13] During the second World War, while Petts served as a conscientious objector, Chamberlain began writing poetry as well as making art.[14] Petts and

Chamberlain separated in 1943. She moved to Ynys Enlli (Bardsey Island) in 1947, where she lived for fourteen years, basing her memoir *Tide-race* on her experiences. In 1958 she published her poetry collection, *The Green Heart*. In 1963, she moved to Ydra, a short boat ride south of Athens, returning to Wales in 1967. She published her novel *The Water Castle* in 1964, her journal *A Rope of Vines* in 1965, *Poems with Drawings* in 1969, and her final book, *Alun Lewis and the Making of the Caseg Broadsheets*, in 1970.[15] She died in 1971 in Bangor, at the age of 57, of an overdose of sleeping pills.

In its formal divisions, *A Rope of Vines* consists of an Introduction and three titled parts – The Good Wells; O Sailors, O Voyagers; and This Island Burns Me – which are sub-divided into numbered chapters of varying lengths. These chapters narrate, in roughly chronological order, Brenda Chamberlain's experiences on Ydra: 'The Good Wells' takes readers from her early days on the island to her removal to Agios Efpraxia, the mountaintop *monasteri* run by nuns; 'O Sailors, O Voyagers' is set during the days she spent at the monastery; 'This Island Burns Me' narrates experiences following her return to settled life on Ydra until the disruption of routines and relationships by political upheaval in Athens.

We learn on the first page of Chamberlain's Introduction that a crisis has occurred: her 'friend Leonidas serves sentence for manslaughter of an English tourist in the port of Ydra' (1). We also learn that Chamberlain is staying at the nunnery. The journal describes her arrival on the island and her emotional and spiritual struggles following the arrest of Leonidas, whose story is told within the larger context of Chamberlain's personal journey from isolation and alienation to a sense of involvement and belonging. From beginning to end, readers are invited to identify the author with the narrator, who on p. 144 is explicitly named 'Brenda'. Besides treating Chamberlain's own experiences, the journal also describes, in vivid detail, the world in which the author finds herself – the people, flora, fauna, dwellings, tavernas, and religious sanctuaries. In the mid-1960s, according to Chamberlain, tourism on the island was confined 'to the port of Ydra and its unreal international set',[16] allowing her an immersion in traditional Greek island culture while living in the interior. Towards the end of the journal, we see signs of transformative changes in Greek life in the years preceding the 1967 military coup.

But while a reader will recognise in *A Rope of Vines* the subject matter and scope within a journal's purview, very soon he or she becomes aware of the absence of expected context and background. One might think that a primary reason for appending an author's Introduction to a journal would be to establish an orienting framework for the main narrative. Chamberlain's Foreword to her earlier memoir, *Tide-race*, provides just such a framework: she explains when she arrived on Ynys Enlli, and why, with whom, and what she found upon arrival.[17] In her Introduction to *A Rope of Vines*, on the other hand, Chamberlain begins *in medias res* by telling the reader she has 'returned' to the 'good mothers of Efpraxia'. In fact, the main function of Chamberlain's brief Introduction is not to provide context but to focus the reader's attention on the *act* of writing and to detail the kind of journal Chamberlain hopes to offer. To this end, Chamberlain invokes Roman poet and philosopher Lucretius and English adventurer and memoirist T. E. Lawrence. In admiration of Lucretius's ability to write 'flowingly and with detachment', she quotes 'a snatch' of his translated work that she had 'copied down' (4). She expresses the wish that she 'could write really well', like T. E. Lawrence, whose words 'in certain passages of *Seven Pillars of Wisdom*' became, for Chamberlain, 'the skin of his adventures in the desert' (4). The Introduction concludes with a defence of the writer and the artist's creative vocation – one 'sneered at' by those with a 'mechanical nine to five job'. From the outset, then, Chamberlain foregrounds for readers her interest in style and technique, the craft of the artist and writer.

Chamberlain mentions off-handedly that by travelling to a Greek island she had 'thought to sink' into 'the dream of classical myth' (83), dismissing with the verb 'sink' and the noun 'dream' her naïve and romantic assumptions about Greek island life. But we are not told what specific conditions of her creative or personal life prompted her 1963 move from Wales to live on Ydra for an extended period.[18] We do not know what family or significant friends she left behind in Wales. No letters or packages are mentioned arriving, giving the impression of almost complete isolation.[19] The journal does not reveal how she obtained a place to live on Ydra or secured her servant, Varvara. Only a few references to time of day, day of the week, the month or year briefly orient the reader. 'This was a Wednesday, of no significance', Chamberlain writes on p. 97, and she expects readers also to find such information insignificant.[20] We might be notified that seasons are passing, 'Spring into summer into autumn' (111), and we might date certain passages from reference to an historic event, as when Chamberlain mentions 'excitement and exultation in the port' on the day a ship 'brought the newspapers with the result of the elections' (119).[21] Along with the absence of clear chronology[22] and explicit time markers, locations are not always identified, and may shift radically. Most action takes place on Ydra, but on p. 103 (for example) we are suddenly in Athens. By withholding contextual markers of time and place, Chamberlain achieves one of her central aims: she forces the reader into direct experience of the present.[23]

Chamberlain intensifies this sense of immediacy by incorporating excerpts from her original notebooks written between May 1963 and May 1964 into A Rope of Vines, without commentary and set off by quotation marks. These might be a single inserted sentence, or an entire chapter (as with chapter 31 on pp. 52–3).[24] Including such excerpts heightens the immediacy of the prose while emphasising Chamberlain's innovative understanding of the journal as a genre that accommodates diverse presentations of reality.[25] The drawings, discussed later in this essay, immerse the reader in a similar immediacy: they are not composite or epic but like sketches in providing highly personalised, non-contextualised, framed scenes from the artist's point of view at a particular moment.

Though readers are deprived of immediate contexts and continuities of time and place, we are supplied with larger and deeper contexts that span historical periods and diverse cultures. These include allusions to ancient and modern writers interwoven through the text. Besides the references to Lucretius and T. E. Lawrence mentioned earlier, she invokes writers as diverse as Thomas Mann (quoting from *The Holy Sinner* for the epigraph to her book), Shelley (24), de Maupassant (52), and Dostoyevsky (80). She draws upon popular elements of Greek myth such as the song of the sirens (110) and Pandora's box (112), but also lesser-known figures such as the 'Dirae screaming for vengeance' (112).[26] We learn from these larger contexts that while Chamberlain appears to be isolated from family and friends, as well as from her own past,[27] she was in touch with extensive systems of meaning, belonging, and creating that to a great extent shape her responses to the de-stabilising, radically 'other' culture and environment of Ydra.

Brenda Chamberlain was attracted to life in isolated environments,[28] but certainly not isolated from writers, books, or that crucial instrument for dissemination of cutting-edge contemporary writing, the literary magazine. In her autobiographical essay in *Artists in Wales*, Chamberlain relates how as a child she would spend great amounts of time 'in the school library, where I was at peace with books, a thick carpet, and silence' (45). In the same essay she writes that while she lived in north Wales, prior to moving to Ynys Enlli,

> Poetry became as precious as bread. I can remember buying
> a new magazine in Bangor (perhaps it was *Poetry London*)
> standing in the street to read it, as a starving person will
> tear the crust from a loaf. *Life and Letters*, *Poetry Quarterly*,
> and many other 'little' magazines were printing new poems
> as they were written, with urgency ... (48)

In her commentary on the making of the Caseg
Broadsheets, Chamberlain confesses to having fallen 'under
the influence' of D. H. Lawrence at the time of her move
back to Wales from London,[29] an influence that may help
account for her desire to experience, as Lawrence did,
cultures and environments not yet overwhelmed by
industrialisation and modernity.[30] She also kept abreast of
writers publishing in the two newly launched vehicles for
Welsh writing in English, *Wales* and *The Welsh Review*,
such as Dylan Thomas, whose prose and poetry were likely
inspirations for the rich, sometimes baroque, style of much
of *A Rope of Vines*.

Though Chamberlain does not include full poems in *A
Rope of Vines*, as she does in *Tide-race*, many of the prose
passages display the density and rhythmic and sonic
qualities of prose poetry: 'Women passed in the first light,
riding-queens moving towards the valley where first I
scented wolves, and the squalor of stinking privies,
carcases, and wet hides. Dogs prowled the morning
puddles, and the river-beds were yellow as lions' (97).
One can see the Hopkinsian 'sprung rhythm' syncopation
of stressed and unstressed syllables in a scansion of the
second sentence: 'Dogs prowled the morning puddles, and
the river-beds were yellow as lions' [/ / V / V / V, V V / V /
V / V V / V, where / is stressed and V is unstressed]. There
is also intricate alliteration in this sentence, particularly of
'p', 'd', 's', 'l', and 'w'. And it does not take too fine an
ear to discern Dylan Thomas's 'fire green as grass' (from
'Fern Hill') echoing behind Chamberlain's 'river-beds ...
yellow as lions'.[31]

Even in remote Ynys Enlli, Chamberlain's house in the

summer was 'filled with visitors, including artists and writers such as Stephen Spender ...'[32] American 'San Francisco Renaissance' poet Kenneth Rexroth, who corresponded with Chamberlain regarding his anthology *New British Poets* (1949) while she lived on Ynys Enlli, credits her for 'advice and correspondence ... valuable to me beyond thanks or estimate'.[33] In his long poem 'The Dragon and the Unicorn', Rexroth writes of an attempt to visit Chamberlain: 'At Aberdaron no boat to / Bardsey too stiff a wind, so / I loaf four days...' But with 'no sign of the wind letting up,' he must 'leave Brenda Chamberlain / To her island of ten thousand birds / And go on to Dolgelley ...'[34]

As a contributor to important literary magazines of her day[35] and a self-described voracious reader of contemporary poetry, Chamberlain would have been familiar with Anglo-American modernists, such as expatriate Americans T. S. Eliot and H.D. (Hilda Doolittle).[36] Possible connections with H.D. are especially intriguing: in its exclamations, sequenced imagistic phrasing, and classical content, Chamberlain's language in *A Rope of Vines* – such as 'O Sea! Thou Ocean, *Thalassa!* Indigo, green of jade, white silver black' (110) – can resemble H.D.'s in a poem such as 'Sea Rose': 'Rose, harsh rose, / marred and with stint of petals, / meager flower, thin ....' Both writers were independent women with life-long affinities for Greek culture and literature. Critic Joseph Bennett found the poems in Chamberlain's first book – published five years before her move to Ydra – to 'have a Mediterranean quality about them; the Furies, the Sirens, are about to appear'.[37] Both Chamberlain and H.D. responded to the Second World War in their writing – Chamberlain through her poem sequence 'The Green Heart' (begun in 1941 and published in *The Green Heart* in 1958[38]); H. D. through her three long poems – *The Walls Do Not Fall* (1944), *Tribute to the Angles* (1945), and *The Flowering of the Rod* (1946) – published together in 1972 as *Trilogy*. Chamberlain and H.D. both published in *Life and Letters To-day*, edited by Robert Herring and H.D.'s partner, Bryher (Annie Winifred Ellerman), who was also the magazine's financial backer. Chamberlain published in the iconic modernist American journal *Poetry* (Chicago),[39] which famously launched H.D.'s career in 1913 by first publishing her poems (courtesy of Ezra Pound). The work of contemporary writers with whom Chamberlain was certainly familiar, or whose influence was generally felt within British and American letters, is perhaps the most important context for understanding her achievement in *A Rope of Vines*, allowing readers to apprehend the text not only as a record of personal experience, but also as a self-consciously literary construct – a multi-faceted conversation with other writers, works, and traditions.

II

While Brenda Chamberlain does not help her readers to apprehend the immediate context for the action in her journal, she does develop a plot – or more accurately, the trappings of a plot. We are told that an English tourist has been killed in the port of Ydra, and Chamberlain confesses to being close to the killer, an Ydriot named Leonidas, charged with manslaughter. Questions arise. How did this tragedy occur? What will happen to Leonidas? Can Chamberlain help him fight the charge or provide comfort? Will the full nature of their relationship be revealed? Will it flourish or wither? These questions, set up early in the text, initially serve as a dramatic pull to keep the reader moving through the narrative. Given the intensity of Chamberlain's feelings for Leonidas as described in the journal, one expects *A Rope of Vines* to explore the relationship fully, but after the first mention on page 1, the nascent plot does not develop: the questions raised are either answered quickly and simply, or never addressed.[40] We don't hear of Leonidas again until p. 46, a third of the way through the book. We are not supplied with the details of his crime and conviction until p. 58, and then only minimally. The journal's over-arching focus is not on Leonidas, nor on Chamberlain's relationship to him, but on how events relating to his arrest disrupt and even unhinge Chamberlain's life. Chamberlain entices the reader with the promise of dramatic action and passionate feelings, but ultimately returns our attention to a different subject: how her writing and art arise out of emotional and spiritual crisis.

Perhaps the main convention of journal writing that Chamberlain challenges in *A Rope of Vines* is the genre's inherent assertion of veracity: conventional journals promise to describe actions that happened, people who existed. But in *A Rope of Vines*, Chamberlain regularly encourages readers to doubt the accuracy of her descriptions. 'It was a secret joke, never spoken of,' she writes, 'that sometime I would write my autobiography, but it should be invented' (56) – an assertion complicated by the fact that a joke – 'something said or done to excite laughter or amusement' (*OED* def. 1) – is by its nature not a secret, but a shared experience. 'Who is this woman I stare at in the mirror?' Chamberlain asks on p. 104: 'Did I invent her, or did she make me up in the glass?' Chamberlain will occasionally distinguish for the reader what is real from what she has imagined; at other times readers must make such determinations for themselves. Some people are real; others might be real but are transformed in the crucible of Chamberlain's imagination, such as the 'young and beautiful nun' Chamberlain fantasises about upon arriving at the monastery: 'Because she is not seen, she can be imagined as fair beyond the loveliest girls who gather at the well as dawn comes over the mountain-shoulder' (14).

Chamberlain begins her autobiographical essay in *Artists in Wales* with a memory of deceiving her brother with a story about her being born in Africa: 'I lied and lied', she writes, 'about the heat, crocodiles, swamps. Alligators turned in strong, smooth water' (44).[41] This strategy of substituting imaginative constructs for mundane reality begun in childhood informs much of Chamberlain's published writings. While the word 'journal' in the subtitle to *A Rope of Vines* leads one to anticipate a 'true story', readers soon realise that fact and fiction, reality and fantasy, the mundane and the mythic are interwoven in service of 'creative truth'. 'Sometimes, truly, it would appear that life as it is called, is part of the world of dreams', Chamberlain tells readers on p. 94. She asks us to accept that products of the imagination can be as real as any string of events that actually occurred.

III

A Rope of Vines presents in detail Brenda Chamberlain's apprehension of the foreign place to which she has moved, but readers are not indulged with many facts about Ydra. We are told that it is an 'island of 3,000 souls and 300 churches' (1), and we learn the names of some villages, tavernas, and monasteries. But we are not informed of exactly where the island is located or given its history. The Greek language is not mentioned, and we have no idea whether or not Chamberlain struggled to communicate with native Ydriots. Chamberlain instead provides us with visual and emotional apprehensions of moments and immediate environments from an intensely personal point of view, fulfilling reader expectations of a journal in providing quotidian detail of Ydra's people, flora, and fauna. 'How could I ever cut myself off from the simple things of the earth?' Brenda Chamberlain asks on p. 53, and on p. 61 writes,

> I am clinging to, seeking out, in whatever form it may take, a normal goodness – a new baby being carried in the sun for the first time, the fishermen dancing at Loulou's *taverna* with Yanis, wine-barrels on the edge of the *agora*, more and more of them being placed there to be hosed out, their

hoops newly painted, ready for the grape-must which will
soon arrive from over the sea, for the new season's retsina.

Some of the most arresting and affecting sections of *A Rope
of Vines* are the minute observations and vignettes, which
precisely, viscerally, and visually capture life on the island:
'An ant passes my foot, dragging a long pink petal' (23); 'A
small pale-coloured donkey brought up the rear, carrying
dead poultry, two on each side tied by the legs and flopping
forlornly their broken necks' (23); 'A praying mantis, going
in the opposite direction, stopped when it saw me, and
turned back for another look. I crouched down, the mantis
reared upright for a closer inspection, before resuming its
journey' (105). In its precision and accuracy, Chamberlain's
prose can be realistic (though never 'journalese'); it can also
be dramatic, passionate, lyric, and surprisingly comic – as
with this wonderful vignette of a husband and wife:

> There was a brown grease-woman in Lamia, a woman
> made to be pinched, and she was cooking camel meat,
> and in between times was with a pole unhitching
> sausages from the ceiling, and I was the whole time
> sinking lower onto the table from the smell of zoo. Under
> a trapdoor her husband descended among the camel-
> carcases, and was unabashed. For him, it was the scent
> of home. (100)

The evocative phrase 'the smell of zoo' is comic but also
highlights Chamberlain's sense of being 'a rare bird flown in
from overseas' (85): the composite 'smell of zoo' would be
recognised only by foreigners (such as Chamberlain) for
whom a zoo is commonplace. While there are no zoos on
Ydra, creatures wild and domestic abound in Chamberlain's
account of life on the island. Part one of *A Rope of Vines*
begins with an exclamation of wonder at an animal of the
sea: 'A dolphin leapt!' (5). Chamberlain especially delights
in the island cats: 'the long-drawn unearthly wails of the
Kala Pigadhia cats, raising up for me too-clear pictures of

nimble bodies squeezing through shut doors, jaws opening meat-safes, the unearthly inventiveness of the half-wild animals, busy at our food supplies' (16).

But while readers do gain a sense of the island's flora and fauna, the writing primarily focuses on the human dimensions of island life. Chamberlain is fascinated by human quirks, our distinctive ways of being: 'One of the nuns likes to lie on her bed in the morning reading the newspaper. I sometimes hear her washing up dishes at the sink in the corridor, and this afternoon I met her eating a honey cake' (77). Chamberlain is a chronicler of social activity, such as the gathering of Ydriot women at the well; she is acutely aware of the squabbles of families, the island's civic and religious rituals, the tense, intense relationships between men and women, the lines separating genders: 'The world of men was suddenly abroad, men on mules, a boy in a pith hat riding a donkey' (26). She is careful to provide names to individuate major and minor characters: her friend Yanis (45), the 'biting boy' Aldo (56), the waiter Michalis (90), Captain Theophanis (93), the boatman Evangelos Limmiotis (110, 111).

Chamberlain often catalogues what she consumes of food and drink – usually configured as gifts that confirm or create relationships. In revealing that her 'breakfast is brought ... by the cheerfully smiling lame nun: coffee, rusks, sheeps' milk with sugar, and a glass of water' (69), Chamberlain conveys to us that she eats alone, but that the nuns are content with her presence in the monastery. She experiences distant, formal, yet affectionate and meaning-ful relationships with them. Meals at the monastery are simple but described in loving detail, as with her midday meal on a Sunday: '*arni psito*, lamb on the knucklebone, strong goat-cheese, macaroni, cheese and tomato sauce, watermelon for dessert' (69). For breakfast one morning while Chamberlain is staying in the monastery, Leonidas climbs up the mountain to bring her 'black cherries, hard-boiled eggs, and a thermos of iced *Demestika* wine' (72).

Iced wine might seem an odd beverage for breakfast, but Chamberlain in this journal is an unabashed lover of wine and the fellowship of friends sharing a bottle. At a *taverna* along the coast at Vlichos she recounts being 'given unlimited retsina, fish, salad, cheese, and dessert was a watermelon' (86). At a party 'to celebrate the winter' she takes pride in having 'killed seven bottles of red wine between us, two Greeks, two Canadians, and myself' (135). Even the camomile tea she sips with her friend Yanis comes 'laced with cognac' (140).

This intense interest in people, names, relationships relates to a central motif of Chamberlain's journal: her search for community on Ydra – an impulse that likely relates to her sense of being both intimately connected with, yet estranged from, her native Wales, a conflicted identity shared by many English-language writers of her generation, including Dylan Thomas and R. S. Thomas.[43] As the journal progresses, Chamberlain shifts her sense of who is 'the foreigner' (54), who a stranger, who a comrade. And while there is never a question that she can belong on the island in the way a native Ydriot belongs, she does form lasting attachments. Two thirds through the journal she feels able to state 'I have a past here' (111); a few pages later she asserts that 'For some years, I have been on the fringe of other people's lives. Now, on this island, I have found my way of life again, having my own table at Graphos', with my friends, my guests' (120). To a great extent, the arc of this story runs from isolation to attachment, from individual existence to connections within a community, signaled by the pronoun shift from the dominant 'I' of the journal's first half, to the increasing use of 'we' and 'our' in the latter half. 'There is a handful of people to hang onto for very life, but they too are leaving with the dying of the sun ... becoming at once other people to us,' Chamberlain asserts near the end of the journal. 'What shall we do with ourselves, now that our friends have gone away?' (138).

If the text emphasises Chamberlain's inner struggles

and her apprehension of the environment as well as cultural institutions and social engagements around her, the drawings emphasise human-made structures within the landscape. Dispersed through the text are 65 drawings, causing the reader to shift from text to drawing and back every few pages – constantly engaging with their interplay, and thus constantly aware of the book as a hybrid construct.[44] Opposite the first page of Brenda Chamberlain's Introduction to *A Rope of Vines* is a drawing of a drinking vessel on the floor of a room before an opened door, through which one encounters a vista of mountains, islands, the sea. Here and in all drawings, the white paper suggests a sun-drenched and sun-bleached background. The drawing extends an invitation for the reader to accompany Chamberlain on a journey via text and drawings into the framed scene, a motif repeated on p. 92.[45] Readers of journals do not expect to confront drawings by the author interspersed through a text, though there is a long tradition of interweaving text and art in English-language literature, including the Caseg Broadsheets. This mixed-media strategy was a consistent feature of Brenda Chamberlain's creative life, and in the late 1960s also included collaborations with a dancer and composer;[46] her only book without drawings is her first, *The Green Heart*.[47]

The drawings in *A Rope of Vines* are not illustrations of the text but parallel expressions of Chamberlain's experience: they tell their own stories while echoing, and interacting with, the written text. While Chamberlain's prose often depicts or refers to human life on the island, only two drawings include people. One of these, on p. 14, features Chamberlain herself, the woman wearing a broad-brimmed hat, dressed in white on a donkey, separate from the two figures in black. The drawings concentrate on houses, tavernas, monasteries rooted within the bare rocks and hills of Ydra, or rising directly from the landscape, as with the design on the title page, where a small structure protrudes from the hillside at an angle. People may, or may not, be inside the structures: Chamberlain's focus in the drawings is not on humans, but on what humans confect for emotional and physical shelter.

As with her prose, Chamberlain's drawings reflect a shifting point of view and temperament: they can be dramatic, lyric, and comic. They convey a balance between design and disintegration, organic unity and instability, human artefact and the natural world, the familiar and the foreign. They are not photographic, and not predictable. Sometimes they present imposing vistas, where buildings are dwarfed by mountains and the bay (43); sometimes they focus on minute particularities. One of the most charming is of a cat in the monastery basking in the sun (77). The drawings of urns can show a slyly female shape (as on p. 55), and indeed, Chamberlain plays with sexuality in the text and in certain drawings. On p. 49, Chamberlain has drawn Leonidas's house (described in prose on the page opposite) with a door shaped like a large phallus – or perhaps not? Her drawings of the convent where the nuns live on pp. 101 and 127 are faced by a hill with a cave – or is it a vagina? Chamberlain herself indulges in such Rorschach-test sightings: 'Seabed-discovered Metéora reared above us, cloud-maddened pillars, evil shapes built of sea-pebbles. A phallus' (98). Like the text, the drawings can be ambiguous, shape-shifting: the one on p. 17 might depict rocks, plants, small trees, buildings, abstract shapes, or a combination of these. In many, Chamberlain demonstrates the technique of linear geometric perspective while simultaneously undermining realistic representation. She creates believable space with distortions, large and small. There are few straight lines; nothing is plumb; upheaval seems imminent. The mountain on p. 131 is a chaos of swirls; the lines on the roof on p. 109 are like waves on a shore. As the text approaches its conclusion, the drawings project the gathering threat against democracy: the window in the house on p. 123 has bars.

Despite the celebration of social structures in the

drawings and of communal activities in the text, Chamberlain does not lose sight of human complexity, our easy transitions from nobility to small-mindedness. She bemoans pettiness in Ydriot village life, and by implication throughout the wider world: '"Dismal world," you wrote. O miserable, dismal world of petty intrigue' (123).[48] Chamberlain's journal moves, inexorably, from her initial sense of separation, to her involvement in islanders' lives, to the journal's final chapters, when Chamberlain introduces the ominous local effects of political upheaval at the national level: 'policemen at every corner, and the threat of police at the entrance to every passageway leading from the port' (126). A few pages from the end of the journal, she confesses to living in fear 'of the police-state' (141). It takes only a slight shift in perspective to see the drawing on p. 132 as depicting not a traditional Greek oven but a tragic mask, with two sloping eyes, a long nose, and a dark, despairing mouth.[49]

IV

A Rope of Vines is both a factual and a fictionalised journal, taking as its subject Brenda Chamberlain's inner and outer lives – and their interactions – on the island of Ydra, exploring her spirituality, capacity for emotional attachment, commitment to the artist's vocation, and longing for community. Chamberlain celebrates, as did Walt Whitman in Song of Myself, the self and self-invention, but also, like Whitman, she celebrates life outside the self: the mercantile, social, work-a-day world, the 'enduring boats, laden with melons and water pots, green peppers, and cattle' (148).[50] In rejecting traditional 'journalese' and 'reportage', Chamberlain has fashioned what she terms a 'cable of vine tendrils [to] anchor the ship of my heart' (116). One vine is Chamberlain's relentless charting of her emotional and spiritual states, involving interplay between real and imagined events and people. A second vine is the richly detailed, poetic prose that resonates with the work of writers Chamberlain admired within and beyond the borders of Wales. And a third is the sequence of fine drawings that comment upon, and diverge from, the written text. Such intertwined elements in this multi-faceted and multi-layered writer/artist's journal create the 'phantasmagoria', to invoke Yeats's formulation, that must be present when 'a poet writes ... of personal life'.[51]

NOTES

1   Her work appears in all major anthologies of English-language poetry from Wales, including Keidrych Rhys's *Modern Welsh Poetry* (1944), Meic Stephens's *The Lilting House* (1969), Garlick/Mathias's *Anglo-Welsh Poetry 1480–1990*, and Dannie Abse's *Twentieth Century Anglo-Welsh Poetry*. Tony Conran asserts that Chamberlain and Lynette Roberts constitute 'the heroic generation of Welsh women writers': *Frontiers in Anglo-Welsh Poetry* (Cardiff: University of Wales Press, 1997), p. 165.

2   In some studies, discussion of Chamberlain is little more than a footnote to, or context for, discussion of Alun Lewis, as in Roland Mathias's *Anglo-Welsh Literature: An Illustrated History* (Bridgend: Poetry Wales Press, 1987), pp. 95–7.

3   Jill Piercy, for example, finds the language in Chamberlain's first poetry collection, *The Green Heart*, to be 'often awkwardly expressed and difficult to read with a glut of hyphenated words': 'Between Two Arts,' *Planet*, No. 68 (April/May 1988), pp. 77–86 (78). Offering a contrary opinion, American Joseph Bennett finds the poems 'ripe, pungent and rich', quoting for illustration a passage with a line containing hyphenated words, 'From the night-sea he fishes for a bright-armoured herring': 'Five Poets', *The Hudson Review*, Vol. 11, No. 2 (Summer, 1958), pp. 302–7 (306). Kate Holman in her Writers of Wales study argues that Chamberlain's writing 'might have profited from a little more humor and detachment, a little less earnestness': *Brenda Chamberlain* (Cardiff: University of Wales Press, 1997), p.

94 (hereafter BC), though a work such as *A Rope of Vines: Journal from a Greek Island* is in fact often humorous – the humour in part deriving from Chamberlain's sense of detachment as a writer/artist and foreigner on a Greek island. Tony Conran does not believe 'her verse to be very important' (*The Cost of Strangeness: Essays on the English Poets of Wales* (Llandysul: Gomer Press, 1982), p. 204) and expresses surprise that 'she has appeared in no fewer than four of our anthologies' (p. 206). Commenting specifically on *A Rope of Vines* (mistitled *A Rope of Sands*), Conran finds it 'much more fragmentary and rootless than [*Tide-race*]' (p. 208). Neglect or disparagement of Chamberlain might in part derive from suspicion of her strategy of using letters from Karl von Laer as sources for her poetry and prose, an 'audacious use', Holman remarks, 'that conflicts directly with our notion of poetry as something original and unique to the poet' ('"So Near, So Far, Brother or Lover": Brenda Chamberlain and the Letters of Karl von Laer', *The New Welsh Review*, No. 2 (Autumn, 1988), pp. 45–54 (48).

4   Brenda Chamberlain, *A Rope of Vines: Journal from a Greek Island* (Cardigan: Parthian, 2009). All further references will be given parenthetically in the essay.

5   David Wills has examined post Second World War writings by British authors who explore the Greek character and way of life. He comments on Chamberlain's hope that in Ydra she would escape 'the dictates of a machine-driven existence' (p. 179) and on her interest in '"oriental" aspects of Greece' (p. 185). 'British Accounts of Residency in Greece, 1945–2004', *Journal of Modern Greek Studies* (May 2005), pp. 177–197.

6   Allison Smith's phrase, in *John Petts and the Caseg Press* (Aldershot: Ashgate Publishing Limited, 2000), p. 18.

7   Kate Holman's phrase ('So Near, So Far', p. 46).

8   Critics characterising Chamberlain and/or her work in gender terms express widely divergent opinions. Tony Brown and M. Wynn Thomas see in Chamberlain 'sexual (and gender) confusion, unfocussed need' (189); Kate Holman speculates that Chamberlain 'often seemed happiest in the company of young people' (BC 5), an opinion echoed by Alison Smith (68). Commenting on Chamberlain's poetry (rather than on her person) in his review of *The Green Heart*, Joseph Bennett finds the style 'curiously masculine', with a 'virile tone' (306).

9   Chamberlain did not characterise her previous book, *Tide-race*, as a memoir, journal, or work of fiction, leaving it to the reader to decide its genre.

10 OED

11 Letter from Chamberlain to John Petts, 9 May 1941, quoted in Smith, p. 52.

12 Critics have differed in characterising Chamberlain's prose books by genre. While most consider *The Water Castle* to be her single novel (for example), Jill Piercy refers to *Tide-race*, *The Water Castle* and *A Rope of Vines* as Chamberlain's 'three published novels' (p. 77).

13 For views on the project, see Brenda Chamberlain's *Alun Lewis and the Making of the Caseg Broadsheets* (London: Enitharmon Press: 1969); Roland Mathias's 'The Caseg Letters – a commentary', *Poetry Wales*, Vol. X (1975), pp. 46–77 (reprinted in *A Ride Through the Wood*); and Allison Smith's *John Petts and the Caseg Press* (Aldershot, Hants.: Ashgate Publishing Limited, 2000).

14 Her first published poem appeared in *The Welsh Review* in 1939 (Holman, p. 6). For a discussion of Chamberlain as artist and writer, see Jill Piercy's 'Between Two Arts', *Planet*', No. 68 (April/May 1988), pp. 77–86.

15 Her play, *The Protagonists,* written during Chamberlain's stay on Ydra, was 'performed at the University College, Bangor, on 11 and 12 October 1968' (Holman, *BC* pp. 63, 64).

16 'Brenda Chamberlain', *Artists in Wales*, ed. Meic Stephens (Llandysul: Gwasg Gomer, 1971), p. 52.

17 Brenda Chamberlain, Introduction, *Tide-race*, (Bridgend: Seren Books, 1987), pp. 13–14.

18 Much of this background is provided in 'Brenda Chamberlain', *Artists in Wales*, pp. 44–54 (52–53).

19 In fact, Chamberlain did receive and send letters and packages, as her original notebooks written on Ydra make clear: '6:30 Sunday evening – my letters just came, by way of the elegant young man in sunglasses with a portfolio under his arm, who delivers the mail with give-away negligence & charm' (from MS 35 21516B, National Library of Wales).

20 Chamberlain was not adverse to establishing clear dates when it suited her purpose: each chapter of *The Water Castle* is titled with a day and month.

21 The election of 19 February 1964 provided a clear victory for Georgios Papandreou and the Center Union Party.

22 Though not pursued as radically as in *A Rope of Vines*, this interest in dispensing with the past is also a theme and narrative strategy in *Tide-race*.

23 In *Alun Lewis and The Making of the Caseg Broadsheets* Chamberlain praises Alun Lewis's writings that convey a sense of immediacy and freshness: to her, Lewis's 'letters speak ... with more immediacy than the poems. ... There is something contrived about the poems, a shade too much "poetry"' (p. 14). Tellingly, 'too much "poetry"' for Chamberlain is not flowery language but language that distances the writer from the subject. Later she remarks that Lewis's 'letters stay alive because the words flowed directly from the mind and brain to the pen' (p. 36).

24 Chamberlain mentions her original notebook in her Introduction to *A Rope of Vines* (p. 4). In her essay for *Artists in Wales*, she also quotes her own prose, identifying the passage as coming 'from a notebook of the time' (p. 47).

25 There are excerpts from her original notebooks written as the events occurred, there are descriptions of events in the present tense that were composed after the events occurred, and there are self-reflexive passages, commenting on the process of composition and on the journal itself.

26 In commenting on this fascination with 'voices of the past', Katie Gramich quotes from a relevant poem by Chamberlain in *Poems with Drawings* (1969): 'the dead whisper with the dead / the living gossip with the dead' (*Twentieth Century Women's Writing in Wales: Land, Gender, Belonging* (Cardiff: University of Wales Press, 2007), p. 122).

27 Though Chamberlain moved to Ydra soon after having lived for fourteen years on Ynys Enlli, Wales is directly referred to only three times: on p. 3 of the Introduction (where she refers to Ynys Enlli as 'my own island'), p. 112 when recalling her childhood in north Wales, and ironically on p. 132, when 'Cardiff or Zanzibar' are posited as being equally foreign. On p. 11 Chamberlain relates a scene in which her servant Varvara is 'shocked' to discover her gutting fish and doing so 'correctly', a skill mastered during the years on Ynys Enlli. 'She would be more surprised', Chamberlain writes, 'if she knew how many fish I have gutted in my life.'

28 In his review of *A Rope of Vines* for *Books and Bookmen*, Norman Thomas notes that both Ydra and Bardsey lie 'about six miles' from the mainland ('Island in the Sun', Oct. 1965).

29 Brenda Chamberlain, *Alun Lewis and the Making of the Caseg Broadsheets* (London: Enitharmon Press: 1969), p. 1.

30 It is worth noting that Chamberlain coined the phrase 'the machine' as shorthand for the de-humanising mechanisation of modern culture well before R. S. Thomas: 'The machine rules them in their safe upper-suburban life ...' (p. 10).

31 'Fern Hill' appeared in Dylan Thomas's 1946 collection, *Deaths and Entrances*.

32 Holman, BC p. 8.

33 Kenneth Rexroth, 'Introduction0 pt *New British Poets* (Norfolk, CT: New Directions, 1949), p. xxxvii. This correspondence is available in the Kenneth Rexroth archive at the University of California, Los Angeles library. In Rexroth's *New British Poets* anthology, Chamberlain keeps company not only with important modern Welsh poets such as Alun Lewis, Dylan Thomas, and Glyn Jones, but also with high profile English, Irish, and Scottish poets of the period.

34 Kenneth Rexroth, 'The Dragon and the Unicorn', *The Collected Longer Poems of Kenneth Rexroth* (New York: New Directions, 1968), pp. 105–6.

35 In the 1940s and 1950s Chamberlain published in a variety of journals, including *The Dublin Magazine*, *Life and Letters Today*, *The New Yorker*, *Poetry London*, *Poetry Quarterly*, *Wales*, and *The Welsh Review*, as well as the anthologies *Modern Welsh Poetry*, *New British Poets*, *New Directions*, and *New Irish Poets*.

36 Kate Holman asserts that Eliot's *Four Quartets* are echoed repeatedly in *A Rope of Vines* (BC p. 59).

37 Bennett, p. 306.

38 M. Wynn Thomas and Tony Brown's 'The Problems of Belonging' in *Welsh Writing in English* (Cardiff: University of Wales Press, 2003), pp. 165–202 (188).

39 'For Alun Lewis', Volume 66, September 1945, p. 303 and 'Midnight Mass', Volume 67, December 1945, p. 137.

40 Indeed, at some point readers might wonder if Leonidas exists only in the pages of *A Rope of Vines* – an issue raised by Chamberlain herself, after questioning her own reality: 'And Leonidas, have I invented him too, because he was

necessary to me?' (p. 104). In her essay for *Artists in Wales* Chamberlain nowhere mentions Leonidas; her stay at the nunnery is unconnected to trauma: 'Almost the first thing I did was to go on muleback to the nearest monastery, a nunnery, with my new friend and maid, Varvara Dashloulike. A few weeks later, I stayed as a guest of the nuns ... Those few days gave me extreme happiness' (p. 52). Furthermore, Chamberlain's notebooks on deposit at the National Library of Wales do not mention a Leonidas or any friend jailed for manslaughter. It is possible that a real person named Leonidas did exist but that Chamberlain provides him with a pseudonym in the published journal. It is further possible that the relationship was real, but that the intensity depicted in the journal is one-sided: experienced by Chamberlain and not Leonidas. In an article for the *New Welsh Review*, Kate Holman quotes friends of Chamberlain on the interplay between invention and reality in her life: '"She lived in an extraordinarily high-powered make-believe world of her own, but was so aware of the world outside ..." says her friend Michael Realkes-Williams. "She thought and thought about things and they became real," confirms Esme Kirby' ('So Near, So Far', p. 46).

41   Chamberlain's childhood invention of a foreign origin for herself foreshadows her adult interest in living in places (Enlli and Ydra) culturally and physically removed from the perspective of her native Bangor.

42   In one of her notebooks, MS 35 21516B, it is a friend identified as 'Bill' who brings the breakfast: 'On the first morning, I went out at about 8 o clock, went a little way along the walls towards the long steps and came face to face with Bill, who said "Hello, you look just the same." He had brought for our breakfast, firm black olives, bread, hard-boiled eggs, & a thermos of red wine – Demestika.'

43   Tony Brown, for example, addresses R. S. Thomas's 'uncertainty of identity and his related searching for a way of life where he can feel more fulfilled, where he can feel at home' in his Writers of Wales study, *R. S. Thomas* (Cardiff: University of Wales Press, 2006), p. 22. See also M. Wynn Thomas and Tony Brown's 'The Problems of Belonging', in *Welsh Writing in English* (Cardiff: University of Wales Press, 2003), pp. 165–202.

44 Chamberlain also used drawings, titled sections, and untitled chapters in *Tide-race*.

45 'Journey', cognate to 'journal', derives from the Old French word *journee*, meaning a day's travel.

46 The dancer was Robertos Saragos; the composer (of electronic music) was Halim el Dabh (Piercy, p. 83).

47 While *The Water Castle* does contain five drawings, Jill Piercy states that 'drawings were prepared to accompany the text but were not used' and that 'Chamberlain felt disappointed that it was not illustrated' (p. 82).

48 This disillusionment echoes the opening exclamation of poem XIII (Part III) of her sequence 'The Green Heart': 'The terrible passions of humanity!' The beginning of an early chapter in *Tide-race* expresses a similar sharp reaction to human passions: 'Terror. Violence. Greed. I was not passing over to a dream life, an escapist's paradise, but to one that whitened the hair and bowed the back, that would raise sea-monsters of hatred and despair' (*Tide-race* (Bridgend: Seren Books, 1987 [first published by Hodder and Stoughton: 1962], p. 56).

49 While the text does not make it clear that the drawing is of an oven, Chamberlain's original notebook MS 35 21516B in the National Library of Wales does, on p. 73.

50 The *Times Literary Supplement* identifies 'Whitmanian rhetoric' in *A Rope of Vines* in its largely positive 1966 review, though the reviewer complains about 'a curious atmosphere of falsity and exaggeration that hangs over even the most insightful passages' (Anon., 'Hélas', *The Times Literary Supplement*, 27 January 1966, p. 67).

51 From *W. B. Yeats: Later Essays*, ed. W. H. O'Connell (New York: Scribner, 1994), p. 204.

Maimed Individuals:

The Significance of the Body in *So Long, Hector Bebb*

Sarah Morse

Ron Berry's vivid and often brutal novel *So Long, Hector Bebb* tells the story of a fictional professional boxer, Hector Bebb, whose life is first defined, and then unravelled, by violence. Hector is the great hope of the Cymmer White Hart boxing club, and after serving a year-long suspension from the sport for improper conduct in the ring, he returns to the gym to train for his career comeback, and we follow his progress through a series of fights as he prepares to challenge for the British middleweight title. The day after he becomes the BBBC Champion, Hector returns to Cymmer, realises his wife's adulterous behaviour, and attacks and accidentally kills her lover in a late night café. Hector flees the town, adopts a new identity, and lives as Joe Williams for seven years before he is discovered. Through the resonant effects of these events Berry's text considers many themes, ranging from de-industrialisation to the wilderness, but this study will consider the significance of the body in the narrative.

Before turning to consider the narrative of the text in detail, it is necessary to reflect on its unusual structure. The novel is arranged in fifty-three chapters, each narrated by one of fourteen narrative voices, a departure for Berry's long fiction which, until this novel, was largely narrated in the third person.[1] Although the narrative arc of the plot is linear, the chorus of voices creates an episodic feel in the narrative as the intimate stream-of-consciousness testimonies deviate from the central plot to expose their own stories and recall earlier times. A reviewer for the *Times Literary Supplement* in 1971 dismissingly observed that the novel creates 'the impression of a confusion of voices', but this confusion is a defining concept of the novel.[2] The various perspectives offered by the different voices expose the fluidity of the concept of narration, an ambiguity which is accentuated and complicated by the narrators also reporting their discussions with each other. Through this device, the reader becomes aware of the centrality of subjectivity in the construction of a narrative, and also the construction of self and identity, as the characters are distorting mirrors of one another. Berry is therefore able to present the complexities of the circle of people that surrounds the White Hart boxing club as the reader negotiates the conflicting first-person reports.[3]

The numerous narrators also enable Berry to address an inequality within boxing: the silence of the boxer. Loïc Wacquant has observed that in debates about boxing – that is, considerations of 'its (im)morality, the brutality it exemplifies and displays, the exploitation it thrives on, and the destruction it spells' – the voice of the fighters themselves is 'invariably drowned out and lost',[4] Wacquant goes on to reflect how the voices of many boxers are also largely absent from, or obscured in, media reports about the sport:

> Testimony about boxing, whether for or against, is characteristically gleaned from the pronouncements of champions, past and present, famous and infamous, as dutifully filtered and refurbished by journalists and sports writers. Occasionally one hears the views of the elite of the coaching corps or those proffered with resounding conceit by top promoters and managers, chief profiteers of this callous commerce of dreams and pain that is professional prizefighting. Only by exception do visions of the Manly art issue from the mouths of the rank and file, the 'preliminary' boxers, club fighters, prospects and contenders, journeymen and opponents, trial horses and bums, who constitute the overwhelming majority of practitioners and without whom the boxing economy would instantly collapse.[5]

It is the voices of these 'preliminary' boxers that Berry imagines in *So Long, Hector Bebb*. The use of multiple first-person narrators facilitates the expression of the testimonies of six boxers past and present, including British and Welsh champions, club fighters, former boxers, and another who suffered a brain injury in a match. Indeed, the boxing narratives (including those of the trainer, Sammy John, a veteran of the sport) constitute over half of the novel's chapters, providing an insight into their understanding of the sport; conversely, the only manager to feature in the novel, Abe Pearson, narrates only four chapters and, as I shall consider shortly, sports journalism is also questioned. The testimony of Bump Tanner, a Welsh champion, subtly expresses the poetry he perceives in boxing, describing the third round of a training bout as the '3rd stanza',[6] while Len Jules's account recalls without irony the 'pure science' he deployed in his first training session with Hector: 'Bap bap bap on his bluddy snout' (*SLHB* 125). Hector's account of his title fight with Jesse Markham reveals the mind games deployed in boxing as he reflects how in the tenth round he 'tormented' his rival, whispering into his ear 'there'll be 5 more [rounds] to go after this one', a reminder which surprises Markham and allows Hector to 'send in a nice right hook low down, safe on the mark' (*SLHB* 83–84). Through the character of the pub landlord and former boxer, Tommy Wills, Berry also finds a means to reveal his awareness of the 'filtered and refurbished' depiction of boxers in the media. When the newspapers begin to report Hector's crime, Tommy reflects on the role of journalists in the representation of experiences within the boxing ring:

> Nobody remembers fight reporters, scores of the bastards who've scribbled their blind ignorance about Dempsey, about our little Jimmy Wilde, or Maxie Baer, or Joe Louis. Parasitic bastards they are without exception. Never tell me any fight reporter, any so-called boxing expert can explain what happens when a boxer's put to sleep. (*SLHB* 117–18)

The space between experience and representation is exposed, and it is this fissure that Berry's text inhabits.

Although Berry's autobiography, *History Is What You Live*, outlines the football career of his youth, there is no acknowledgement of a similar experience of boxing.[7] Nevertheless, Berry convincingly occupies the minds of the pugilists as the voices meticulously recount the often unseen aspect of boxing, namely the training and the associated self-discipline and dedication it requires. The text outlines how much of the boxers' time is spent training, describing the efforts of the athletes in the gym, but also suggesting the relative brevity of the boxing matches. In one chapter, Hector details his early morning jogs with Sammy, recording the specifics of the activity over a series of paragraphs, and reflecting on his mental preparations: he notes that his competitor is 'fixed in [his] mind like a battery ready for flattening' (*SLHB* 28). In contrast, the same chapter recounts Hector's first match after his suspension in two short sentences: 'Pete Rider went in 3. He didn't cost much puff' (*SLHB* 29). Hector's next two fights are described in a similar manner: Joe Myers 'lasted 4. After him, George Dill went in the 8th' (*SLHB* 30). Training underscores how boxers rely on, and are defined by, their bodies. As Kath Woodward observes:

> Boxing bodies are highly regulated and self-disciplined through a set of routine practices and mechanisms so that the body becomes the inscribed surface of events combining the body practices and the traditions to which they belong. Boxing bodies are disciplined and regulated through techniques of the self.[8]

It is Sammy who provides an insight into such 'techniques of the self', reflecting on the boxer's reliance on his body and his self. He observes how:

> Fighters undertake loneliness. Welsh fighters bawling the national anthem, hearts steaming *hwyl* like hot flannels,

they're no better off. Eager teenagers coming into the game, that's the first lesson they learn. After the shouting's over you drop back into your own private skin. Then you feel empty. It's what you've got to live with, the emptiness. No slap-happy butties sharing pints, fags, victory hours, fillies, weekend hobbies. Inside the ropes the law says him versus yourself. (*SLHB* 48)

Despite the very public performance of the boxing match and the camaraderie of training, the boxer exists in his 'own private skin' and is defined by the inherent rivalry of the sport. The boxer always stands alone. The 'emptiness' that Sammy perceives is the solitary and independent nature of boxing, but also the experience of negotiating this sense of combat and solitude in life outside the ring; the 'emptiness' of the return to a normal, mortal role, after performing as a hero.

It has been observed that despite the apparent glamour of the ring, boxing is evidently a 'working-class job', a means of 'earning a living or, to be more precise, of augmenting other sources of income by exchanging the only tangible asset that those bereft of inherited wealth and educational credentials possess: their body and the abilities it harbours'.[9] As the character Tommy Wills outlines, by the end of his boxing career he was 'fighting to put up the bond' for a lease on a public house in Tosteg, as it was a reliable and accessible means of earning a wage. It is the relation of body and capital that I next wish to consider. As Berry's text accurately records, boxers are largely drawn from a working-class background – the White Hart boxers are employed as draymen and labourers. Kath Woodward argues that such class-based interpretations follow Pierre Bourdieu's assertion that 'the body is the most indisputable materialization of class taste'.[10] Woodward reflects that:

Bourdieu has argued that working-class bodily types constitute a form of physical capital that has a lower exchange value than that which has been developed by the ruling classes. Working-class people have more limited access to the means of converting physical capital into cultural capital and their physical capital is predominantly devalued. Thus boxing could be seen as a largely male, working-class engagement in converting physical capital.[11]

This conversion of physical capital into economic capital is evident in *So Long, Hector Bebb*, and it is through the character of the manager, Abe Pearson, that Berry considers the theme. It is noted early in the novel that Abe 'planned Hector's career as if the boy dropped out from a polythene bucket. Nothing malicious, simply indifference to Hector as a person' (*SLHB* 19). Abe himself reinforces this, remarking that Hector is a 'high grade machine', rather than a person; he is a means of producing capital wealth through his success in the ring (*SLHB* 23). Nevertheless, although reduced to a machine, Hector's body is central to this economic potential. Sammy recalls Hector's first training session at the White Hart as a teenager, and his first meeting with Abe. He describes how

> Abe waddled out of the office, examined the boy's hands, ran his fingertips over his eyebrows, reached down to the spinal knobs at the back of Hector's neck, and offered him a cigarette.
>   Hector said, 'Sammy reckons you want to see me in action.'
>   'G'wan then, strip off,' Abe said. (SLHB 123)

The importance of Hector's body is emphasised as he is judged by his physicality, but this is juxtaposed with Abe's waddling. Unlike the boxers he manages, Abe relies not on his own body to earn money, but on the success of the boxers, and as such, he consumes their physicality.

This scene moreover brings into focus how boxing is a union of the body and economic capital. Viewed through the corporeal/capital lens, it is evident that in de-industrialised south Wales, 'crafty old' Abe Pearson occupies a position analogous to that of the exploitative colliery owner, and the boxers echo the position of the colliers. Indeed, there are further analogies between these conventionally masculine activities. Boxing, like coal mining, is not only defined by the physicality of the action, but it is a 'highly skilled activity that requires mastery of a complex and multi layered corpus of knowledge', and reading *So Long, Hector Bebb* in the context of Berry's other writing exposes this facet of the sport.[12]

The significance of the body in boxing resonates throughout the text, as the corporeality of the other characters is also explored. Abe's grotesque corporeality is emphasised throughout the novel. Described by his wife Bella as a 'fat old pig', who grunts, as he was 'born for grunt-grunting, [being one of] these porky men' (*SLHB* 134, 64), his portrayal through the narratives of the other characters focuses on his greed, once more emphasising his role as an exploiter of the economic potential of bodies. This is reinforced by the frequent references to Abe's acts of consumption and ingestion. In an early scene, a sparring session between Hector and Bump Tanner escalates into 'a right bash-up' as they aggressively attempt to settle a disagreement (*SLHB* 32). Flesh becomes a motif of the encounter as Bump's lips are described as 'stretched like raw meat' (*ibid.*), an image that emphasises the primitive quality of the encounter, as does the description of the female audience as 'squawking like African parrots.' Abe enters the gym to investigate the commotion with 'gravy blobbing at the corners of his mouth'. Berry once more exposes the dynamic of body and capital as Abe is again physically and metaphorically consuming a product of his engineering. This image is later echoed when Sammy John remarks how Abe is 'always dragging cigar smoke with big chews of protein mushed inside his mouth. It's second nature to him, this kind of ignorance. His head treats his body like a waste pipe' (*SLHB* 76). His body is thus reduced to a vehicle of consumption and ingestion.

Although Abe is representative of base consumption, his appetite does not extend to sexual voracity and he preaches 'anti-sex mania' to the White Hart boxers (*SLHB* 69). It is through many of the female characters of the novel that Berry explores the sexual nature of bodies. Sue John, Jane Saddler, Bella Pearson and Millie Bebb all reflect on the sexual aspects of their relationships. Like the boxers, the female characters too are defined by their corporeality. Sue is a hairdresser, dedicated to maintaining the cosmetic appearances of both her female clients and herself. Indeed, Sue appears to be perfect, as Bella reflects: 'sometimes I think if I was a man I'd fall for Sue. She's ever so independent in her ways. Ever so, you'd scarcely credit. Morning, noon and night she's perfect' (*SLHB* 43). The pristine appearance conceals, and perhaps compensates for, Sue's anxieties. The 'PRIVATE' aspects of her chapters reveal that she yearns for children, the absence of which she expresses through the biology of her body: 'We never missed. Never. I wish I could miss. Once, twice. Twice makes positive, absolutely sure. Can't now. Shan't ever now. Too old.' (*SLHB* 53). Sue believes that her body has failed her ambitions to have a family, but a recollection featured in one of her husband's monologues suggests that this is not the case. Early in the novel Sam John recalls Sue's sexual assertiveness:

> Originally it was an impulse, Sue lugging me across to the studio couch every Sunday afternoon after dinner, dominating the opening gambit you might say. Because impulses become habits, I winded her. Cruel necessity poignant as drowning kittens, ramming me knee into her stomach. (*SLHB* 18)

At first it appears that Sam retaliates against his wife's initiation of the regular intimacy. His violent action reveals that he reverts to his boxing past as he attempts to reassert his dominant masculinity, but closer examination of the passage reveals an ambiguity. The action suggests a subtle brutality: the analogy of the 'poignant drowning of kittens' implies that perhaps the knee to the stomach was an attempt to cause his wife to miscarry, a 'cruel necessity' due to their regular Sunday afternoon habit.

If Sue fits the image of the dutiful good wife (albeit without children), both Bella and Millie inhabit the stereotype of the lascivious, adulterous, and dangerous wife – those who possess the agency and the will to cuckold their husbands. Bump Tanner informs the reader of the history of Abe Pearson's wife: 'Bella Will (not May) they tabbed her around Cymmer town. Years ago though, years now', suggesting her obvious sexuality (*SLHB* 69). Bella's marriage, however, is a rather chaste relationship, largely due to Abe's varicocele; she tells Sue that: 'My Abie's hopeless, helpless, useless!' (*SLHB* 104). Like Sue, Bella also faces an act of aggression in her marriage, but it is an act against her that she transforms into a sense of self-empowerment. Once again contrasting Abe's grotesque body to that of a body beautiful, in this instance, the Chinese Bends-toned body of his wife, Berry examines Abe's exploitation of power. It is Bella's body – and therefore her agency – that Abe seeks to maim when he burns his wife with a cigar, as he punishes her for attempting to persuade him to undergo an operation to remedy his varicocole, and therefore re-engage his sexuality. Bella recounts:

> He dabbed his cigar on my lovely white thigh.
> 'G'wan. Give us a scream' he says.
> I wept myself to sleep. It was quite good for me too, in a way pure relief. All Monday I felt like singing. ... Now I'm perfectly resigned to him and his varicocele thing. I'm free to come and go. As if I was a man. Neither do I have to worry about him being jealous. Abie can't take revenge like Millie Bebb's raving animal. There isn't enough physical element in my husband to do so, even make the attempt. For instance, that cigar, I wanted him to feel guilty, share some of my emotional distress, besides which a tiny scar for life isn't very important. (*SLHB 134*)

Bella uses her body against Abe. In using her physicality she realises the lack of a corresponding 'physical element' in her husband. It is evident that she believes that Abe's varicocele has emasculated him, but her act of manipulation, which culminates in the 'tiny scar', empowers her as it is a visible testimony of Abe's abuse, and an emblem of the apparent threat she poses to his authority. She uses her sexuality to exploit her husband's vulnerability, and she declares that she will adopt male behaviour, 'free to come and go' to fulfil her want, and this masculine trait is heightened as it is the White Hart boxer, Bump Tanner, a signifier of raw masculinity, that Bella first selects for an extra-marital relationship.

Hector's wife, Millie, is also defined by her body and its sexuality. At the beginning of the novel, the reader is made aware of the perceived agency of Hector's wife as Sam outlines how Sue 'dropped [Hector] when he married Millie. Her nice quiet boy grew horns and hooves in front of her eyes' (*SLHB* 16). Sue loses the surrogate son she has clothed, fed and cared for to an openly sexual younger woman. The apparent danger that Millie represents is further emphasised by Sam John's description of her visits to the White Hart gym:

> Millie wore red nylon fitting her like sprayed enamel. We had to ban her from the gym. Always theatrical, this girl, always on the verge of man-eating. ... When Millie came to the gym our boys grafted like Bedlingtons fed on bullock's blood. Hector'd have to be a buck stoat to manage, which he isn't, can't be, impossible due to his nature. ... Hungry Millie, she's always been his nuisance. (*SLHB* 46)

Millie is reduced to a sexual machine in a similar manner to the way her husband is presented as a fighting machine. The red 'sprayed enamel' conjures the bodywork of a car rather than a woman, and the connotations of power and danger further emphasise the impact of Millie's overt sexuality.

Indeed, Millie's female sexual agency is presented as though it is a mystical force – the man-eater's presence encourages the boxers, already signifiers of a powerful masculinity, to become exaggeratedly masculine as they train like 'Bedlingtons fed on bullock's blood'. But even this phrase suggests more of Millie's assertive and dangerous sexualised femininity than the masculinity of the boxers, as it is the blood of castrated bullocks, rather than bulls, that the boxers seem to have consumed.[13] Like Bella, Millie also finds herself in a sexless marriage. She describes her husband as a 'semi-eunuch' and despairs of her situation: 'Any pathetic wife who watches the moon from her bedroom window night after night has my full sympathy. It makes a woman feel out and out sick' (*SLHB* 91).

Millie cannot reconcile the different aspects of Hector that she encounters inside and outside the boxing ring. Her accounts of Hector's fights emphasise the sexualised elements of his performances: 'you only got to watch him stalking like a panther in his knicks and boots. You'd think him terrific. Ramping-tamping for a husband is what I mean' (*SLHB* 36). But her descriptions of her intimacy with Hector reveal that he is a 'Panther inside the ring, bash-bash-bash, and shivering finicky as a little cock robin once in a blue moon, I mean under the sheets' (*SLHB* 91). Hector's masculinity is distinct from his sexuality, as a reported conversation between the two characters reveals. Mille notes that Hector's asexuality 'defied human feelings', and that:

> I warned him often, 'Hector, you're acting contrary to nature, neither is it safe for you to do the dirty on our married life', and then he'd come back with, 'I'm a professional fighter not a professional effer' – using that expression. Before long I went out and about for company. (*SLHB* 36–7)

Although Hector implies that his masculine energies are directed into his boxing career, the matter of his sexless nature is ambiguous, as a scene early in the novel illustrates. In keeping with his 'anti-sex mania', Abe Pearson is keen to ascertain how Hector conducts himself. Soon after meeting the young boxer he asks Sammy whether Hector 'Chase[s] after the skirts at all? Can he behave hisself in public?', once more establishing sometimes conflicting elements of boxing, the discipline and the overt expression of masculine power (*SLHB* 13). Meanwhile, as Hector showers after a sparring session with the White Hart veteran Len Jules, his apparent shyness is questioned. Hector stands with his back turned to Len, which prompts him to question Hector's heterosexuality: ''Dear oh dear, 'ere's a little fairy in yere. Come unwell 'ave you, darlin'?' (*SLHB* 15). Hector reacts by punching Len twice, 'left hook, shovel hook, dumping Jules in the rim of the bath', but the question of his sexual orientation remains. Sam reports that when he and Hector next meet with Abe, the matter is raised once again:

> 'Len Jules started it, Mr Pearson. He tried to make out I was a poof or something. I can take a joke as good as the next, but Len got too pers'nal. No call for that.'
> 'Are you laddie?' squeaked Abe, fatly immobile, his scrapey voice threatening like rust.
> I said, 'He's as normal as I am. Len's got a mad sense of humour. I'd hang one on him and all if he insulted me.'
> Abe did Shylock with both palms. 'I'm enquiring off the boy Sammy.' (*SLHB* 15–6)

Hector does not answer the question. It is irrelevant to his success as a boxer, but the issue is never resolved.

The novel also uses the lens of the body to consider violence. Through the characters of Prince Jenkin Saddler, Mel Carpenter, Vic Crane and Hector, Berry examines the victims, perpetrators and effects of aggression. Prince and Mel signify the victims of violence as they are both maimed bodies: Prince bears the scars and wounds of war, and Mel lives with a brain injury he suffered during a match with

Hector. The soldier-warrior figure, in combination with the boxing-heroes, allows Berry to consider the liminal, and sometimes morally ambiguous, distinction between controlled, accepted aggression and instinctual, transgressive violence. Prince Jenkin embodies the role of acceptable aggression, but his scars and amputation signify something of the uncanny. His disfigurement also unsettles the female characters: Sue describes him as 'a peculiar gentleman. Something gone wrong with him only she didn't know what exactly, apart from the empty sleeve and scarred face', and Bella too is disconcerted: 'That awful man from the farm. Dreadful person, just staring, staring, stripping me down to the skin with his eyes' (*SLHB* 113, 66). Prince Jenkin's maimed body is emblematic of the unseen horror of war that the characters cannot comprehend. It is Sammy who first suggests that Prince Jenkin's appearance reveals and exposes an unacknowledged aspect of humanity:

> He had dark brown eyes, dry, flat dark as flakes of chocolate, the left side of his face gouged from cheekbone to jaw, faintly mapped purple, pale purple. Usually he left his artificial hand contraption in the car. You couldn't imagine Prince enjoying a social function, those metal falsies grabbing and pouring condiments over his vittles. Maybe we're all of us left cripples ourselves, I mean the way our ordinary cripples scrimp along in the rat race. (*SLHB* 75)

Prince Jenkin's appearance exposes an emptiness that the other characters obscurely sense, but never acknowledge or confront.

Like Hector, Prince Jenkin stands apart from the norm, a shared aspect that, once more, the perceptive veteran of boxing, Sammy, first observes: 'The man's different from the rest of us, though you [Hector] got a touch of it in you too, boyo.' (*SLHB* 74). Prince Jenkin also comes to acknowledge Hector's difference:

'The man is exceptional Jane, he's designed outside of
rote, that stale so-called chemistry, the jiggery-pokery of
what it takes and means to be a man.'
'Hyperbole,' I said. 'You are trying to glorify mundane
reality.'
'He accepts me for what I am,' the lonely hand rising,
lifted slack-palmed against his chest.
... 'I feel we shall soldier on, two maimed individuals
as it were, side by side.' (*SLHB* 121)

There is the suggestion that both Hector and the war
veteran have glimpsed something in the violent scenes they
have enacted: indeed, the brutal energy of Hector's fights is
expressed in their description as 'real massacres' (*SLHB*,
123). Later in the novel, Hector seems to convey this sense
of the uncanny in his accounts of experiences in the hills
above Tosteg and Cymmer. The shift to the near-wilderness
landscape sees Hector step out of society and return to an
earlier means of solitary existence; he is imagined as a
character of his wild habitat. Described as possessing an
'aboriginal certitude' and as a primitive 'geared to survival',
he is a figure who seems to belong in the environment of an
earlier time (*SLHB* 153). The indigenous quality of Hector
is emphasised as he is seen to enact the 'meaningless,
familiar passion of a man matched to his environment' as he
works the land, tending to the livestock and hunting with
Prince (*SLHB* 151). It is in this setting that the most violent
scene in the novel occurs. Attempting to survive on the hills,
Hector must hunt for food. As a ewe and her lamb graze
near the abandoned colliery, he realises the prospect of a
hot meal and decides to kill the sheep, an act presented as
a primal act of opportunism:

I heard her hooves on the fallen stones. As her black nose
came level I hit her one CLUNK, like wood on wood.
Flinging out to full length I grabbed her hind legs. She
was trapped. But I lost true sight, everything fuzzy and
Roman candles firing inside my chest. Strength came in
spasms, although I robbed myself, the lamb bleating,

bleating, tormenting my mind. Blood splashed over my trousers. Heavy drops of rain began to fall. By and by, dead lamb, unconscious ewe, me straddled over her, both of us quite still. (*SLHB* 194)

The violence is enacted in an unwilled wild frenzy; Hector loses 'true sight', and seems only to become aware of his actions as the blood stains his trousers. The phrase 'I robbed myself' again suggests that Hector undoes aspects of himself as he bludgeons the ewe; indeed, the primal violence contrasts with the controlled aggression and skill he exhibits in the boxing ring. The sense that Hector steps out of himself in the frenzy is further underlined by his reflection that the lamb has been torn to pieces: 'bits left of him, poor mite' (*SLHB* 196). In observing the carcass of the lamb, and burying it, Hector distances himself from his violent actions and returns to more civilised behaviour. It is this boundary between conscious control and subconscious wildness that Prince Saddler also appears to have transgressed. Mel Carpenter, too, has glimpsed this boundary. His fractured language, in particular his reduction of a hymn into an impolite, syllabic form (the refrain 'Onward Christian Soldiers, marching as to war, / with the cross of Jesus marching on before' is rendered as 'arse stew or, wee thack crass awe Jee-hee-hee-zuz mar chin none beef hoar!' (*SLHB* 100) suggests that he is trapped in the transgressive and primitive space.

The exposure of this narrow boundary between the civilised and the barbaric encourages the reader to perceive the wildness of the other characters in the novel: in their obvious sexuality and apparent thrall to biology, Sue, Bella and Millie all reveal a primal nature. The uncivilised aspects of the civilised society are also exposed, for example in the narration of Vic Crane's violent attacks on young girls, which Hector describes as 'He did a bad thing to that young girl. Pushed her face into a wire netting fence', and reflects that 'there's no root blame. No remedy either. ... Everybody failed, Vic being untameable. Not his fault' (*SLHB* 30). For a character familiar with the aggression and violence of boxing, it is an unusually coy manner in which to describe a brutal act. As such, the timid description suggests a more depraved act of sexual violence. The reactions to Hector's act of 'legitimate husband's revenge' against his wife's lover, Emlyn Winton (*SLHB* 52 also reveals how deplorable violence can be accepted. Tommy Wills, a pub landlord and former opponent of Hector, reflects that Hector should have marked Millie for life, 'put her nose out like mine is. What's the satisfaction in duffing the bloke?', proposing that domestic violence is a legitimate response to infidelity (*SLHB* 117).

The focus on the body in *So Long, Hector Bebb* allows Berry to reveal that Hector is not the only 'trained animal' to reside in the Cymmer community. The motif of boxing reveals the infrastructures of society that contain and conceal the latent wildness of humanity and, as the chorus of voices reports, the effects of transgressing these boundaries resonate. As the novel concludes, it is useless for the residents of Cymmer to offer 'so long to Hector', as his actions have unravelled their veil of civilised, acceptable, behaviour.

NOTES
1   Berry's 1968 novel *Flame and Slag* saw Berry experiment with some first-person narration through the device of a character's private journal. The narrative structure of *So Long Hector Bebb* is reminiscent of William Faulkner's *As I Lay Dying*, an aspect of the text that deserves further investigation.
2   *Times Literary Supplement*, 1 January 1971, p. 5.
3   The heterogeneous narration also allows Berry to ventriloquise first-person female voices for the first time, a device which facilitates the articulation of feminine identities, as well as masculine, an aspect I shall return to consider later in this analysis.
4   Loïc Wacquant, 'The pugilistic point of view: How boxers think and feel about their trade', *Theory and Society*, 24, 4, pp. 489–535, (489).

5   Wacquant, p. 490.

6   Ron Berry, *So Long, Hector Bebb* (Cardigan: Parthian, 2005 [1970]), p. 34. Henceforth referred to in the text as *SLHB*.

7   Ron Berry, *History Is What You Live* (Llandysul: Gomer, 1998), p. 147.

8   Kath Woodward, *Boxing, Masculinity, and Identity: The 'I' of the Tiger*, (London: Routledge, 2007), p. 68.

9   Wacquant, p. 501.

10   Pierre Bourdieu, *Distinction: A Social Critique of the Judgement of Taste*, p. 190, cited in Kath Woodward, p. 36.

11   Woodward, p. 36.

12   Wacquant, p. 503.

13   It is worthwhile examining how Millie's appearance declines after the death of Emlyn and the disappearance of Hector. She is still defined by her body, but it is a grotesque one.

'It Was Forbidden, Strictly Forbidden':

Contesting Taboo in Bernice Rubens'
I Sent a Letter to My Love

Michelle Deininger

Spanning twenty-four published novels, Bernice Rubens' fictions represent an eclectic mix of styles, genres and subjects. Born in Cardiff in 1928, of Lithuanian-Jewish descent, she enjoyed a successful writing career extending over forty years, including winning the Booker Prize for *The Elected Member* (1969), until her death in 2004. While many of these novels deal with issues directly related to her Jewish heritage, notably *Brothers* (1983), which traces the survival of four generations of a Jewish family, some, such as *Yesterday in the Back Lane* (1995) and *I Sent a Letter to My Love* (1975), contain Welsh settings. Despite her obvious interest in writing about Wales, critical material on Rubens has tended to focus on her place as a Jewish writer, or as a Jewish writer within British culture, rather than within Welsh culture specifically.[1] Yet, at the same time, she does not sit entirely easily within the emergent category of Welsh writing in English, perhaps on account of the way in which, as critics such as Katie Gramich have noted, she 'tend[s] to compartmentalize her works into those dealing with Jewish relationships and those which are set in Wales'.[2] It would clearly not, then, be possible simply to re-label Rubens as a Welsh writer without ignoring some problematic questions about her writing and also effacing a significant part of her cultural and imaginative heritage. Instead, her fictions are situated at a particularly fruitful intersection of identities – not just the 'divided sensibility' that has been discussed by historians such as Dai Smith, of being both British and Welsh, but a multiple, complex and necessarily hybrid synthesis of a traditionally marginalised Jewish identity within this already multifarious context.

Not only does the content of her fiction cause difficulty in determining where she fits as a writer, but the way in which she writes causes similar dilemmas. Thus, critics have drawn attention to her 'unique' style[3] and the 'maddening refusal [of her writing] to fit neatly into any single category'.[4] There is, then, something intrinsically discomfiting about her writing because she cannot be successfully classified or pigeonholed. If we focus on the novel in question, *I Sent a Letter to My Love*, this sense of unease, of discomfort, constantly confronts the reader through the text's content, themes, imagery and, especially, language. Set in the 'one-eyed'[5] seaside town of Porthcawl, the novel depicts the struggle of siblings Amy and Stan Evans, and their close friend, Gwyneth Price, against the overwhelming tediousness of their everyday existence. Having suffered from rickets in childhood, Stan, now in his fifties, is confined to a wheelchair. His younger sister, Amy, who has never married nor even experienced any kind of sustained sexual or romantic relationship, is his primary carer. Gwyneth, the third member of this peculiar triangle, is still a virgin despite her advancing years.

Much of the novel's tension and drama revolves around Amy placing an advert in the personal column of the local paper under the pseudonym of 'Blodwen Pugh'. Instead of the numerous potential suitors that Amy anticipates rescuing her from her life of drudgery caring for Stan, she receives just one reply – from her brother. The second part of the novel traces their increasingly sexualised correspondence and the impact their burgeoning relationship has on them as individuals, as siblings, and on their friendship with Gwyneth. By the end of the novel, a marked shift has taken place – Stan has ended the relationship with 'Blodwen', choosing instead to marry Gwyneth, while Amy has taken to her bed in the grip of an 'emotional paralysis' (202). The novel ends, as it begins, with a desolate image of 'screech[ing]' gulls, while Amy lies dying on the bedroom floor, surrounded by the scattered love letters, material evidence of the deception that she had so desperately hoped to hide from Stan.

The very subject matter of the novel, a quasi-incestuous correspondence between brother and sister, should alert the reader to the fact that Rubens is not afraid to tackle topics that many writers would typically avoid. The novel is, as a whole, constantly probing the nature of social taboos and the impact these taboos have on ordinary people, and, most importantly, transgressing and contesting those taboos. One of the ways the text achieves this is by the examination and unpicking of taboo words, including – but not limited to – swear words. Ranging from 'cripple' to the phrase 'Fuck, fuck', these words are predominantly uttered, contrary to type, by the frumpy, middle-aged Amy. At the same time, the central female characters, Amy and Gwyneth, construct an alternative vocabulary to describe and manage aspects of the changing world around them that are, in their opinion, taboo – such as women wearing trousers or advertising themselves in lonely hearts' columns. These taboos are all in some way connected back to the body and sexual desire – either physically or psychologically. As the earlier reference to 'cripple' may suggest, the text is also concerned with disability, especially the needs, wants and desires, especially sexual desires, of the disabled body – desires which, traditionally, have been either ignored or considered taboo. Given the novel's complex exploration of taboo and its wide-ranging implications, it is perhaps unsurprising that any theoretical perspective used to discuss it will be correspondingly complex and multifaceted. Indeed, it has been necessary to draw on elements of sociolinguistics, psychoanalysis, the intersection of feminist, postcolonial and disability theories, and even fashion history to attempt to assemble some kind of usable framework with which to explore the novel.

Forbidden Words

Perhaps one of the most initially striking aspects of the novel is its preoccupation with obscene, offensive or forbidden words. Seemingly unconcerned by social conventions regarding polite and proper language, Amy Evans swears frequently throughout the novel, using the phrase 'Fuck, fuck' on many occasions. One especially shocking use of this obscenity occurs when Amy attempts to steal a frame, containing a likeness of the imaginary Blodwen Pugh, from a photographer's shop in Porth. Slowed down by a 'long hesitation' (97) and mounting fear, she is caught in the act by a small girl. Although Amy is able to talk her way out of trouble, she is publicly accused again by the little girl on the bus home. When the child and her mother get off, Amy slyly waits until the bus pulls away and then, as she turns to look out the window, she strikes back:

> She poked out her tongue, so far it hurt, and put her fingers to her nose at the same time. 'Fuck, fuck,' she mouthed to the little girl and her astonished mam, and felt vastly better for giving them something to gawp about. She'd had the last word, for the bus drew away before they could retaliate even in gesture. (103)

Within the field of sociolinguistics, the issue of perceptions surrounding how much women swear has been the subject of some scrutiny. For example, Tony McEnery notes:

> One might imagine that males use bad language more than females. Indeed it has been suggested in the past – especially in research in the 1970s – that swearing was a behaviour engaged in more frequently by males than by females ... it is still ... a widely held folk belief in Britain that men swear more often than women. This is clearly not the case.[6]

In the context of the 1970s, then, the depiction of a woman swearing challenges the assumption that such taboo language is only exploitable by men. Furthermore, an 'old woman' (97) like Amy is not supposed to be swearing, and especially not at small children. As McEnery also notes, older people as a group, especially of Amy's age, use this type of language least, 'avoid[ing] the largest number of BLWs [bad language words] as a consequence'.[7] While the theft of the frame is described as 'almost an act of defiance' (97), Amy's obscene language can be viewed as equally rebellious. Her language, and especially her resulting sense of empowerment, can be read as a type of resistance that seeks to undermine stereotypes of women, especially older women, as polite and self-effacing.[8]

Amy's swearing is perhaps even more prevalent in her youth. It is difficult to avoid constructing a psychoanalytic reading of this behaviour as the text repeatedly points towards Amy's foul-mouthed disobedience being directly related to her mother's coldness towards her. Even the relationship depicted, albeit only fleetingly, by the mother and daughter in the photographer's shop contains more solidarity and warmth. When the reader's attention is first drawn to Amy's rude vocabulary, it is when her mother publicly humiliates her. While the angelic Stan is allowed to wander onto the beach so that the weekend picnickers can 'stare and wonder at his beauty', Amy is swiftly removed as her mother 'guide[s] her away from others' opinion', while 'pinch[ing] her stubby nose' (8). This physical underlining of Amy's 'squat' nose, 'stubbed onto her face like a plasticine afterthought' (4), clearly causes Amy much emotional anguish. She responds to her mother's public rejection of her by 'hurry[ing] down to the sea, saying over and over again, "Fuck, fuck"' (9). Research into the motivation behind swearing has revealed that 'Most cussing is an emotive reaction to anger, frustration, or something unexpected and usually, but not necessarily, undesirable.'[9] Indeed, it is been demonstrated in studies of the brain that

> Swearing and cussing ... is almost certainly a function of
> the right hemisphere of the brain for a majority of the
> population, whereas normal language functions are
> carried out by and in the left brain. The right brain deals
> with emotions.[10]

Swearing, then, is effectively hardwired into the emotional
rather than the rational aspects of the psyche, suggesting
that Amy's fondness for obscenity runs deeper than a
desire to shock or misbehave. It can, instead, be read both
as a means of release and as an anguished plea for
attention and affection.

Later, Amy encounters a man the text repeatedly refers
to as 'the pussy-man' (14), presumably a paedophile, who
offers her money to 'come in the fields', an invitation
which is revised to 'Fourpence to have a look at [her] pussy'
(13). She tells him he can 'have a look for a million
pounds' (13) but warns that her mother will be along
shortly. Undeterred, the 'pussy-man' replies: 'I'll wait for
your mam, then ... P'raps she'll show me *her* pussy for
fourpence' (13). There are several key preoccupations at
work in this disconcerting exchange. First, even as a young
girl, Amy's sense of self-worth is clearly already damaged.
She does not believe she is worth that much, as her mother
has 'conditioned her to knowing her value as less than
nothing' (13). Second, she tells the man with 'utter
conviction' that 'Our Mam hasn't got a pussy' (13),
underlining the text's anxieties about the denial and
repression of bodies as sexual entities, not least women's
bodies – issues that we will return to later. Third, the
exchange brings to light Amy's 'lexicon of words without
meaning' (10), which, aside from 'pussy', include words
such as 'sickly child' and 'rickets' (6). This gap in meaning
in Amy's 'lexicon of words' again underlines a predominant
theme in the novel – the anxieties associated with
confronting words that have come to be taboo. When Amy
asks 'What's a sickly child?' (6), her mother 'simply
stretche[s] across and slap[s] her face' (6). Similarly, when

she asks 'What's rickets?' she has to 'dodg[e] her mam's outstretched and stinging palm' (6). In his study of swearing, Timothy Jay notes:

> Parents try to tell their children that using dirty words openly is not permissible and rules of etiquette are observed. Breaking the rules can result in physical punishment, such as a slap in the face or having a mouth washed out with soap.[11]

In the text, words such as 'cripple' and phrases such as 'sickly child' take on the same offensive connotations as actual swear words and are punished accordingly. As they are never properly explained to Amy, they remain elusive and undefined. Amy herself remains somehow excluded from this type of vocabulary, and is then severely limited in the way she can articulate taboo subjects later in life.

'Oh, there's disgusting': Articulating Repressed Desires

If these forbidden words have a negative, punitive association for Amy, it is little wonder that for other aspects of her life, especially as a grown woman, she develops an alternative way of talking about taboo subjects. One particularly interesting example can be found in the text's discussion of women wearing trousers. Women of Amy and Gwyneth's generation, born during the 1920s and 1930s, would have seen an increasing number of women adopting trousers as a mode of dress for use in sport, leisure activities or on holidays. However, as fashion historians have noted, during the 1930s trousers for women 'were not considered acceptable to many people in other more formal situations such as work, for evenings, or shopping and sightseeing in town'.[12] Trousers would then be associated in the minds of women of Amy's age with a certain frivolity, informality and leisure. By the 1960s, French designers such as André

Courrèges had ensured that unisex apparel such as the trouser suit became extremely fashionable. Indeed, Porthcawl boasts a 'posh shop on the pier', Pugh's, that stocks 'dresses made in Paris, and trousers too' (63) and it is because of these exotic associations that Amy chooses the name Pugh for her alter ego, Blodwen. The idea of women wearing trousers suggests not just frivolity and leisure but the changing way women can construct their identity in public. The female body in trousers is unhindered in carrying out practical tasks, is much more physically defined, and is, therefore, more obviously noticeable as a sexual body. For Amy at least, however illicit their associations, trousers represent the possibility of escape and freedom – of an opportunity 'to change the non-style she had worn all her life' (65).

In contrast to the static insularity of Porthcawl, Amy wants something different, something more fulfilling. Struggling through another morning of the same 'tired repetitive ... dialogue' that Amy, Gwyneth and Stan share every day in the Evans' kitchen, Amy 'suddenly ... crave[s] some change' (35). She disrupts the monotonous exchange by refusing to speak her usual lines. On another morning, she goes a step further and changes her lines completely, musing that she will grow her hair long or even perm it. It is her last suggestion for self-reinvention that floors both Gwyneth and Stan as she declares: 'Might even buy myself a pair of trousers ... They're all the rage now' (51). Completely taken by surprise, Stan laughs while Gwyneth has fears about Amy's 'sanity' (51). Amy knows that the only way of saving face is to 'pretend that it had all been a joke' and so 'join[s] in their laughter' (51), but this does not detract from the fact that her disruption of their usual roles and lines is a form of resistance, of reforming the shape of their relationship. For Gwyneth, the idea of trousers can only be suitably described with the word 'Disgusting' (51). This, the text points out, has become an 'overworked word' and that 'considering [Gwyneth] and Amy shared it equally, it was a wonder it had not lost all its meaning' (51). This word, then, appears to be very closely related to Amy's lexicon of words without meaning – it has to do so much work, cover so many subjects, that it risks having no actual meaning at all. Yet despite this risk, the word acts as an outlet for feelings which have been repressed or are impossible to articulate in any less general terms – Amy and Gwyneth are 'able to pronounce it with such venom and such spleen' (51) of which both have 'ample supply' that this word 'could have done overtime for ever without losing one iota of its rage' (52).

When both women muster the courage to wear these 'disgusting' trousers, it is Gwyneth in fact who has been far more transgressive. When the three go on a picnic to the beach, she slides down a sand dune and frays the seat of her trousers so badly that the others can see the 'blistered and trellised evidence of Gwyneth's secret' – that 'Gwyneth "Intacta" Price wasn't wearing any knickers' (136). This revelation gives Stan the opportunity to give vent to his increasing sexual appetite by calling out 'Seen your bum, I did … Your red bum', while 'relishing' this word's 'filth like a child' (136). What is significant about this scene is that Stan has been able to master a vocabulary for his changing sexual desires that is, as yet, unavailable to the women. Much like his stamp collection, which is in fact camouflage for his assortment of pornographic photographs, Stan has access to an alternative way of approaching his sexuality. While he can use words like 'bum', the women have not yet been able to seize anything beyond 'disgusting'. In fact, it is this very word which Amy exclaims when she discovers the pornography, although this is partly to 'offset the enjoyment of her viewing' (77). 'Disgusting' provides a means, however inadequate, to give voice to both women's subconscious desires.

While Stan eases his sexual frustrations under the cover of his so-called stamp collection, articulating the word 'disgusting' is, sadly, the closest Gwyneth comes to any kind of sexual fulfilment. When Amy admits to her that she gets 'a bit of fun from reading' the lonely hearts column at the back of the paper, albeit carefully qualified with 'Disgusting it is' (48), the reaction provoked in Gwyneth is far from calm. The text continues:

> 'Oh, there's disgusting,' Gwyneth said. 'Marriages are made in heaven, not in newspapers. Isn't that right, Stan?' ... Gwyneth screwed the paper into a ball, wringing it with anger. 'Disgusting,' she spat, wringing it tight again. And when no more filth could come out, she dropped it exhausted into the basket. 'Disgusting,' she almost screamed. It was the nearest Gwyneth 'Intacta' Price would ever come to an orgasm. (49)

This description evokes an earlier scene in which Amy, having read the newspaper, with increasingly frequent references to its content being 'disgusting' (the personal columns being 'the most disgusting of all'), wonders to herself 'what the world [is] coming to' but 'half fear[s], and more than hope[s], that she too could be swept along by the filthy tide that engulfed it' (34). While Amy finds some sort of satisfaction through her textual relationship with Stan, a way through the 'dark corridors of joy' which for both her and Stan their 'separate disorders had forbidden' (128), Gwyneth remains, apart from some bottom-pinching and general teasing from Stan, unfulfilled. Moreover, as the text ends while she is marrying Stan, the sex that would presumably follow remains forever displaced beyond the novel's conclusion. There is a sense, then, that both women are ill equipped to deal with a society which, in a rapid state of post-war change, has begun to recognise and advocate a more liberal sexual identity for women.

Taboo Bodies

The novel's engagement with the issue of unfulfilled sexual desire also extends beyond the failure of language adequately to describe experience, and questions what sort of bodies can be represented as having these impulses, lusts, and needs. Disabled bodies are intrinsically 'taboo' within the conventions of what constitutes 'normal' within society. Physical disability is often a visible marker of difference from the average human body, whether through genetics, disease or accident. Freud discusses how 'Anyone who has violated a taboo becomes taboo himself because he possesses the dangerous quality of tempting others to follow his example' and so is 'truly contagious in that every example encourages imitation, and for that reason he himself must be shunned.'[13] There is a sense that the disabled body, made taboo by being different, is also somehow contagious. Even Amy, when she becomes gripped by paralysis at the end of the novel, is assumed by other people to have 'caught it from Stan' (210). Concomitant with this idea of contagion is a deep-seated fear of discernible mortality. As Stan realises, when looking at the wooden arm of Gwyneth's amputee brother, Huw, there is the palpable presence of death in bodies which do not comply with society's standards – Huw's wooden arm 'call[s] attention to the death in him, to his part-by-part dissolution' (82). In the light of these preconceptions about disability, it is not difficult to see why the sexual needs and desires of disabled bodies are supposed equally taboo. Working against these negative connotations, the novel attempts to construct identities that are far more complex and, at times, affirmative.

As we have already explored, 'cripple' is a forbidden term, a 'taboo in the house' (89) of Stan and Amy's youth. Even in middle age, the word has lost none of its negative associations for Amy. When Stan declares 'There's many a girl in Porthcawl would have me, cripple or no' (104), Amy 'shudder[s]', presumably in revulsion or shock. The word connotes dirt, especially in the imagery of the word 'drop[ping] from his lips, as lightly as a crumb from her sponge cake', detritus which Amy 'would have liked to [have swept up] with her dustpan so that it was all nice and tidy as it had been before' (104). This imagery of consumption resonates with the text's earlier presentation of Stan's 'relish' for the word 'bum,' his 'predilection' for which 'fe[eds] on its constant use' (136).[14] Stan will no longer accept Amy's refusal to acknowledge this description of his condition, insisting that it is time they both 'faced the facts' (104). Moving on from the image of the spilt food, the language takes on a distinctly sexual flavour as Amy imagines how 'In no time the carpet would be covered with his ejaculation' (104). The word 'cripple' becomes a kind of self-arousal, even verbal masturbation that will leave 'a permanent stain that no amount of cleaning ... would remove' (104). This sexualised vocabulary is further underlined when Amy finally articulates these 'terrible words' herself: '"You're a cripple," she shouted, and her anger excited her to repeat it. "A cripple. Always was. Always will be."' (105). She then describes herself as 'an old maid' which Stan repeats as 'Old maid Amy Evans, ... always was, always will be' (105). This use of 'approved labellings', of naming each other into acceptance, stirs up 'the beginnings of liberation' (105). No longer bound by these categories, this act of articulation takes on a deeper significance – of the capacity to live beyond the limits that their social roles of 'cripple' and spinster ascribe them, and to value the bodies that have been branded by these terms.

The theme of disability has a wider focus than just Stan's wheelchair-bound body. In her own way Amy is just as damaged as her brother, particularly in terms of her sexual self-esteem. The latter has been defined as 'the value one places on oneself as a sexual being, including sexual identity and perceptions of sexual acceptability'.[15] A recent study has demonstrated that when sexual self-esteem is 'damaged, the individual's self-view, satisfaction with life, capability to experience pleasure, willingness to interact with others and ability to develop intimate relationships may be limited'.[16] This description clearly has much bearing on the way Amy is presented in the novel. For instance, she cannot look at herself in the mirror in Pugh's, deciding that 'It would take a monumental act of heroism to face a mirror unclothed' (66). She has only ever had sex once, with a French soldier whose name she did not even know (she refers to him, pitifully enough, as 'Parlee Voo'), and it is only in her later years that she is able to open up and love properly, although not through a conventional relationship.

It has been suggested that damage to sexual self-esteem can occur when an individual has been 'harshly insulted and embarrassed'.[17] Looking back at Amy's past, to the episode on the beach where her mother tugs at her nose, unwilling to exhibit her purportedly ugly daughter to the Sunday picnickers, it is clear to see where Amy's unhappiness with her appearance stems from. However, it is perhaps the incident that occurs when Amy finds herself pregnant by the nameless French solider that consolidates this sense of self-loathing. Desperate for a bottle of gin to induce a miscarriage, she goes to the American Forces camp, 'prepared to give them a feel in the blackout, and a bit more if that was the going price for a bottle of gin' (39). However, she has not reckoned with them examining her 'in the cruel light of their torches', as one of the soldiers shines one 'brutally into her face' (39). They give a 'low and long whistle' which both she and they know is a 'catcall' (39), which, by definition, is intended to express sexual attraction or admiration. The words used to describe their actions, such as 'cruel' and 'harsh,' suggest a kind of psychological, if not sexual, assault, while the 'catcall' is meant to be derogatory and humiliating – instead of inviting her to join them, they throw 'the torch at her feet' and turn their backs on her, 'laughing' (39). What is especially interesting about reading Amy in the light of these theories about sexual self-esteem is that the study in question proposes that a severe lack of this esteem 'can constitute a disability that significantly interferes with the individual's functioning'.[18] It would not be so great a leap, then, to suggest that Amy is as disabled as Stan, through her self-perception as ugly, fat and unlovable. It would also follow that Amy is just as imprisoned by the society in which she lives as Stan is – physiologically unscathed, but psychologically damaged, perhaps irreparably. At the same time it situates Amy's sexual needs and desires as being as taboo as Stan's.

Strategies of Resistance

While the text draws attention to some negative aspects of psychological and physical disability, it seems far more concerned with striving to evade, resist and even rewrite disabled bodies and to defuse the taboos surrounding them. Exploring these textual strategies involves drawing, albeit from a literary perspective, on linguistic theories regarding the notion of 'face', as well as the concept of politeness theory. Erving Goffman has described the term 'face' as 'the positive social value a person effectively claims for himself [sic]' and 'an image of self delineated in terms of approved social attributes'.[19] Developing aspects of Goffman's theories, Penelope Brown, in her work on politeness theory, has questioned the traditional assumption that women are, on the whole, more polite than men, arguing that, in fact, 'the relationship between the status of women and the politeness or formality of their speech is by no means as simple and straightforward as has been assumed'.[20] Consideration for others' feelings is bound up in the notion of face, Brown argues – 'desires to not be imposed upon (negative face), and desires to be liked, admired ratified, related to positively (positive face)'.[21] She goes on to describe 'positive politeness' as an attempt to 'disarm threats to positive face' while 'strategies of negative politeness' are

essentially avoidance-based, and consist in assurances
that the speaker recognizes and respects the addressee's
negative face and will not (or will only minimally)
interfere with his or her freedom of action.[22]

What is especially interesting about Brown's arguments is
that she attempts to posit two further hypotheses at the
end of her article, one of which is particularly valuable in
discussing *I Sent a Letter to My Love*. Brown argues that
'Deference (and, in general, negative politeness) prevails if
and where people are in a position of vulnerability or
inferiority in a society. Hence women in an inferior, less
powerful position than men will be likely to use more
negative politeness.'[23] As a disabled individual, Stan is
situated in a similarly marginalised position to women –
vulnerable because of his physical frailties and deemed
inferior by those around him. The taxi driver at Coney
Beach, for example, 'babie[s] him as automatically as he
would have shouted at a foreigner, for both in his eyes were
retarded' (53). In terms of self-effacing modes of
politeness, the reader will perhaps be reminded of Stan's
line throughout the novel, 'There's good you are to me,
Amy' (23). The parallels between Stan's vulnerable position
as a disabled person and that of other groups become more
apparent as Brown goes on to argue:

> However if women are so inferior as to have no face at all
> (like children, or beggars, or slaves, who in many
> societies are treated as having no face), the particular
> strategies of negative politeness they use will be different
> than in societies where women are accorded some social
> esteem.[24]

Within Brown's hypothesis, it could be argued that there is
space for marginalised or peripheral identities, people who
have no face to speak of, to adopt different types of
strategies within social interactions, allowing them to stand
outside the accepted norms of polite behaviour, and

perhaps even to subvert those strategies. They can, in a sense, claim a position of power outside the rules of the dominant discourse. The recurring invocation of 'There's good you are to me' is a case in point when it resurfaces at the end of the novel, this time with a very different twist. Unable (or simply unwilling) to make preparations for Stan and Gwyneth's wedding, the bedridden Amy parrots her brother's line: 'There's good you are to me, Gwyneth' (205). This is not, however, straightforward mimicry. The text is emphasising the reversal in roles – Gwyneth has become the carer, taking on Amy's role, while Amy has taken on the identity of the weakened, disabled body hitherto associated with her brother.

As we have seen, the disabled body has connotations of contagion and death but there are ways in which this position of supposed vulnerability is rewritten as a position of power. Early on in the novel, Amy wonders to herself whether Stan is hiding something behind the screen of his 'saintly smile' and whether he has 'all his life ... colonised and hated [his parents] for creating and making such a puppet of him' (74). The significance of this ambiguous word 'colonise' becomes altogether clearer, however, by the end of the novel, as the reader begins to realise that Stan has been in a position of power all along. Arguably suggesting a sense of exploitation and forcible appropriation, the word denotes a subtle shift in the power relations at work in the novel. As Foucault has argued, 'power is tolerable only on condition that it mask a substantial part of itself. Its success is proportional to its ability to hide its own mechanisms.'[25] Stan's position has been similarly masked throughout – not the puppet, but the puppeteer, pulling the strings of the other characters to attain his desires. A prime example of this can be traced back to the stamp collection for which Stan asks Amy to buy him a registered envelope every week. Amy feels 'angry' that he has 'pulled such a fast one on her' (78) for so many years, as she has been unwittingly adding to his collection of 'dreadful couplings underneath his mattress' (78). When Amy herself becomes paralysed, she does not feel in a position of weakness, but instead feels 'like a conqueror' (203). She not only appropriates Stan's phrases but also the 'colonising power of a cripple' (p. 203), suggesting that this perceived position of infirmity has its own covert strategies of power. Moreover, the text has rewritten the disabled body as a nexus of power – power which is not fixed and monolithic but shifting, relational, and, ultimately, subversive.

It is evident from this examination of *I Sent a Letter to My Love* that taboo functions within the text in complex and myriad ways. Taboo language is extremely important, whether in terms of the emotional response affixed to swear words, or the power relations at play in complexes of taboo words that exclude or include those who try to speak and understand them. There is a strong gender bias regarding who has the power to master new vocabularies and the fact that Stan can employ new words to describe his sexual awakening, while the women have to endure the inadequacy of 'disgusting', underlines the text's engagement with the problems women face in grasping power, both in and through language. At the same time, this word does of course allow the female characters access to a limited, though meaningful, language of sexuality. This limited language underlines the text's preoccupation with the way in which women like Amy and Gwyneth are ill-equipped, particularly linguistically, to deal with changing standards in society which encourage and enable women to embrace themselves as sexual beings with legitimate needs and desires. While the position of women is actively questioned, it is the text's persistent undermining of the negative connotations of disabled bodies that is perhaps the most radical aspect of the entire novel. These bodies can move beyond the labels that have been ascribed to them, beyond being crippled or deformed, whether mentally or physically, and can aspire to the kind of meaningful sexual relationships that have so long been viewed as taboo. Moreover, the text insists on the validity of providing space for marginalised identities, the destabilisation of the weakness traditionally ascribed to them, and, especially, the rewriting of these identities as sites of power.

Clearly, the intricacies and implications, however provisional and cursory, of the significance of taboo in *I Sent a Letter to My Love* bring to light a large number of issues that demand further exploration in future criticism on Rubens. At the same time, this particular novel could be considered as a powerful intervention in the dialogue between feminism, postcolonial theories and disability studies. Indeed, the representation of marginalised identities in the novel resonates strongly with the parallels Rosemarie Garland Thomson has emphasised 'between the social meanings attributed to female bodies and those assigned to disabled bodies', including 'exclus[ion] from full participation in public as well as economic life'.[26] In the growing corpus of texts in the field of Welsh writing in English, there are many examples of bodies which have been damaged, dismembered or born disabled. Drawing on the work of postcolonial critic Ato Quayson, Stephen Knight notes that various texts 'bring forward to consciousness the images of disability that have had a covert presence in the post-war imagination'.[27] Quayson himself points to the way in which colonialism can be viewed as having been a 'major force of disabling the colonized from taking their place in the flow of history other than in a position of stigmatized underprivilege'.[28] In Quayson's work, images of disability seem to be the metaphorical scars or vestiges of anxiety that linger in literary representations of countries hit hardest by colonialist subjugation. While Wales could not be easily compared with the countries Quayson examines, such as Rwanda or Sierra Leone, it could be argued that the Welsh experience still exhibits some of those same scars.

However, in *I Sent a Letter to My Love*, these images of disability are working not as barely perceptible reminders of subjection, but as a subversive rewriting that has the capacity to imagine power emanating from the margins.

NOTES

1 Critical work within Wales tackles this issue much more explicitly. See, for example, Stephen Knight's *A Hundred Years of Fiction* (Cardiff: University of Wales Press, 2004) and Katie Gramich's 'Both In and Out of the Game: Welsh Writers and the British Dimension', in *Welsh Writing in English*, ed. M. Wynn Thomas (Cardiff: University of Wales Press, 2003), pp. 255–77.

2 Gramich, 'Both In and Out of the Game', p. 265.

3 Nicholas Le Mesurier, 'Surviving the Earthquake', *New Welsh Review*, 18 (Autumn 1992), pp.26–9 (26).

4 Hana Sambrook, 'Bernice Rubens', in *Contemporary Novelists*, 7th edn, eds Neil Schlager and Josh Lauer (Detroit: St James Press, 2001), pp. 861–2 (862).

5 Bernice Rubens, *I Sent a Letter to My Love* (Cardigan: Parthian, 2008), p. 38. All further references are to this edition and are given in the text.

6 Tony McEnery, *Swearing in English: Bad Language, Purity and Power from 1586 to the Present* (London: Routledge, 2006), p. 34.

7 McEnery, *Swearing in English*, p. 46.

8 Fruitful parallels could be made with Erica Jong's consciousness-raising novel, *Fear of Flying* (London: Vintage, 1973), which features a female protagonist who regularly swears.

9 Keith Allan and Kate Burridge, *Forbidden Words: Taboo and the Censoring of Language* (Cambridge: Cambridge University Press, 2006), p. 78.

10 Allan, *Forbidden Words*, p. 78.

11 Timothy Jay, *Cursing in America* (Philadelphia: John Benjamins, 1992), p. 32.

12 Katina Bill, 'Attitudes towards Women's Trousers: Britain in the 1930s', *Journal of Design History*, 6:1, pp. 45–54 (49).

13 Sigmund Freud, *Totem and Taboo*, in *The Origins of Religion*, tr.

James Strachey (London: Penguin, 1990), pp. 43–224 (p. 86).

14   Gwyneth, as a sexual being, on the other hand, is associated with rotten food. Amy refers to her as an 'overripe virgin who had put it all by for this day [of her wedding to Stan]. Open it tonight ... and you'll find it's all gone bad. Kept it too long you did, girl. Now it's not fit for human consumption' (p. 211).

15   Kathleen S. Mayers, Daniel K. Heller, and Jessica A Heller, 'Damaged Sexual Self-Esteem: A Kind of Disability', *Sexuality and Disability*, 21:4 (Winter 2003), pp. 269–82 (270).

16   *Ibid.*, p. 269.

17   *Ibid.*, p. 270.

18   *Ibid.*, p. 269.

19   Erving Goffman, 'On Face-Work: An Analysis of Ritual Elements in Social Interaction', in *The Discourse Reader*, eds Adam Jaworski and Nikolas Coupland (Abingdon: Routledge, 1999), pp. 306–20 (306).

20   Penelope Brown, 'How and Why Are Women More Polite: Some Evidence from a Mayan Community', in *Language and Gender: A Reader*, ed. Jennifer Coates (Oxford: Blackwell, 1998) pp. 81–99 (82).

21   *Ibid.*, p. 84.

22   Brown states that '[t]he classic negative politeness strategies are characterized by self-effacement, formality, restraint, where potential threats to face are redressed with apologies for interfering or transgressing' (p. 85).

23   *Ibid.*, p. 98.

24   *Ibid.*

25   Michel Foucault, *The Will to Knowledge*, tr. Robert Hurley (London: Penguin, 1998), p. 86.

26   Rosemarie Garland Thomson, 'Theorising Disability', in *Relocating Postcolonialism: A Critical Reader*, eds David Theo Goldberg and Ato Quayson (Oxford: Blackwell, 2002) pp. 231–69, (231).

27   Knight, *A Hundred Years of Fiction*, p. 185

28   Ato Quayson, 'Looking Awry: Tropes of Disability in Postcolonial Writing', in *Relocating Postcolonialism*, eds David Theo Goldberg and Ato Quayson pp. 217–30, (228).

Further Reading

Primary Texts A:
selected other works by featured authors

Abse, Dannie, *A Poet in the Family* (London: Robson, 1984 [1974]).
—— *Welsh Retrospective* (Bridgend: Seren, 1997).
—— *The Presence* (London: Hutchinson, 2007).
—— *New Selected Poems* (London: Hutchinson, 2009).
Berry, Ron, *This Bygone* (Llandysul: Gomer, 1996).
—— *Collected Short Stories*, ed. Simon Baker (Llandysul: Gomer, 2000).
—— *History Is What You Live* (Llandysul: Gomer, 1998).
Chamberlain, Brenda, *The Green Heart* (London: Oxford University Press, 1958).
—— *Tide-race* (Bridgend: Seren Books, 1987 [1962]).
—— *The Water Castle* (London: Hodder and Stoughton, 1964).
—— *Alun Lewis and the Making of the Caseg Broadsheets* (London: Enitharmon Press, 1969).
Davies, Rhys, *A Human Condition: The Selected Short Stories of Rhys Davies* (London: Heinemann, 1969).
Edwards, Dorothy, *Winter Sonata* (London: Wishart & Co., 1928).
Evans, Margiad, *The Wooden Doctor* (Dinas Powys: Honno, 2005 [1933]).
—— *Autobiography* (Oxford: Basil Blackwell, 1943).
—— *The Old and the Young* (Bridgend: Seren, 1998 [1948]).
—— *A Ray of Darkness* (London: John Calder, 1978 [1952]).
Humphreys, Emyr, *A Toy Epic* (Bridgend: Seren, 1995 [1958]).
—— *Outside the House of Baal* (London: Eyre & Spottiswoode, 1965; revised and reprinted, Bridgend: Seren, 1996).
—— *Land of the Living* novel sequence: *Flesh and Blood, The Best of Friends, Salt of the Earth, An Absolute Hero, Open Secrets, National Winner, Bonds of Attachment* (Cardiff: University of Wales Press, 1999–2000 [1971–91]).
—— *Unconditional Surrender* (Bridgend: Seren, 1996).
—— *The Woman at the Window: Twelve Stories* (Bridgend: Seren, 2009).
[Jones, Lewis: *Cwmardy* and *We Live* are Jones's only published works of fiction.]

Rubens, Bernice, *The Elected Member* (London: Eyre & Spottiswoode, 1969).
—— *Brothers* (London: Hamish Hamilton, 1983).
—— *Yesterday in the Back Lane* (London: Little, Brown & Co., 1995).
Williams, Raymond, *The Fight for Manod* (London: Chatto and Windus, 1979).
—— *Second Generation* (London: Hogarth, 1988).
—— *People of the Black Mountains: Volume 1, The Beginning* (London: Paladin, 1990).
—— *People of The Black Mountains: Volume 2, The Eggs of the Eagle* (London: Paladin, 1992).
—— *Who Speaks for Wales? Nation, Culture, Identity*, ed. Daniel Williams (Cardiff: University of Wales Press, 2003).

Primary Texts B:
works by selected Anglophone Welsh writers not featured in this volume

Aaron, Jane, ed., *The View across the Valley: Short Stories by Women from Wales* (Dinas Powys: Honno, 1999).
Adams, Sam, ed., *The Collected Short Stories of Roland Mathias* (Cardiff: University of Wales Press, 2001).
Azzopardi, Trezza, *The Hiding Place* (London: Picador, 2000).
Beagan, Glenda, *The Medlar Tree* (Bridgend: Seren, 1992).
Beale, Anne, *Rose Mervyn of Whitelake* (London: Hurst and Blackett, 1879).
Bennett, Anna Maria, *Anna, or Memoirs of a Welch Heiress* (London: William Lane at the Minerva Press, 1785).
—— *Ellen, Countess of Castell Howell* (London: William Lane at the Minerva Press, 1794).
Brito, Leonora, *dat's love* (Bridgend: Seren, 1995).
Bush, Duncan, *Glass Shot* (London: Secker and Warburg, 1991).
Davis, Elizabeth, *Betsy Cadwaladyr, a Balaclava Nurse: The Autobiography of Elizabeth Davis, edited by Jane Williams (Ysgafell)* (Dinas Powys: Honno, 2007 [1857]).
Chatwin, Bruce, *On the Black Hill* (London: Picador, 1982).
Coombes, B. L., *These Poor Hands: The Autobiography of a Miner Working in South Wales* (Cardiff: University of Wales Press, 2002 [1939]).
Davies, Lewis, *Work, Sex, and Rugby* (Cardiff: Parthian, 1993).

Davies, Peter Ho, *The Welsh Girl* (London: Sceptre, 2007).

Davies, Stevie, *Kith and Kin* (London: Phoenix, 2004).

—— *The Eyrie* (London: Weidenfeld & Nicolson, 2007).

Davies, W. H., *Autobiography of a Supertramp* (Oxford: Oxford University Press, 1980 [1908]).

Dearnley, Moira, *The Watery Glass* (Llandybïe: C. Davies, 1973).

Dillwyn, Amy, *The Rebecca Rioter* (Dinas Powys: Honno, 2001 [1880]).

—— *A Burglary* (Dinas Powys: Honno, 2009 [1883]).

Ellis, Alice Thomas, *Unexplained Laughter* (London: Penguin, 1986).

Evans, Caradoc, *My People* (Bridgend: Seren, 1995 [1915]).

—— *Capel Sion* (Bridgend: Seren, 2002 [1917]).

—— *My Neighbours* (Aberystwyth: Planet, 2005 [1920]).

—— *Nothing to Pay* (Manchester: Carcanet, 1989 [1930]).

Evans, George Ewart, *The Voices of the Children* (Cardigan: Parthian, 2008 [1947]).

Evans, Stuart, *The Caves of Alienation* (Cardigan: Parthian, 2009 [1977]).

Gallie, Menna, *Strike for a Kingdom* (Dinas Powys: Honno, 2003 [1959]).

—— *The Small Mine* (Dinas Powys: Honno, 2000 [1962]).

Goodwin, Geraint, *The Heyday in the Blood* (Cardigan: Parthian, 2008 [1936]).

—— *The White Farm and Other Stories* (London: Jonathan Cape, 1937).

Griffith, Llywelyn Wyn, *The Way Lies West* (Bath: Cedric Chivers, 1969 [1945]).

Griffiths, Niall, *Sheepshagger* (London: Jonathan Cape, 2001).

Gunning, Elizabeth, *The Orphans of Snowdon* (London: H. Lowndes, 1797).

Gwyn, Richard, *The Colour of a Dog Running Away* (Cardigan: Parthian, 2005).

Hardy, Elizabeth, *Owen Glendower, or, The Prince in Wales* (London: Richard Bentley, 1849).

Hatton, Ann Julia ('Ann of Swansea'), *Cambrian Pictures, or, Every one has Errors* (London: E. Kerby, 1810).

James, Siân, *A Small Country* (Bridgend: Seren, 1999 [1979]).

—— *Storm at Arberth* (Bridgend: Seren, 1995).

—— *Not Singing Exactly* (Dinas Powys: Honno, 1996).

—— *Love and War* (London: Piatkus, 1997).

Jones, Glyn, *The Valley, the City, the Village* (Cardigan: Parthian, 2009 [1956]).

—— *The Learning Lark* (Llanrwst: Gwasg Carreg Gwalch, 2005 [1960]).

—— *The Island of Apples* (Cardiff: University of Wales Press, 1992 [1965]).

—— *The Collected Stories of Glyn Jones*, ed. Tony Brown (Cardiff: University of Wales Press, 1999).

Lewis, Eiluned, *Dew on the Grass* (Dinas Powys: Honno, 2007 [1934]).

—— *The Captain's Wife* (Dinas Powys: Honno, 2008 [1943]).

Llewelyn, Michael Gareth, *White Wheat* (London: John Murray, 1958 [1947]).

Llewellyn, Richard, *How Green Was My Valley* (London: Penguin Classics, 2001 [1939]).

Machen, Arthur, *The Terror: A Fantasy* (London: Duckworth, 1917).

—— *The Great God Pan* (Cardigan: Parthian, 2010 [1913]).

Meredith, Christopher, *Shifts* (Bridgend: Seren, 1988).

—— *Griffri* (Bridgend: Seren, 1991).

Merriman, Catherine, *State of Desire* (London: Macmillan, 1996).

Morgan, Clare, *An Affair of the Heart* (Bridgend: Seren, 1996).

More, Olivia, *The Welsh Cottage* (Wellington, Salop: Houlston & Son, 1820).

Norris, Leslie, *Collected Stories* (Bridgend: Seren, 1996).

Parry, Catherine, *Eden Vale* (London: John Stockdale, 1784).

Prichard, T. J. Llewelyn, *The Adventures and Vagaries of Twm Shon Catti* (Cribyn: Llannerch, 2005 [1828]).

Raine, Allen, *Queen of the Rushes* (Dinas Powys: Honno, 1998 [1906]).

—— *A Welsh Singer* (London: Hutchinson, 1897).

—— *Torn Sails* (London: Hutchinson, 1898).

—— *Garthowen* (London: Hutchinson, 1900).

—— *A Welsh Witch* (London: Hutchinson, 1902).

Richards, Alun, *Dai Country* (Cardigan: Parthian, 2009 [1973]).

—— *Home to an Empty House* (Cardigan: Parthian, 2006 [1973]).

—— ed., *The Second Penguin Book of Welsh Short Stories* (Harmondsworth: Penguin, 1994).

Robinson, Emma, *Owen Tudor: An Historical Romance* (London: Routledge, 1857 [1849]).

Sheers, Owen, *Resistance* (London: Faber, 2007).

Sinclair, Iain, *Landor's Tower* (London: Granta, 2002).

Spooner, Louisa Matilda, *Gladys of Hurlech: A Romance of Welsh History* (London: Charles Skeet, 1858).

Thomas, Bertha, *Stranger within the Gates* (Dinas Powys: Honno, 2008 [1913]).

Thomas, Dylan, *Collected Stories* (London: Everyman, 1993).

—— *Portrait of the Artist as a Young Dog* (London: Everyman, 1993 [1940]).

Thomas, Henry Elwyn, *Where Eden's Tongue Is Spoken Still* (London: George Bell; Newport, Mon.: H. R. Allenson, 1904).

Tobias, Lily, *Eunice Fleet* (Dinas Powys: Honno, 2004 [1933]).

Trevelyan, Marie, *From Snowdon to the Sea: Stirring Stories of North and South Wales* (London: John Hogg, 1895).

Trezise, Rachel, *In and Out of the Goldfish Bowl* (Cardigan: Parthian, 2000).

Vaughan, Hilda, *The Battle to the Weak* (Cardigan: Parthian 2010 [1925]).

—— *Her Father's House* (London: Heinemann, 1930).

—— *The Soldier and the Gentlewoman* (London: Victor Gollancz, 1932).

—— *Pardon and Peace* (London: Macmillan, 1945).

—— *Iron and Gold* (Dinas Powys: Honno, 2002 [1948]).

Vaughan, Richard, *Moulded in Earth* (New York: E. P. Dutton, 1951).

Williams, Charlotte, *Sugar and Slate* (Aberystwyth: Planet, 2002).

Williams, Mallt and Gwenffreda, a.k.a. 'The Dau Wynne', *A Maid of Cymru: A Patriotic Romance* (London: Simpkin, Marshall & Co., 1901).

Selected Secondary Texts

Aaron, Jane, *Nineteenth-Century Women's Writing in Wales* (Cardiff: University of Wales Press, 2007).

Aaron, Jane and Chris Williams, eds, *Postcolonial Wales* (Cardiff: University of Wales Press, 2005).

Bohata, Kirsti, *Postcolonialism Revisited* (Cardiff: University of Wales Press, 2004).

Brown, Tony and Russell Stephens, eds, *Nations and Relations: Writing Across the British Isles* (Cardiff: New Welsh Review, 2000).

Davies, John, Jenkins, Nigel, Baines, Menna and Lynch, Peredur I., eds, *The Welsh Academy Encyclopaedia of Wales* (Cardiff: University of Wales Press, 2008).

Dearnley, Moira, *Margiad Evans* (Cardiff: University of Wales Press, 1982).

—— *Distant Fields: Eighteenth-Century Fictions of Wales* (Cardiff: University of Wales Press, 2001).

Garlick, Raymond, *An Introduction to Anglo-Welsh Literature* (Cardiff: University of Wales Press, 1972).

Gramich, Katie, *Twentieth Century Women's Writing in Wales: Land, Gender, Belonging* (Cardiff: University of Wales Press, 2007).

Green, Diane, *Emyr Humphreys: A Postcolonial Novelist?* (Cardiff: University of Wales Press, 2009).

Hechter, Michael, *Internal Colonialism: The Celtic Fringe in British National Development, 1536–1966* (London: Routledge & Kegan Paul, 1975).

John, Angela V., ed., *Our Mothers' Land: Chapters in Welsh Women's History 1830–1939* (Cardiff: University of Wales Press, 1991).

Jones, Glyn, *The Dragon Has Two Tongues*, ed. Tony Brown (Cardiff: University of Wales Press, 2001 [1968]).

Knight, Stephen, *A Hundred Years of Fiction* (Cardiff: University of Wales Press, 2004).

Lloyd, David T., ed., *Writing on the Edge: Interviews with Writers and Editors of Wales* (Amsterdam: Rodopi, 1997).

Lloyd-Morgan, Ceridwen, *Margiad Evans* (Bridgend, Seren, 1998).

Llywelyn, Dorian, *Sacred Place, Chosen People* (Cardiff: University of Wales Press, 1999).

Mathias, Roland, *Anglo-Welsh Literature: An Illustrated History* (Bridgend: Poetry Wales Press, 1986).

—— *A Ride through the Wood: Essays on Anglo-Welsh Literature* (Bridgend: Seren, 1995).

Meredith, Christopher, ed., *Moment of Earth: Poems and Essays in Honour of Jeremy Hooker* (Aberystwyth: Celtic Studies Publications, 2007).

Osborne, Huw, *Rhys Davies* (Writers of Wales Series) (Cardiff: University of Wales Press, 2009).

Pikoulis, John, *Alun Lewis, A Life* (Bridgend: Seren Books, 1991 [1984]).

Prys-Williams, Barbara, *Twentieth-Century Welsh Autobiography* (Cardiff: University of Wales Press, 2004).

Rothkirch, Alyce von and Daniel Williams, eds, *Beyond the*

Difference: Welsh Literature in Comparative Contexts (Cardiff: University of Wales Press, 2004).

Smith, Emma, *Masculinity in Welsh Writing in English: The Cases of Lewis Jones, Glyn Jones, Gwyn Thomas and Ron Berry* (Saarbrücken: VDM Verlag, 2009).

—— ed., *The New Companion to the Literatures of Wales* (Cardiff: University of Wales Press, 1998).

Thomas, M. Wynn, *Internal Difference: Literature in Twentieth-Century Wales* (Cardiff: University of Wales Press, 1992).

—— *Corresponding Cultures: The Two Literatures of Wales* (Cardiff: University of Wales Press, 1999).

—— ed., *Welsh Writing in English* (Cardiff: University of Wales Press, 2003).

Williams, Raymond, *The Welsh Industrial Novel* (Cardiff: University College Cardiff Press, 1979).

—— *Politics of Modernism: Against the New Conformists*, ed. Tony Pinkney, 2nd edn (London and New York: Verso, 2007).

almanac
Yearbook of Welsh Writing in English

almanac
Yearbook of Welsh Writing in English

almanac
Yearbook of Welsh Writing in English

Information for Contributors

Correspondence and contributions for publication should be addressed to the editor: Dr Katie Gramich, School of English, Communication and Philosophy, Cardiff University, Humanities Building, Colum Drive, Cardiff, CF10 3EU (email: GramichK @cf.ac.uk). The *almanac* publishes essays on literary topics, not on purely Welsh historical matters. While its primary concern is the study of Welsh writing in English, papers on Welsh-language authors, written in English, will be considered; the Yearbook will also consider papers which relate the two literatures of Wales or discuss the literatures of Wales in international, comparative contexts. Papers should not normally exceed 8,000 words in length.

Manuscripts (two copies) should be typed on one side of the page, double spaced, and produced according to the current MHRA Style Guide. Include a computer disk with the hard copies, and note the word-processing programme used. All contributions will be refereed. While a decision will be made as expeditiously as possible, allow three months for a decision. Contributors of published papers receive two complimentary copies of the issue in which their paper appears. The *almanac* web page, which includes information on past issues, is at:

http://www.cardiff.ac.uk/encap/journals/periodic/welshwrit.html

LIBRARY OF WALES

The Library of Wales is a Welsh Assembly Government project designed to ensure that all of the rich and extensive literature of Wales which has been written in English will now be made available to readers in and beyond Wales. Sustaining this wider literary heritage is understood by the Welsh Assembly Government to be a key component in creating and disseminating an ongoing sense of modern Welsh culture and history for the future Wales which is now emerging from contemporary society. Through these texts, until now unavailable, out-of-print or merely forgotten, the Library of Wales brings back into play the voices and actions of the human experience that has made us, in all our complexity, a Welsh people.

The Library of Wales includes prose as well as poetry, essays as well as fiction, anthologies as well as memoirs, drama as well as journalism. It complements the names and texts that are already in the public domain and seeks to include the best of Welsh writing in English, as well as to showcase what has been unjustly neglected. No boundaries limit the ambition of the Library of Wales to open up the borders that have denied some of our best writers a presence in a future Wales. The Library of Wales has been created with that Wales in mind: a young country not afraid to remember what it might yet become.

Dai Smith
Raymond Williams Chair in the Cultural History of Wales,
Swansea University

LIBRARY OF WALES
FUNDED BY

Llywodraeth Cynulliad Cymru
Welsh Assembly Government

CYNGOR LLYFRAU CYMRU
WELSH BOOKS COUNCIL

LIBRARY OF WALES

SERIES EDITOR: DAI SMITH

WWW.LIBRARYOFWALES.ORG

LIBRARY OF WALES
titles are available to buy online at:

PARTHIAN

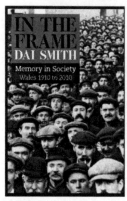

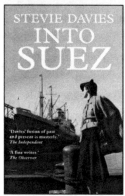
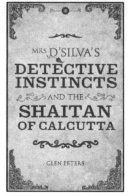

www.parthianbooks.com

Lightning Source UK Ltd.
Milton Keynes UK
21 January 2011

166114UK00001B/10/P